The Making of a Digital World

Evolutionary Processes in World Politics Series
Series editor: William R. Thompson, Indiana University

The Historical Evolution of World-Systems, edited by Christopher Chase-Dunn and E. N. Anderson (2005)

Puzzles of the Democratic Peace: Theory, Geopolitics, and the Transformation of World Politics, by Karen Rasler and William R. Thompson (2005)

The Making of a Digital World: The Evolution of Technological Change and How It Shaped Our World, by Joachim K. Rennstich (2008)

The Making of a Digital World

The Evolution of Technological Change and How It Shaped Our World

Joachim K. Rennstich

palgrave
macmillan

First published in 2008 by
PALGRAVE MACMILLAN™
175 Fifth Avenue, New York, N.Y. 10010 and
Houndmills, Basingstoke, Hampshire, England RG21 6XS
Companies and representatives throughout the world.

PALGRAVE MACMILLAN is the global academic imprint of the Palgrave Macmillan division of St. Martin's Press, LLC and of Palgrave Macmillan Ltd. Macmillan® is a registered trademark in the United States, United Kingdom and other countries. Palgrave is a registered trademark in the European Union and other countries.

ISBN-13: 978–1–4039–7448–8
ISBN-10: 1–4039–7448–9

Library of Congress Cataloging-in-Publication Data

Rennstich, Joachim K.
    The making of a digital world : the evolution of technological change and how it shaped our world / Joachim K. Rennstich.
       p. cm.—(Evolutionary processes in world politics series)
    Includes bibliographical references and index.
    ISBN 1–4039–7448–9
      1. Social change. 2. Social evolution. 3. Technological innovations—Social aspects. 4. Globalization. I. Title.

HM831.R46 2008
303.48′201—dc22   2007027280

A catalogue record for this book is available from the British Library.

Design by Newgen Imaging Systems (P) Ltd., Chennai, India.

First edition: March 2008

10 9 8 7 6 5 4 3 2 1

Printed in the United States of America.

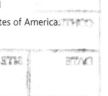

To my parents

CONTENTS

List of Figures   ix

List of Tables   xi

Acknowledgments   xiii

One   Thinking about Globalization—an Introduction   1

Two   An Evolutionary Theory of Globalization   26

Three Drivers of Global Change—Leading Sectors of the
       Informational Network Economy   71

Four   Drivers of Leading Sector Change—the Role of States,
       Organizations, and Individuals   135

Five   Drivers of Leading Actor Change—Interstate
       Rivalry at the Systemic Level   165

Six   The Continuation of Change of the Global Complex
       System—an Outlook on Its Future Development   198

Notes   212

References   228

Index   253

LIST OF FIGURES

2.1	Generational Leadership Long Cycle	30
2.2	Global Complex Systems—Schematic	33
2.3	Complex Global System Development Matrix	52
2.4	System Leadership Transition	58
3.1	IT-share (%) of Equipment Investment, United States, 1960–1996	96
3.2	Semiconductor Sales ($ million), 1976–2002	97
3.3	Internet Growth, Users and Share of World Population, 1995–2002	103
3.4	Internet Host Survey Count, 1981–2002	103
3.5	Number of Base Pairs (billions) and Sequences (millions) in GenBank Database, 1982–2001	125
4.1	B/C Matrix of Organizational Interaction Forms	147
4.2	Cellular Organizational Structures	151
5.1	Major Power Rivalries, Major Power Wars, and Rivalry Environments, 1494–2000	173
5.2	Number of Major Power Rivalries in Maritime Commercial Rivalry Environment, 1494–1640	188
5.3	Number of Major Power Rivalries in Transition Phase 1 and Industrial Production Phase Rivalry Environment, 1640–1815	189
5.4	Number of Major Power Rivalries in Industrial Production System Rivalry Environment, 1740–1914	190
5.5	Number of Major Power Rivalries in Transition Phase 2 and Digital Commercial System Rivalry Environment, 1914–2000	191

LIST OF TABLES

2.1 Hypothesized Relationship between Learning
Long Cycle, K-waves, Global Lead Industries, and
Network Phases (All Years CE)   41
2.2 Phases of World System Evolution, McNeill,
Wallerstein, Buzan and Little, and Modelski   43
2.3 Extended Evolutionary World Politics Model of
Process of Globalization, 930–2080 CE   45
2.4 Evolutionary World Politics Matrix, Modern
Era, 930–2230 CE   49
3.1 ICT Equipment Investment in OECD countries,
Percentage of Nonresidential Gross Fixed Capital
Formation, Total Economy, 1980–2000   94
3.2 Contribution of IT Equipment to Growth in Capital
Equipment, United States, Percentage, 1993–1998   95
3.3 Number of Internet Hosts (gTLDs Adjusted) and
Web Sites, per 1,000 Inhabitants, July 1997–July 2001   104
3.4 Key Global Telecom Indicators for the World
Telecommunication Service Sector, 1991–2001,
US$ billions (Adjusted for Inflation)   107
3.5 Mobile Subscribers in OECD Countries, 1990–1999   112
3.6 Mobile Subscribers, Worldwide, 1995–2001   114
3.7 Broadband Penetration, Subscribers per 100 Inhabitants,
2002–2006   122
3.8 National Shares (in percentage) of the Total Number
of Publications in the Biotechnology and Applied
Microbiology NSIOD Journal Category, 1986–1998   130
3.9 International Strategic Biotechnology Technology
Alliances with at Least One Partner Based in the
United States, 1980–1998   132

5.1   Major Power Rivalries   168
5.2   Major Global Wars, 1494–2000   177
5.3   Global Complex System Rivalry Environments,
      1190–2000   179
5.4   Main Characteristics, Global Complex System
      Rivalry Environments, 1190–2030   185
5.5   Summary of Summary Statistics for Major Power
      Rivalries, Major Powers, Major Power Dyads, and Rivalry
      Environments   194
5.6   Analysis of the Effect of Rivalry Environments on
      Number of Rivalries per Year   195

ACKNOWLEDGMENTS

In the course of writing this book I have run up many debts of gratitude and it is my great pleasure to acknowledge them here. In the first place, my thanks are owed to William Thompson whose unrivalled intellectual rigor, breadth of knowledge, and sharpness of mind has never failed to open up new intellectual paths for me to venture on (as well as countless holes in my argument). No other teacher has ever presented me with such wealth—of knowledge, devotion of time, attention, and guidance—in such an extraordinarily generous and noble fashion. It is because of him that this work marks not an end but rather a beginning of many new endeavors.

My deep appreciation extends to the following colleagues, Karen Rasler, Jeff Hart, and David Audretsch. How this work could have been completed without their generous advice and critical assistance I know not. I am especially grateful to Sharon La Roche and Scott Feickert who were generous in lending their assistance and encouragement during my entire time at Indiana University.

The responsibility for the opinions conveyed in these pages is, of course, mine alone. However, the ideas themselves were developed, often challenged, and refined in the course of many exchanges with fellow colleagues and friends, old and new. In particular, I would like to mention: Giovanni Arrighi, Volker Bornschier, Chris Chase-Dunn, Claudio Cioffi-Revilla, Michael Colaresi, Catherine Daily, Ulrich Erlhof, Clark Gibson, Nathan Griffith, Albrecht v. Harder, Kimberly Mealy, George Modelski, Ursula Rennstich, Julian Westerhout, and Nathan Zook. The team at Palgrave has provided me with much appreciated guidance and assistance along the editorial process—this book would have been lacking in substance and style without their hard work and dedication. I also owe much gratitude to

Meghan Teich, who has constantly reaffirmed me in my endeavors. Finally, my largest debt remains to my parents. Their unquestioning support and more importantly, their guidance and boundless love have never failed me. No words could ever adequately express my gratitude.

CHAPTER ONE

Thinking about Globalization—an Introduction

Introduction

Globalization has become a buzzword so widespread in use and meaning that its use as a conceptual tool becomes increasingly questionable. Originating in French and American writings in the early 1960s, the concept of globalization has been used to capture everything from global financial markets, the internet, and the "flattening" of the world (Friedman, 2006) to the destruction of the Amazon rain forest and the sex trade in Southeast Asia, yet providing little substantive insights in terms of globalization as a theoretical construct.

Despite the vast number of pages printed on the subject, most works are concerned with a descriptive analysis of globalization as a *phenomenon*, whereas there seems little work aiming for an overarching framework and analysis of globalization as a theoretical construct. An even greater problem is the ahistoricism that marks this literature. Far from searching for the roots of the globalization process and trajectories in former interactions between social agents, globalization is often believed to be uniquely tied to our contemporary context. In this view, globalization is the result of modern day telecommunication, the development of high-speed travel, and the ubiquity of information on a global scale.

As a result, little has been achieved in terms of a coherent analytical research project or even a deeper understanding of the process itself. Thus Guillén (2001a, 238) concludes his comprehensive review of the globalization literature with the remark that

> definitions and timing aside, one of the persistent problems afflicting the study of globalization is that it is far from being a uniform, irreversible, and inexorable trend. Rather, globalization is a fragmented, incomplete, discontinuous, contingent, and in many ways contradictory and puzzling process. (see also Gilpin and Gilpin, 2000; Giddens, 2000; Guidry et al., 2000; Held et al., 1999)

To resolve this "contradictory and puzzling process" is the aim of this work. To do so this book aims to provide answers the following questions: is there something inherently novel and/or unique about modern (digital) technologies that renders our insights from past patterns of transformation useless? Is globalization as we experience it today thus a stage in an ongoing developmental process or a unique occurrence in history?

Here we argue that globalization—defined as the process of increasing width and depth of interaction and interdependence among social units in the global world system—is essentially evolutionary in its form and a as a result has its roots in earlier periods of time. Broadly following Modelski's (1990; 2000; see also Modelski and Thompson, 1996) conceptualization, globalization in our view comprises a set of coevolving processes: global *economic* evolution (of trading systems and world markets); global *political* evolution (of nation–state systems, world power competitions, and international organizations); *democratization* (i.e., the formation of a potential democratic community); and the creation of a *world public opinion*[1] (through media and learning processes). The ultimate agents of these processes are individuals and organizations sponsoring and advancing innovation that results in the formation of global layers of interactions. These agents act in a structural environment that provides certain possibilities of action (and denies others). The organizational logic of these structures is not based on some pre-destined trajectory or goal but rather the result of *self-organization* that is a characteristic of (some) complex systems.

The central question of this book can thus be formulated as follows: do the past patterns of global system development still hold true for its current transformation or are we are witnessing a structurally different development, whether technologically induced or the result of its increased complexity? In order to answer this question, this work stresses the following developments:

- the development of a *global system* (drawing on complex systems theory) and its relationship with the development of *external* and *internal network structures*;

- the evolutionary trajectory of technologies and their effect on the development of *technological styles*;
- the impact of external and internal network structures on the evolutionary development of technological styles;
- the relationship of nested economic and political coevolving processes and their role in the development of a more slowly, coevolving social process, extending existing frameworks in an effort that views globalization ultimately as cultural process driven by human agency; and
- the impact of digital technologies on these processes.

It is important to emphasize that here we do not argue that globalization (i.e., the global system process) in its current stage is the same or even resembles (in relative terms, however measured) earlier stages at any given earlier point in time. Such an assertion would indeed be impossible to hold up not only empirically but also theoretically. Given our assessment of the development of the global system as an evolutionary, complex system process, only the opposite can be true. The current stage of the global system process is unique and unprecedented in many ways: for example its geographic reach, its complexity, and its level of interconnectedness, to name just a few characteristics. However, the same holds true for earlier stages. The core of this work is thus not so much a study of the outcome of the global system formation process, but rather the process itself.

This study demonstrates that we are indeed witnessing a major transformation of the global system. It shows, that this transformation is indeed part of a long-term set of coevolving global system development processes, which is neither entirely unique nor unprecedented. The dynamics of the transformation are echoing those of past global system change. Technology plays, as it has done in previous transformations, a crucial, yet not deterministic role. It enables, drives, and manifests the development of what Perez (1983; 2002) calls a new *technological style/ revolution* or a new socioeconomic environment, for the industrial period more commonly referred to as *Fordism*. This technological style, however, interacts and depends for its development (or lack thereof) as much on the social, political, and cultural environment in which it operates as much as it influences these environments.[2] To make sense of the implications of the development of a new technological style thus requires us not only to identify the key technologies (making possible and driving the development of new leading sectors) enabling this new socioeconomic environment. It also makes it necessary for us to place the role of technology in a broader, historical context.

The lack of attention to this broader historical context is the reason why most existing globalization analyses misrepresent, misunderstand, and misinterpret current transformations. This study is unique in putting current changes not only in a historical context but also in a more systematic and empirical fashion, unpacking the global political, economic, social, and cultural implications of this change. Identifying distinct phases in the global system development it demonstrates the resemblance of past commercial networks with emerging digital networks (contrasting them with industrial production systems). Thus this work advances existing evolutionary models and provides new tools for the analysis of our modern day world. It employs these tools to explain how globalization affects the micro- and macrostructures of national economies, the world economy as a whole, the dispersion of power in the global world system, and its impact on major global war.

Much discussion in the globalization debate, either implicitly or explicitly, surrounds the issue of agency in a changing economic environment. Often the perceived loss of human agency is seen mainly as the result of technological change. Here, we focus on the role of agency where it is most clearly perceptible in processes that essentially drive the global system process: the rise and fall of leading sectors, the rise and decline of world powers, and the long movements of world opinion. On the basis of the existing framework of the Evolutionary World Politics (EWP) Matrix, the book extends this framework, both theoretically and conceptually. In doing so, it provides a special focus on and interprets current transformations as part of the unfolding of a set of separate, nested and coevolving long-term processes. The study pays special attention to the decline of the previous leading sectors and the subsequent rise of new leading sectors based on informational technologies. It provides a new theoretical and conceptual understanding of the decline and rise of world powers during transition phases and the formation of a new *world opinion* in the form of a new sociopolitical and technological paradigm, here referred to as the informational network (iNet) economy.

After a review of the more general globalization literature, this chapter continues with a review of the more long-term oriented global system literature, followed by a review of evolutionary approaches concerned with the development of the international political economy. The chapter then concludes with an introduction of the theoretical model employed in this survey, followed by a summary of the individual chapters.

Major Trends in the Globalization Literature

Originating primarily in sociology journals in the mid-1970s and continuing in the economics and political science literatures, the number of publications on *globalization* dramatically rose, especially since the mid-1980s and thereafter (see the excellent study of the development of the globalization literature by Guillén, 2001a). By contrast, the anthropological and historical literatures, have produced surprisingly less research on the subject. Not only the sheer number of works is remarkable, but even more so is the diversity of authors and schools that have contributed to it, ranging from mainly qualitatively oriented social theorists (with some authors avoiding entirely the effort to invoke any form of empirical research) and postmodernist scholars on the one end to management consultants and business school writers, highly quantitative empiricists and economists, and even the occasional politician waging into the debate.

The definitional problems associated with the term *globalization* are reflected in the wide range of definitions and conceptualizations to be found in the sociological, political science, economics, and other literatures. Most would intuitively agree with Held et al. (1999, 16), who define globalization as a "process driven by—and leading to—increasing crossborder flows of goods, services, money, people, information, and culture." Others, such as the sociologist Anthony Giddens (1990, 64) emphasize the decoupling (*distanciation* in Giddens' words) between time and space as one of the major attributes of globalization. In similar fashion, Mittelman (2000), a political scientist, and Harvey (1989), a geographer, stress the effects of globalization on the dimensions of space and time; these authors, however, see the *compression of space and time* and subsequently a *shrinking* of the world, as major outcomes of globalization.

The development and various forms of global flows[3] seem the major focus of other writers, such as the influential work of the sociologist Manuel Castells. Castells sees the informational aspects of the globalized economy as its major characteristic, as it enables an economy with "the capacity to work as a unit in real time on a planetary scale" (Castells, 1996, 92). Whereas some authors employ a special emphasis on global production networks (see Reich, 1991; see also Dicken, 1992; Gereffi, 1994), others see globalization not so much driven by old flows of trade and investment (e.g., Gilpin, who defines globalization as the increasing interdependence of national economies in trade, finance, and macroeconomic policy, see Gilpin, 1987, 389) but by new flows of

increasing technological scale and information flows (Kobrin, 1997).
Guillén (2001a, 236; 2001b) aims to combine the perspectives of
Robertson (1992), who stresses not only Harvey's and Mittelman's
dimensional compression but also the intensification of the conscious-
nesses of the world as a whole and Albrow (1997, 88), who emphasizes
globalization as the "diffusion of practices, values and technology that
have an influence on people's lives worldwide" as part of his definition
of globalization as "a process leading to greater interdependence and
mutual awareness (reflexivity) among economic, political, and social
units in the world, and among actors in general."[4]

In his empirical study of the literature, Guillén (2001a) has identified
five key debates capturing the broad spectrum of social, economic,
political, and cultural themes of main interest to social scientists engaging in the subject (see especially Table 2 for a summary in Guillén,
2001a, 242–43), three of which are at the center of this work as well.
The most basic of these concerns the very fact if globalization is indeed
occurring[5] or not.[6] The second major debate in the globalization literature concerns the question, whether globalization leads to a greater
convergence[7] or rather entrenches or even worsens existing imbalances
within the global economy.[8] A third issue reflected in the literature is
the effect of globalization on the authority of nation-states. Whereas
some authors argue for the increasing loss of control,[9] others argue that
the power of the nation-state can be preserved despite the supposed
effects of globalization.[10]

Existing contributions to the debate surrounding globalization differ
the most in respect to (1) the conceptualization of globalization; (2) its
causation; (3) its periodization; (4) the impact globalization has on
various levels of human interaction; and finally (5) the trajectories of
globalization. Both, those who embrace the concept, as well as the
skeptics, tend to conceptualize globalization mostly as a fully integrated
global market, with convergence in social, cultural, and political spheres
(i.e., a singular condition or "final destination") as a measure for some
degree of globalization. Where they differ, is the outcome of their
analysis: whereas the supporters find plenty of evidence for high-level
integration effects of globalization, the skeptics argue that the lack of
true integration and convergence toward a single market proves proponents of globalization wrong.

Lately, there seems to be a growing consensus in the more analytical
literature that globalization is not a single phenomenon, but rather a
process, neither novel nor uniquely tied to contemporary developments
such as the widespread diffusion of communication technology. Yet,

while most studies discuss either the economic impact or the political consequences of the globalization process, there still exist only few studies that analyze globalization from a broader, more holistic and historical perspective. Especially the historical trajectories of globalization beyond the twentieth or nineteenth century and the dynamics between the political, economic, cultural, and social dimensions of the globalization process are often neglected or only marginally taken into account. Fortunately, this lack of a broader conceptualization and analysis of the globalization process is starting to be addressed in the literature.

Historical and Long-term Studies of Globalization

The rise of attention to the increasing visibility of the manifestations and effects of globalization has focused interest in many social science research traditions, but mainly so (or at least rooted) in sociological research, often summarized as the *world systems* school.[11] A basic divide separating analytical approaches to world system history concerns the discussion whether the year 1500 CE marks an important watershed or not.[12] Some authors, such as Wallerstein, widely attributed to be the founder of the world system research program but by far not the only (or arguably first) writer with a more holistic approach to the study of international relations, identify a unique modern world system emerging after 1500 CE.[13] Increasingly, however, world system historical analysis stretches beyond the "magical" (but for many authors far too Eurocentric, see e.g., Frank, 1998) 1500 CE mark.

Broadly conceived, four major schools of thought have emerged that challenge the view of the 1500 CE-threshold: Some authors argue for a continuing *world system* (e.g., Frank and Gills, 1993). For these authors, our current world system has its systemic origins in 2700–2400 BCE, a single world system as a result of the division of labor in the form of center-periphery and hinterland and intersecting hegemonies and superhegemonies. This school employs a long-term economic focus on constant capital accumulation with *A/B phases*.

A second school argues for the comparative study of *world systems* (Chase-Dunn and Hall, 1997; 1991; Frank and Gills, 1993). In this view, the systemic origins of (different) kind of world systems reaches as far back as 10000 BCE (for kin-based systems), whereas the division of labor in this view is not marked by a dichotomous core and periphery/hinterland structure, but consists of a three-layered, core—semiperiphery—periphery structure. The rise and composition of hegemons in this view vary by the respective predominant *accumulation mode*, their main determent for differences in various (and sometimes coexisting) world systems. As a result, this school place their long-term economic foci on various accumulation modes and their transitions, rather than the *long-wave* approach with A/B phases. A few studies have employed data analysis of city sizes as evidence but as a result of the differences in the "system-modes" and the time period covered analysis is mainly theoretical.

A third view identifies an engulfing world system (e.g., Wilkinson, 1987; 1993), placing the systemic origins around 1500 BCE and sharing the view of a threefold division of labor in the form of a core-semiperiphery-periphery structure. Here, the world system is led by dominant powers and parahegemons and the long-term economic foci are highly based on the constancy of capital accumulation with A/B phases. Data applied concentrate mainly on city sizes.

A fourth view applies an evolutionary approach to the study of the world system as we experience it today and argues for an evolving world system (e.g., Modelski and Thompson, 1996). Modelski and Thompson place the systemic origins of the world system at around 3500 BCE and view the division of labor primarily in the form of center-hinterland rather than a core-periphery structure. In this view, its current economic active zone leaders and the long-term economic foci rest on radical innovation waves mainly influence the world system. This school also employs a much more rigorous emphasis on empirical justifications of their developed theories and places an emphasis on the application of statistical data, concentrating and applying data on leading sectors (K-waves), naval concentration, city- and population-sizes.

For other social scientists[14] engaging in historically oriented work, the barrier of the 1490s "cut-off-date" marking the emergence of the modern world proved too high for many a historically oriented writers to overcome (as a result of one's view of world history, the definition of capitalism and its rise in the world system, or the significance and development of the "European miracle"). Earlier approaches, founded in the dominating international relations paradigmatic tradition of realism,[15] have sought to analyze change either focusing on certain *events* (i.e., temporally discrete happenings), *processes* (i.e., the modes and types of change), or *structures* (or ecology of action in the words of one author, see Rosenau, 1995) and have been recently reviewed in great detail by Dark (1998). In similar fashion, a few international relations theorists (Ruggie, 1983; Cox, 1986; Ashley, 1986)[16] began to look to historical sociology in the early 1980s as a way to bring history back into their discipline and paradigmatic evaluations, a development that has gathered some momentum recently.[17]

Here we follow largely the evolutionary school of thought for our study of the development of the world system. The findings of all of the authors discussed above provide useful insights into the processes of innovation and diffusion of technology (in a broad sense, encompassing not only material technologies but also processes), the development of leading sectors, and the developmental path of these dynamics. Taken together, they mark important contributions to the development of a framework of the process of long-term change of the evolution of a globalized world system. A major premise of this study is the argument that globalization is better understood in terms of global system development, in our view an evolutionary process in the making for an extended period of human history. To make this case, we must show that the current processes usually identified with globalization are part of a *longue durée*. We must demonstrate that these changes resemble past patterns of change and are but a part of a new cycle in the long-wave of world politics. To do so, we now focus our discussion more closely on evolutionary approaches.

Evolutionary Approaches—an Overview

Despite the multitude of evolutionary approaches in the social sciences we can identify a number of core assumptions that build the basis of the approach. The special emphasis on change is probably the most commonly associated factor of evolutionary approaches. So it is not surprising that assumptions regarding variation and selection are crucial concepts for the evolutionary paradigm. An evolutionary paradigm does not limit itself to a focus on a certain set of actors or level of analysis but allows a flexibility that enables us to focus on various levels or actors, even simultaneously. What matters are the different formats of a given unit of analysis and their development over time. For example, at a certain point in time there might exist a number of technologies as a result of economic innovation or variations in the types of states.[18] At a subsequent time, some of the variations of the given unit might have vanished or declined in importance in relation to other units.[19] Thus, the crucial question is why one approach has been favored and selected over the others. From an evolutionary viewpoint the answer lies in the feedbacks between ecologies and actors: as environments and actors change, so too do the probabilities that some approaches will survive or prove more successful than others, while others will wither or even disappear. As discussed earlier, of interest is not simply change in itself, but rather the interaction between changing elements.

Change, then, is a constant phenomenon rather than a disruption from the norm. Rather than searching for some forms of equilibria, evolutionary frameworks aim to identify and understand the dynamics of the system and its subsystems. It is important to remember the underlying argument, that change in this context is neither linear and constant, nor completely random. This would render any study useless or at least highly speculative. Change appears in a variety of shapes and sizes. Whereas some changes can have large, immediate effects, other changes develop their impact gradually and more incrementally.

Also, the interaction and feedback effects in the system have an important impact on the timing of change. Often a number of previously insignificant and incremental changes can suddenly grow in importance and scope and quickly diffuse throughout the system when paired with new innovations. For example, over the course of history we repeatedly see major inventions occurring relatively unnoticed and remaining insignificant elements of change. They only gain in significance if and when placed in an appropriate socioeconomic environmental context before they develop into major innovations. Thus, we can state that depending on the type of change, as well as the time point in which those changes occur, those changes are likely to lead to different outcomes. What becomes crucial from an evolutionary perspective is to uncover the pattern of change within the system of interest, in our case the development of the global world system.

By taking into account the element of change in a systematic manner we are far better equipped to understand (and explain) current global macro- as well as microdevelopments and their near-term future effects than with a simple linear extrapolation of past values into the future. Employing an evolutionary approach to the study of globalization we are able to describe with a high degree of confidence the whole picture of a possible new wave of the globalization process albeit only parts of the puzzle have established themselves firmly now. This, however, does not imply a deterministic manner of analysis or interpretation.

The Spectrum of Evolutionary Approaches

Evolutionary frameworks (outside of the natural sciences) early on advanced in economics but have been increasingly adopted in other social sciences as well. They have emerged as a powerful tool to study complex social processes involving a wide array of factors (such as geography, technology, but also institutions, commercial developments, financial flows, warfare, etc.). In political science, evolutionary theories have become particularly influential on scholars interested in the study of the part of the International Relations literature that is devoted to the study of the international political economy as a way to overcome the limitations of institutional approaches. Whereas most neo-institutional approaches to industrial innovation and competitiveness in the international political economy literature focus on national variations of institutional capacity for the creation and diffusion of technological innovations,[20] other approaches have focused on the sectoral level of analysis. Economists have of course significantly influenced this strain of research. Here we shall focus on the strand of economic literature with the most impact on international political economy studies, namely evolutionary economics.

Evolutionary Economics

A unifying characteristic of evolutionary economics has, from the beginning, been its criticism of neoclassical economic theory.[21] In the tradition of Schumpeter (1933; 1942; 1989; 1994), the work of Nelson and Winter (1974; 1982; 2002; see also Nelson et al., 1973) and others[22] challenged the static framework of neoclassical economics and proposed an evolutionary framework instead. In contrast to the foci on allocation of scares resources and of economic equilibrium of the neoclassicist, evolutionary economist postulate that economic activities involve continuous disequilibrium and dynamic processes of change involving the creation of new resources. The ultimate outcome of this change remains unpredictable in advance; the major focus of theory must therefore be on the process of change. To counter neoclassical assumptions and theories, evolutionary economists have been developing an alternative theoretical foundation with which to analyze economies and economic change.[23]

Most evolutionary economic approaches[24] in one way or another refer back to the various contributions from Schumpeter (see also Kuznets, 1940).[25] Schumpeter attempted to deny the incorporation of mechanistic influences—such as *force*, *equilibria*, and similar concepts—into the field of economics. Schumpeter's theoretical reasoning was mainly concerned with the problems of change (i.e., evolution). Rather than searching for equilibria, the *cycle* or *organic process* of capitalist development should be explained by an industrial mutation—if I may use the biological term—that incessantly revolutionizes the economic structure from within, incessantly destroying the old one, incessantly creating a new one. This process of Creative Destruction [capitalization in the original] is the essential fact about capitalism (Schumpeter, 1942, 83).

Far from supporting a simplistic Spencerian type of evolutionism (whom Schumpeter accused of combining "naïve laissez-faire" with a simplified version of Darwinism, see Schumpeter, 1994, 773), Schumpeter's approach nevertheless can be described as an evolutionary conception. First, the economy is perceived as an organic whole, propelled by a process of development with endogenous mutations. Second, the capitalistic process is seen as nonmechanistic and path-dependent.[26] In sum, the permanent tendency of the dislocation of the center of gravity of the system and the complex interaction of the different cycles account for an original form of instability, generated within the system itself. Schumpeter's system is thus a system of self-generating complexity and instability, in which the equilibrium concept (although present) only retains a very subsidiary role.

Both theoretically and methodologically, Schumpeter aimed to bridge existing statistical (applying the concept of Kondratiev waves) and historical approaches (in his treatment of the cycles in business cycles), combining them both (Schumpeter, 1933) in a *long-wave* approach. Schumpeter looked especially to the work of a young Russian economist, Nikolai Kondratiev, an internationally influential Russian economist during his time (the first part of the twentieth century), for applied research on reasoned history and statistics. Kondratiev's decisive contribution was the presentation of the hypothesis of long-waves in capitalist development, referred to as Kondratiev or K-waves. For some time, these K-waves represented an important topic in the research of economics and—ironically—has seen a regular rise and decline in interest ever since.[27]

In 1922, Kondratiev published a book formulating, more or less in passing, the long-cycle hypothesis based on his inspection of some statistical series (see Makasheva et al., 1998). Kondratiev claimed that there were long periods of upswings and downswings in historical data, roughly lasting fifty years each. Continuing his research on this phenomenon, he went on to recognize some major transformations in productivity forces (for example, such as the *new industrial revolution* driving the change from the second to the third long-wave), and identified four empirical laws (see Kondratiev's 1926 paper on forecasting in Kondratiev, 1998):

- some years before the beginning of a new long cycle, important changes occur (potentially as much as twenty years before) in

technological innovation, monetary circulation, and the role played by new countries;
- wars and revolutions (i.e., class struggle) are more intense in the upswings;
- agricultural depressions are more intense in the downswings;
- and the downswings of the shorter (economic and/or business) cycles are more intense in the downswings of the long cycle, and the reverse also is true.

Although Kondratiev dismissed the possibility of a precise forecast, he insisted on the need to employ both, historico-comparative as well as statistical methods of induction into historical data, with induction being the sole method capable of increasing the level of understanding of such data.

During the strong postwar growth period characterized by a seemingly indefinite exponential expansion, claims about long cyclical patterns of intense structural change seemed theoretically unjustifiable and practically nonsensical. A dominance of mechanistic theories and models, propelled by new statistical opportunities, erased any concern about these "mysterious" movements of an evolutionary development of capitalism. The revival of the program occurred nonetheless. After the major economic turn experienced in the previous decade, in the 1980s CE the research on long-waves gathered momentum again, in such contributions as Perez (1985; 1986; 2002) and Kleinknecht (1987).[28]

The neo-Schumpeterian approach put forward by Rostow (1952; 1960; 1971; 1978) features quite prominently in the political sciences and particularly so in the early development literature. In contrast to many other writers interested in long-cycles, Rostow argues for a linear growth model in the world economy, characterized by "boom and bust" cycles of growth and contraction marking his *stages of growth* (Rostow, 1952; see also Rostow, 1971). Rostow defines these stages (which all states must undergo in their economic development) as: (i) traditional (preindustrial); (ii) transitional or preconditions for *takeoff* (proto-industrial); (iii) takeoff (industrialization); (vi) drive to maturity; and finally (v) the search for quality (beyond consumption).

These stages, according to Rostow, are based on a theory of production and evidence for fifty-year long-waves can be found on commodity prices. Long-wave fluctuations then can only understood by focusing on

- the dynamics set off by the development of what Rostow identifies as new *leading sectors* (characterized by the introduction and progressive diffusion of new technology);

- the dynamics set off by changes in profitability of the production of raw materials and foodstuffs (either as an effect of prices or new technology), including effects on investment in new territories and mines, or capital movements, interest rates, terms of trade, and domestic international income distribution; and
- the dynamics set off by long-waves of international or domestic migration, or other population dynamics affecting demand for housing, size and composition of the workforce, and so on.[29]

Rostow (1978, 109–10) identifies two principal kinds of trend periods. First, periods during which agricultural and commodity prices (but also prices more generally) and interest rates are rising (or remain relatively high compared to previous and subsequent periods), agriculture is expanding rapidly, and income distribution tends to shift in favor of agriculture and profits, while urban real wages are under pressure. Second, Rostow identifies periods when these trends are reversed (i.e., sinking agricultural and commodity prices and interest rates, contracting agricultural production, and relatively high urban wages). His insistence on a linear unfolding of this process has been the main target of criticism leveled against his work, a criticism often based on a skewed or simplistic notion of his theory, as was his focus on prices and wages (a much more substantiated criticism). However, it must be noted that Rostow's contribution remains important especially in regard to the development of an evolutionary framework: His work has renewed the focus on the significance of leading sectors for the dynamics of capitalistic socioeconomic systems as well as on the importance of viewing dynamics as an endogenous process of capitalistic socioeconomic systems.

A similar concern about leading sectors as a crucial driver for long-waves is shared by van Duijn (1983). He argues, that growth follows a life cycle pattern and thus comprises of S-shaped phenomena. In this view, basic innovations give rise to new industrial sectors that develop in an S-shaped life cycle pattern in their demand for the development of a new infrastructure. Both, demand and supply will overreach: excess accumulation of physical stock, as well as the leveling off of demand in the innovation-incorporating sectors will accentuate the overexpansion of the capital sector, leads to long-wave downturn, until the newly emerging leading sector starts a new long-wave. Van Duijn's life cycle resembles that of the standard product life cycle: (1) birth/introduction stage (innovation) > (2) growth stage > (3) maturity > (4) saturation > and eventually (5) decline.

Frameworks for the analysis of the dynamics and change in sociopolitical system more prominently reflected in the international political economy literature include Dosi's *technological paradigm* (1984; see also Dosi et al., 1988; 1998) and Freeman and Perez's concept of *technoeconomic paradigm* (1998; see also Freeman and Soete, 1997) as well as Perez's *technological style* (Perez, 1983), later captured in the term *technological paradigm* and finally *technological revolution* (Perez, 2002). Three major evolutionary approaches to technological and institutional change have evolved in the international political economy literature: (1) the flexible specialization approach; (2) the regulation approach; and (3) the neo-Schumpeterian approach.

The Flexible Specialization Approach
The flexible specialization approach conceptually distinguishes between two ideal types of industrial production, mass production and flexible specialization (see Piore and Sabel, 1984; Hirst and Zeitlin, 1991; Zeitlin, 1995; Sabel and Zeitlin, 1997). The argument is based on the assumption that the difference in type of industrial production results in different types of institutions and governance structures. Furthermore, technological choice in this view must be endogenized within a sociocultural process (with the emphasis being on social innovation and to a lesser degree on embodied technology). Piore and Sabel emphasize the distinction between two *ideal types* of industrial production, namely (1) flexible specialization and (2) mass production.

The predominant type of industrial production has a significant impact on the nature of institutions and governance structures. In this view, craft production (flexible specialization) with its emphasis on general-purpose machinery and skilled labor, is characterized by relatively low-fixed capital costs and thus more flexible investment capabilities, promoting specialized small- and medium-sized firms in associated external networks. Mass production relies far more on dedicated machinery and relatively unskilled labor, is characterized by high-fixed costs that sink in investment for a significant time, and fosters large, internally integrated corporations, restricting competition and tending toward oligopolistic markets.

In this perspective, technological choice originates within a sociocultural process. Therefore, the emphasis lies on social innovation and only secondarily on embodied technological innovation. At rare turning points (so-called industrial divides) active choices by the social actors in the direction of either type of production are then manifested in a variety of institutional settings and tend to consolidate into an epoch-making standard favoring either mass production or flexible specialization (Piore and Sabel, 1984). This sociocultural process remains relatively autonomous. Governance structures are shaped through the sociopolitical processes, rather than the result of an environmentally driven selection fitting a technology-induced logic.

Social Structures of Accumulation
(SSA) and Regulationist Schools

Rooted in the neo-Marxist tradition,[30] the social structures of accumulation (SSA) school defines capitalism as a wage-labor system of commodity production for profit. In order to overcome purely Marxist analyses, the SSA school proposes an intermediate or meso-level of analysis (between the capitalist system and the individual worker), historically based, and focusing on the logic of *long swings* and *stages* of capitalism. In this view, macrodynamic analysis should begin with the (external) political-economic environment affecting individual capitalists' possibilities for capital accumulation, consisting of all the institutions that impinge upon the accumulation process, and referred to by SSA scholars as the social structure of accumulation (Kotz et al., 1994).

Similarly rooted in the neo-Marxist tradition, the French regulation school argues that the combination of institutional forms, the wage relation, dynamics of the relations among social groups and classes, regimes of accumulation, and modes of regulation defines the mode of development. Theories of regulation make growth and crisis, along with their spatial and temporal and variability, the central questions of economic analysis and connect these phenomena with the prevailing forms of social organization (Boyer, 1990).

What unites the regulationist schools and the SSA school is a concern for precise definitions, a study of the nature of the changes, and the evolution of those sequences. Also, both schools are very reluctant to accept any cycles or waves underlying these sequences, although long-wave analysis shares many common features. However, the heavy emphasis both (neo-Marxist) schools make on the selection of market-arrangements and institutions mainly through the focus on the social relationship structure of the capitalist system, have left them open to a considerable degree of criticism. While an important subsystem, social relational structures are not the only dynamic coordination processes affecting the evolution of the world system acting as a selection mechanism. A much broader framework can be found in the following approaches, rooted in the neo-Schumpeterian tradition.

Neo-Schumpeterian Approaches

The work by Freeman and his collaborators (Freeman, 1983; 1986; 1987a; 1987b; 1996; Freeman and Perez, 1988; see also Perez, 2002; Freeman and Soete, 1990; 1997; Freeman and Louçã, 2001) has taken these insights further and merged them together in a broad framework. Following Schumpeter's approach, Freeman employs a long-wave framework that addresses not just technological innovation but also other variables outside of the purely economic realm. He and his collaborators identify five "successive industrial revolutions" in the last two and a half centuries, which are the result of clusters of innovation resulting in *New Technology Systems* (Freeman et al., 1982; see also Perez, 1983; 2002).[31] These New Technology Systems encompass not only technological systems, but also institutional, social, and cultural ones.[32]

These works are based on the argument that nonlinear complex models are necessary to address the duality of dynamic stability (around the attractors, in a region bounded by the availability of material resources, labor, or technological capacities) of systems that are nevertheless structurally unstable (inducing switches of regimes emerging from changes in the structure). Therefore, according to Freeman and Louçã (2001, 118–19), evolutionary models must address the central features of real economies: capitalism is unstable and contradictory, but it controls its process of accumulation and reproduction and breeds new developments and new phases of dynamic stability (not to be misunderstood as an equilibrium).

In order to understand this evolutionary process, it is thus necessary to focus on the *coordination processes* amongst its units.[33] These social coordination processes are based on two related sets of variables: (1) the technological, scientific, economic, political, institutional, and cultural subsystems and (2) the semiautonomous variables connecting those subsystems are the crucial causal determination for the business cycles and the long-wave movements in real historical development. They constitute the central focus of Freeman's work.[34]

Especially the work of Perez (1983; 1985; 1986; 2002) is important for the understanding and conceptualization of institutional as well as technological change underlying the model developed in this work. According to Perez, system changes cannot take place except through a combination of profound social, organizational, as well as technical innovations, unfolding over an extended period. Perez thus provides a significant theoretical underpinning of the role of K-waves in the transformation not only of new technology systems but also of the types of long-waves in the world system (through its subsystems) as a whole.[35]

The innovative clustering (both temporally and geographically) observable repeatedly in world history leads to successive patterns of change in technology, in industrial structure, and, indeed, also in the wider economic and social system. Taken together, these changes create a new *technological style* marked by new institutional and social arrangements. As these new technologically induced but then broadened constellations emerge, spread, and ultimately dominate the world economy, they eventually are supplanted by a newly emerging phase (in this view during the second K-wave of an Industrial Revolution phase).

In addition, according to Perez, new products based on the availability of these key factors and some complementary inputs have the potential to stimulate the rise of other new industries (i.e., *carrier branches* such as cotton textiles, steam engines, railways, electrical products, computers, etc.). Their rapid growth and great market potential push the growth of an entire economy through the development of a new infrastructure. This infrastructure provides not only demand (in terms of its physical development) but also facilitates and stimulates the growth of both, carrier and motive branches.

Perez furthermore argues, that the structural transformations arising from these new (lead) industries, services, products, and technologies is accompanied (and in a feedback effect also facilitated) by the combination of organizational innovations needed to design, use, produce, and distribute them. Gradually a *common sense* of managing and organizing emerges as the outgrowth of the selection of institutional innovations that best fit the new sociotechnological environment. Perez calls this new approach to management and organization as *technological style* or alternatively *new technoeconomic paradigm*. Once this new style has grown and demonstrated its effectiveness, according to Perez, it sets in motion dynamics beyond the sociotechnological realm, affecting cultural and political systems, society, government, the general culture as well as the composition of business firms.

Such dramatic processes in the form of a widespread structural and organization change are hardly gradual or smooth. Strong resistance from vested interests born out of the previously dominant technological style and manifested in sociopolitical and well as cultural institutions and norms meets them. The downswing of a long-wave (i.e., the phase in which a new technological style emerges and the existing one has matured) is thus one of great turbulence: rapid growth and profitability of newer firms and industries clashes with slowing growth and declining trends (or stagnation), resulting in sociopolitical conflict over the appropriate regulatory regime. This clash is unevenly distributed over all levels, from individuals, as well as on the group level (i.e., firms, other organizations) as well as on the state level. Some of these agents will be immediately and deeply affected, others after a considerable time lag, and yet others hardly at all.

Perez's concept assumes the need for a "clash" between the old and the new system to bring forward the new technological style as well as political and social realignments.[36] This concept invokes the idea of a punctuated equilibrium of evolutionary development, mainly associated with the work of Gould (2002; see also Gould, 1980; 1989; 1993). Challenging the common interpretations of Darwin's view of evolution as a linear and progressive process, and arguing against the view of evolution as a *ladder* or a *cone*, Gould (1989, 32) instead argues that evolution simply "is adaptation to changing environments, not progress." Rather than gradually emerging, change can be dramatic and sudden, taking the form of "punctuated equilibrium." Stages of relative slow movement and little change are interrupted by sudden and dramatic changes. Such broad exogenous change (i.e., punctuation) will lead to a spur in radically new forms, in other words the clustering of innovation demonstrated by Schumpeter and the neo-Schumpterian school.[37]

Criticism of Evolutionary Approaches

A view often encountered in critiques of structuralist approaches is the accusation that the structures directly determine outcomes, when in fact structures are merely generating impulses and possibilities that may (or may not), given a set of certain conditions, lead to certain results. Harvey (1982) for example uses the analogy to a living organism to make this point. Whereas DNA (deoxyribonucleic acid) can trigger the development of the needed organs for growth, it cannot assure that all the conditions of growth will be in place: for example, malnutrition can stunt the brain, iodine deficiency can cause the thyroid to fail, and so on. Similarly, capitalist relations of production are a generative structure that may, for example, stimulate credit mechanisms that allow for larger investments in production facilities, more extensive infrastructure, greater continuity in sales, which in turn have positive feedback effects on capital accumulation. However, this credit system can malfunction, setting off a financial crisis that interferes with the production process. So, rather than arguing for a deterministic outcome through structure, evolutionary studies instead examine the *evolutionary drive* (Allen and McGlade, 1987; see also Allen and Sanglier, 1981; Allen et al., 1992) inherent in all systems, that creates what Allen (Clark et al.,

1995) has called *possibility space*, or the range of potential options for change open to the system and its parts.

The work of Snooks (1998b), an Australian economist who strongly argues against an evolutionary approach, provides a good example of the criticisms often put forward by historically oriented writers.[38] Although he spends an entire chapter (Snooks, 1998b, Chapter 4) on evolutionary theory and even devotes an entire book to debunk the "myth" of social evolution (Snooks, 1997) he fails to offer an accurate description of evolutionary models. Evolutionary understood in this way includes a linear path-dependency that implies a static development rather than a dynamic one and completely denies or ignores the importance evolutionary theory puts on the interaction between the units and the environments in which these changes take place. Whereas path-dependency certainly is an important feature of evolutionary studies, these paths are dependent on the environment in which they unfold.

The intervals between these great waves, according to this view, were not the outcome of a cyclical process, but the result of a break between strategies, "sometimes exaggerated by exogenous shocks" (Snooks, 1998b, 135). Thus, Snooks sees no evolutionary development from one "strategy" to the next in the conquest > commerce > technological change sequence but mainly a process driven by exogenous factors such as chance:

> This strategic sequence of conquest...cannot be regarded as inevitable or automatic. Had the final exhaustion of the commerce strategy in the mid-eighteenth century not coincided with the exhaustion of the wider neolithic technological paradigm...and the subsequent transition via the Industrial Revolution to the industrial technological paradigm, then the strategic sequence would have been conquest > commerce > conquest, as it often was in ancient history...The strategy chosen depends on the physical and social environment communicated to decision-makers through changing relative factor prices. Clearly, this is not an evolutionary system. (Snooks, 1998b, 135)

This conclusion (see also Snooks, 1996; 1997; 1998a) is puzzling, as it is not at all contradictory to an evolutionary analysis. Large changes of this kind can—and repeatedly have done so in world history—greatly change prior paths of development of system-units by favoring forms formerly disadvantaged over other forms more successfully prior to the change in the environment. Neither does an evolutionary analysis of the globalization process entail a linear development, nor does it promote automatic or inevitable sequences, as Snooks seems to attribute to them.

Here we argue that an evolutionary approach provides us with a better understanding of the implications of certain developments in certain moments of time because it provides us with a roadmap of the dynamics of systems. This implies two other foci in evolutionary approaches: time and multidimensionality (Thompson, 2001a). It is rather obvious, that one cannot engage in evolutionary studies without engaging in historical studies of change. Evolutionary analysis weaves together the life cycle analysis of various elements of the system, taking into account the ecological context in which those cycles unfold, since none of these processes do take place in an isolated spectrum. From this follows that evolutionary studies of globalization cannot be limited to, say, changes in world trade, the change in actors, such as states, or the change in forms of political interactions. The complexity, interactions and feedback effects, interdependencies, and coevolution of subsystems make it necessary for students of the globalization process to look at all these issues (and others) simultaneously (Thompson, 2001a).

Approach and Structure of This Book

The major premise underlying this work is the assumption that the global system process, as many other process involving social units, is essentially an evolutionary complex system process. Therefore, it is necessary to apply a holistic view of the process, making use of more narrow, detailed analyses, focusing on the political, economic, social, and cultural aspects of the globalization process along these core dimensions of globalization. Such a perspective is provided by Modelski's EWP model, which has been applied in Modelski and Thompson's (1996) major contribution to the study of long-term sociopolitical and economic development. Their framework is empirically tested (and testable) and provides us thus with a convincing basis for further exploration of the global system process.

This book argues that the globalization process is a nonstatic and cyclical process with changes (increase) in the level of integration (over time) and the structure of the system. Whereas a repetitive pattern of cyclical change (rise and fall of a sociopolitico leader) does indeed exist, the element of structural change and especially the implications of this structural change on the emerging global system as a whole is a significant and crucial part of this pattern. The rise of the global system can be broken down into several distinct phases and the identification and systemization of these phases and patterns are important for the analysis of the current changes and path-dependent structures of the international political economy.

The main contributions of this study to our understanding of the globalization process are twofold. First, it advances the theoretical tools needed for its analysis. Second, it employs these tools to test the continued relevance of past patterns of global system development given the rise of digital technologies.

The aim of evolutionary studies in general is to overcome this separation and identify the pattern of change that includes events, processes, and structures and thus requires the need to study their interactions and feedbacks over time simultaneously. Based on Modelski (1990; 2000) and more specifically Modelski and Thompson (1996), this work develops a framework that allows to model the development of the world system as a global complex system. It argues that the evolving global system comprises of not a single process, say increased interdependence or trading networks, but of a set of nested processes. In this view, globalization can be separated into four nested sequences of cultural, social, political, and economic elements and defined as the formation of a planetary organizational framework and might best be viewed as a spectrum of four processes.[39]

Here, we concentrate specifically on the process of global political and economic coevolution, always in the broader context of the underlying extended evolutionary model. Therefore, this study contributes further evidence to the argument that the processes of global political evolution and global economic evolution are closely intertwined and consist of long-waves of worldwide commercial and industrial arrangements. These long-waves reflect movements in the world economy process in breadth and scope, both geographically and organizationally. Politically this process resulted in moving *active zones* and a pattern of change in the leadership position of states even at the global level with the ability to shape global organization. Economically the result is a pattern of shifting economic paradigms shaping the long path of growth for the global economy.

The work demonstrates that the current global transformations taking place mark not a disruption of previous developments, but rather a new evolutionary phase consistent with earlier steps in the global system process, unfolding in a similar fashion as previous phases. The impact of digital technologies on the geographical and demographical aspects of the global system is at the empirical center of this study. These technologies have a significant and altering effect on the systemic nature and access to the global system, geographical aspects (e.g., physical formation of social, political, economic, or cultural structures; factors of production; also demographical aspects). Most importantly, however, despite their unique characteristics, these digital technologies still bear the same path-dependent structural features as previous new technologies shaping the global system development. While we can manifest significant change in the nature of spatial aspects (and its implications on the global system), other aspects such as the phenomenon of social and economic clusters are still crucial features of the global system. In other words, whereas we identify major transformations of the global system due to the impact of new, digital technologies, the process of global system development remains unchanged and thus consistently evolutionary in nature.

An important aspect of this new phase in the evolutionary process of the global system is the change of the systemic structure from a predominantly industrial and manufacturing-driven environment to a networking-environment (here referred to as the global digital network environment). However, it also important to notice similarities of the new digital network structure with the networking-structure (here referred to as the global maritime trade network environment) of earlier phases of the evolutionary globalizing process. Whereas in predominantly production-oriented environments of the industrial phase the control of internal flows (and thus the buildup of internal networks) remained crucial, the environments of the earlier maritime trade network and the new digital network are characterized through their great reliance on external networks.

As outlined earlier, this work applies an evolutionary approach to the study of globalization and aims to combine the insights of a variety of research traditions and literatures in order to explain and analyze the currently evolving new structures by putting the changes into a historical context, employing past trajectories to evaluate current changes and develop a framework for the future development of globalization. The first part of the book develops a framework for the analysis of the globalization process, and discusses earlier contributions in the study of the international political economy. This work conceives of the world system as a singular one and, following Modelski (2000), understands globalization as a set of intertwined processes.

This research is based on the notion that an evolutionary approach provides the best analytical framework to analyze past and current developments and develop a model that allows projections for the likely future development of the globalization process and its impact. It will discuss the advantages and disadvantages of this framework in contrast to other existing ones and further develops existing evolutionary approaches with a main focus on the political-economic structure of the globalization process but also on the cultural and social aspects of it. The following chapters provide different forms of empirical evidence for the four major aspects of globalization, namely political, economical, societal, and cultural processes.

Chapter 2 lays out the basic assumptions underlying the analysis provided in this book. In doing so, it first specifically discusses the assumptions underlying questions of agency, complex systems theory, as well as the EWP matrix that builds the fundamental theoretical and empirical basis of our analysis developed here. It then continues to present in greater detail the global complex system matrix we employ in the remainder of the book for our empirical analysis, with a focus on the role of network structure for the development of economic and political leadership within the global system process.

Chapter 3 takes a closer look at leading sectors as drivers of global change. It contrasts the three main network structures that have characterized the evolution of the global world system so far, with a special emphasis on the analogies between the two external network structures, the earlier maritime trade network and the newly evolving digital network, which includes not only digital components but also physical assets, integrated into the digital network (such as production centers, network centers, etc.). It provides a comparison between the maritime trade routes and the modern telecommunication and information technology (IT) networks, their backbone character for the world system networks and an analysis of the structure of these networks. The chapter begins with the identification of new leading sectors of the newly developing technological style. These leading sectors include networking and the information and communication technology complex; biotechnology and life sciences; as well as environmental and new power technologies. Together, they constitute the development of a new commercial and organizational arrangement, here referred to as the informational network economy (iNet economy). It concludes the analysis of this new technological style with a discussion of the special economics of networks including the role of network externalities, protocols and standards within the networks, the role of monopolies, and the increasing importance of questions surrounding intellectual property and patents. It also presents a collection of statistical data, both in numerical and graphical form, and identifies the newly emerging leading sectors that are the basis of a new technological style. Following the example of Modelski and Thompson (1996), it presents growth data of leading sector technologies that match past patterns of the development of K-waves and ultimately long-cycles of socioeconomic leadership in the global system process. In doing so, it enables the location of the geographic distribution of leading sector development. The United States is identified as the emerging new (and old) leading great power in the global system. Thus, the newly developing leading sectors do not only follow in their developmental pattern that of previous leading sectors.

Chapter 4 looks at the impact of the new technological style on the main agents in the inner core of the global system development: states, organizational entrepreneurial structures, and individual agents. It introduces a new framework for the analysis of enterprise structures in external and internal network-based global system environments. First, the Venetian and Genoese trade network systems, the Dutch network systems, the British family business structure, and the U.S. Fordist system are briefly contrasted with one another. This follows a more detailed analysis of the emerging new structure and the emergence of what it is here referred to as informational digital *tissues*.

Chapter 5 focuses on the effects of the structural changes in the global system on the global political system and examines more closely the issue of international conflict, and more specifically the question whether we should expect the number of rivalries in the twenty-first century to rise, to remain steady, or even to fall and why so. This chapter uses the earlier introduced categorization of *contexts* in the form of global long-cycle environments and extends them by identifying long-cycle rivalry environments in which interstate rivalries take place. Combining the framework of the leadership long cycle and the concept of rivalries it identifies global long-cycle environments that determine to a large degree the way rivalries are established, how they "behave," and how they end. It employs both a quantitative analysis of the proposed effects of the different systems, as well as descriptive data analysis. It concludes, that the number of strategic rivalries can be expected to remain relatively low, the number of commercial rivalries, however, is very likely to increase significantly in the not too distant future.

The concluding chapter 6 summarizes the major findings and provides a further speculative outlook in the likely future development of the global world system process.

CHAPTER TWO

An Evolutionary Theory of Globalization

Introduction

Two major flaws characterize most globalization studies: the tendency to interpret current social, economic, and political transformations as unique and unprecedented occurrences in human history as well as a limited focus on the perceived agents of these transformation. The lack of attention not only to a broader historical but also to a structural context is the reason why many existing globalization analyses misrepresent, misunderstand, and misinterpret current transformations. Another limitation concerns their focus on a limited set of actors or processes as a result of their paradigmatic orientation, especially in the International Relations literature. Whereas liberals will focus mostly on group actors such as multinational corporations, and other nongovernmental organizations (NGOs) and intergovernmental organizations as primary actors of transformative change, realists will center their analysis of globalization around states as the core actors, just as Marxist and post-Marxist approaches will favor an analysis primarily based on the unequal structure of the world system. While all these approaches provide useful insights into individual parts of the globalization, they lack a comprehensive, multilayered view of the entire global system process.

Building upon the growing literature of evolutionary social scientific approaches reviewed in the previous chapter, this work puts forward a model that allows us to systematically and empirically test current transformations in a historical context and from an evolutionary perspective. This enables us to overcome the limitations of other paradigms and provides us with the needed flexibility to understand the coevolution of political, social, economic, and cultural processes leading to the changing world we find ourselves in.

Identifying distinct phases in the global system development and demonstrating the resemblance of past commercial networks with emerging digital networks (contrasting them with industrial production systems), this work advances existing evolutionary models and provides new tools for the analysis of our modern day world. It employs these tools to explain how globalization affects the micro- and macro-structures of economies, the dispersion of power in the global world system, and its impact on major global war. The following section discusses the paradigmatic assumptions underlying our analysis and lays out in greater detail the evolutionary model that builds the basis of this study.

Assumptions

One of the major advantages of the use of an evolutionary framework is the ability to facilitate a multitude of approaches as part of a common model. These approaches might have different foci in their inquires and can also be rooted in different (social) scientific traditions. We can combine the insights garnered from evolutionary economics illustrating the problems of competition, innovation, and technological change with findings from evolutionary psychologists and their inquiries into cognitive decision-making processes, and the epistemological insights into scientific progress as steered by repeated trials and error-elimination procedures.

Like Dark (1998), Modelski (2001) suggests the need to view an evolutionary, world politics program as a *human species* approach (i.e., taking into account the individual as the ultimate arbiter and important level of analysis) and viewing world politics as a process of organization and reorganization of the human species as a whole (see also Devezas and Modelski, 2003). In this view, global politics promotes the evolution of new forms of political and social organization (manifested in institutions in a broader sense). As Modelski points out, it is not nations or national societies that evolve, but it is policies, strategies, and institutions, that provide coping mechanisms to a changing environment. Thus, both Modelski and Dark imply the need to focus on the relationship between the initial units of analysis (i.e., *individuals*) to other units of analysis (i.e., *systems* comprising various levels, from small groups of people to the global networks of relationships visible in contemporary world politics), that is, the interaction processes between the various subsystems.

A world system, in this view, is conceived of as the social organization of the human species, viewed as one population. This population exists in either an organized or unorganized state, united by basic institutions such as cities, writing, states (or state systems), technologies, and inter-subsystem networks such as trading networks. This notion of the world system (or super world system) is not too different from the ones proposed by other authors basing their analysis on a world historical basis. It also comprises the basis of the development of what we refer here to as the global complex system.

However, there does exist a wide degree of different identification of the composition of its population (e.g., system identity, the level and existence of interaction between its subsystems, its evolutionary development, etc.). The *singular* perspective is based on the concept of a Kantian *universal history* of mankind and relies to a large degree on the writings of McNeill (1991; 1967; see also Pomper et al., 1995). McNeill argues that the various human cultures have experienced a significant degree of interaction among each other at every stage of their history (and never more so than during great transformations of the world system). This view contrasts with a *plural* perspective, of a number of (more than twenty) separate civilizations pursuing essentially independent careers (Toynbee, 1934; see also Huntington, 1996).

Such a species concept implies interdependence among its members because of its close common origins. Thus, while they constitute important elements of the world system, the mere existence of linkages (such as trade networks, flows of communication or technology, migration, etc.) cannot be the central focus of an evolutionary framework defined in such terms. In order to demonstrate the existence of a single (world) system, however, we need to be able to identify institutions that potentially or actually have species-wide impact and significance. In other words, we need to focus our attention on the issue of agency and social structure in such a world system.[1]

Agency

The framework employed in our model focuses on structural change of global scope, on two principal levels of structure: (1) major institutional change (e.g., the rise of the market economy); and (2) organizational change (e.g., the emergence of global organizations in tandem with the nation state). It also takes into account the role of agents (i.e., the individual, groups, etc.), as it acknowledges that social change is driven by innovations from these agents. The long cycles of global politics (driving global political evolution, see Modelski and Thompson, 1996) and in particular the dynamics of K-waves (both discussed earlier in great length) are prime examples of such innovation agency and its effect on structural change.

Change is necessarily at the heart of an evolutionary model. However, given the scope of the analysis (in terms of levels of analysis, temporal and geographical orientation, as well as areas of inquires), it is impossible to focus on all effective processes with equal weight. Yet, what changes (or rather structures of change) are important? Any generalization must be simplifying while preserving its value as an explanatory tool for a wider range of questions. Thus, the main goal of such an evolutionary model must be to unravel the main change processes that drive the system and provide a point of reference over a multitude of levels of analysis and areas of inquiry.

The global complex system framework proposed here is based on the following *evolutionary logic* that explains the creation of *possibility space* or in other words the potential options for change open to the systems and its parts (see Clark et al., 1995). This evolutionary logic driving the global system process is based on the following set of epistemological assumptions of evolutionary economics, which also build the basis of this work (see Andersen, 1994, 15):

- agents (e.g., individuals, groups, organizations, etc.) can never be "perfectly informed" and thus have to optimize (at best) locally, rather than globally;
- an agent's decision making is (normally) bound to rules, norms, and institutions;
- agents are to some extent able to imitate the rules of other agents (imitation), to learn for themselves (learning), and are able to create novelty (innovation);
- the processes of imitation, learning, and innovation are characterized by significant degrees of cumulativeness and path-dependency (but may interrupted by occasional discontinuities);
- the interactions between the agents take place in situations of disequilibria and result in either successes or failures of commodity variants and method variants as well as of agents; and
- these processes of change are nondeterministic, open-ended, and irreversible.

One critical component in this process of order-structuring is generational cohorts as a key subsystem of collective learning, which includes not only the capacity for adaptation, but also for innovation. Figure 2.1 graphically summarizes the preservation and transmission sequence that make up generational learning in the context of the larger global complex system process. On the basis of innovations originating in new forms of sociotechnological behavior of the first (pre-K-wave) generation of innovators, the following second (K-wave) generation, groomed in this new environment, transforms these innovations into a coherent sociotechnological paradigm based on the predominant leading sectors of this first part of an evolving long cycle. The third (K-wave) generation, while still enjoying the spoils of the high returns on the leadership in this increasingly adapted sociotechnological paradigm remains "stuck" in it, unable to adapt to emerging new, alternative sociotechnological innovations, and allowing new socioeconomic innovations to arise in alternative and geographically separate clusters. Rather, this generation builds on the success of the previous leading sector innovations (and

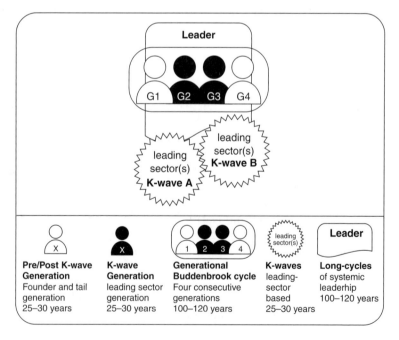

Figure 2.1   Generational Leadership Long Cycle

K-wave), employing the *carrier technologies* of the previous K-wave to develop a second set of leading sectors utilizing this technological infrastructure (see for a discussion of this sequence, e.g., Hall and Preston, 1988). This leaves the fourth (post K-wave) generation witnessing the rise of challengers to this established order and eventually the emergence of a new sociotechnological paradigm often outside its domain of control.

Sociopolitical and economic change seen in this light is always a historical, dynamic process involving the use as well as the creation of resources (as diverse as simple objects, techniques, and knowledge, or even entire social organizations). It is important to note that first, this evolutionary logic is driven, as noted above, by human agency. Second, however, this agency takes place and is embedded in a social and technological context. In other words, whereas the driving logic (the need for optimization of tasks as part of human agency) of this process remains the same, its context changes, constituting a *social learning algorithm* of evolutionary change that is at work at all levels of the global system process (from the individual to the change of the global system as a whole). This process can be understood as self-organization, a feature of emerging order without an external (or internal) orderer.

The arguments developed here rest on the assumption that thinking of the global system as a complex, self-organizing (mostly) social system allows us to step outside the constraints of the study of the institutions and processes that "produce" globalization[2] and instead enables us to analyze the underlying logic that drives, curtails, and reinforces these processes. Here we offer a framework that combines complex system analysis with an evolutionary theory of global system development. We therefore discuss the issue of complex systems in greater detail in the following section.

Complex Systems

Complex systems analysis offers us insights into the way systems establish *order* without a singular or initial ordering entity. Yet an order (or developmental logic) does emerge in such systems, based on feedbacks resulting from trial and error, adaptation, and system-wide learning, resulting in a system that features *self-organization* (for an excellent summary of the relevant literature, see Devezas and Corredine, 2002; 2001; see also Auyang, 1998).[3]

Here we argue, that globalization understood as a long-term social system (involving economic, political, and cultural processes) forming a global social world resembles such an emerging ordered system without a single orderer. No single power, whether an empire, state, or any other unit, has transformed the human social world over the past 500 or 1,000 years (or any other period) into the world we experience today. Rather, globalization thus understood has been the result of a number of reoccurring processes of trial and error, adaptation, system-wide learning and thus: a complex system based on the principle of self-organization.

Employing the general lessons derived from the study of complex systems, it is possible to identify the general (or meta) developmental logic of the long-term globalization process while at the same time leaving room for divergent schools of explanations on the factors that influence important order-structuring factors such as learning or adaptation in the system.

All sociopolitical forms derive ultimately from human agency. We therefore need to focus on the link between the individual, the structure, and the system, in other words decision making (whether constrained or freely made). However, with increased sociopolitical complexity comes greater need to manage information. This, so Dark (1998, 121–22), leads to the following internal dynamic: complex sociopolitical systems will unavoidably increase in complexity, with the consequence of a higher rate of decision making. As a result, the need for more efficient information processing rises, in order to respond to decision-making requirements produced by its own degree of complexity and the structures it employs. This *complexity dynamic* not only increases at first the opportunity for sociopolitical innovation to occur, but also the potential instability (see also Devezas and Corredine, 2002; 2001; Devezas and Modelski, 2003).

As the complexity of the system increases, the range of possible decisions promoting further growth will decrease. In other words, an increasingly complex system will become increasingly *path-dependent and* lose its adaptive flexibility. Unhindered hypercoherent *option-narrowing* will eventually precipitate collapse, which will be a sudden occurrence. In other words, sociopolitical complexity will rise to the point of *edge of chaos*.

Dark (1998) and Devezas and his collaborators (Devezas and Corredine, 2001; 2002; Devezas and Modelski, 2003) discuss the relationship between innovation and systemic development as being based on information processing and decision making and prompted by inter-action, generating a successional model of endogenous sociopolitical change, where the successor system might follow a similar trajectory to that of the system which it replaces, collapsing itself in time and being replaced by yet another sociopolitical system. Progression takes place stochastically through trial and error, random nonaverage fluctuations. In this process, the system *self-organizes* and learns to configure and reconfigure itself toward increasing efficiency and in this manner with each iteration it performs some activity better. Each stage corresponds to a given structure that encompasses previous self-organization, learning, and the current limitations (Devezas and Corredine, 2001, 22).

Figure 2.2 captures this process schematically. The arrow indicates the increases and decreases in complexity and the rate of information processing over time. The dotted boxes graphically represent the types of networks predominant in the relationship structures of agents.

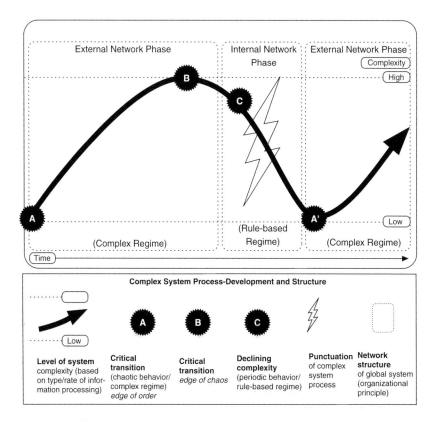

Figure 2.2   Global Complex Systems—Schematic

External networks represent relationship structures typical of chaotic behavior as the process of self-organization is in the exploratory phase. Internal networks represent organizational structures that represent and reinforce established modes of behavior.

At point A the emerging system has a wide range of *possibility space* (understood as the potential options for change open to the system and its parts, options for change, latent in any situation, may or may not be chosen by actors, and may exist only within a limited range of possibilities, see Clark et al., 1995). This period is characterized by a high rate of *chaos* or *chaotic behavior* (i.e., a system not based on learned rules of behavior) and thus a system that follows the logic of a *complex regime* (i.e., without explicit rules). Over time, the complexity of interactions increases significantly and thus the need for an increase in capacity for information processing. The best way agents can cope with this need is through the establishment of rules of behavior (learning) for parts of their interactions to increase their rate of information processing efficacy.

As a result, the possibility space within the system decreases further and further, until it reaches the point (point B in figure 2.2) of a *critical transition* or the *edge of chaos* (i.e., when the system will enter decline mode and the rate of change will begin to slow down and eventually decline). However, the more complex the system becomes–that is, the less chaotic it is and the narrower the possibility space becomes—the more liable it is to collapse. This collapse takes place in the form of a selection of the *fittest* (i.e., the variety best able to adapt to the environmental needs) organizational and institutional variance, as the possibility space for change begins to close and the system becomes hypercoherent.

Point C in figure 2.2 represents this point. It marks the beginning of the punctuation of the complex system process in which a transition to a decline mode (in terms of complexity) will occur. At this point, the old system is in a state of *hypercoherence*[4] and is marked by a largely rule-based decision-making form of adaptation to the needs of coping with a high level of complexity. The enhanced path-dependent trajectory of this system has switched to a rule-based regime, and a dynamic of decreasing complexity. In other words, it has established a specific mode of system-organization with established rules that agents facilitate in their tasks. While maximizing the efficiency of the need for information processing and adaptation to this newly formed environment, other factors (such as new social and technological innovations) continue to transform the global system as a whole and thus soon provide a new need for adaptation that renders the previous optimized system less effective. The need for new forms of adaptation to the global system-induced challenges to agents emerges (point *A'* in the figure 2.2) and the previous rule-based regime is being transformed into yet another complex regime.

Change in complex systems, whether in the direction of greater or lesser complexity, produce a trajectory or *historical path*, limiting future options and thus becoming path-dependent in this way. As a consequence, complex systems as the ones observed here—the nested global economic, political, social, and cultural processes that form the world system we identify as the global complex system—exhibit a tendency to self-organization, that is the endogenous ordering into hierarchies giving them a system-wide form. Thus, these complex systems exhibit *morphogenesis* (i.e., the development of an organism or of some part of one, as it changes as a species) based on processes that are partly independent of agency, although they require agents to both initiate them and enact them (understood as the potential options for change open to the system and its parts, see Dark, 1998, 106). The way the interrelationships between parts of the systems are established (i.e., the structure of the networks) thus becomes crucial for our understanding of the dynamics of these coevolving structures.[5]

Figure 2.2 graphs the relationship between the rate of changes in system complexity and predominant system network structure. As complex sociopolitical systems will inhibit an internal dynamic that leads them to increase in complexity, the rate of decision making must, necessarily, keep pace with this increased complexity (in order to remain efficient in terms of its need for task-optimization). In our model, during the rise in complexity of a system, it is characterized by an external network structure. During point *B* (in figure 2.2), the point of hypercoherence or the *edge of chaos*, the network structure switches its orientation to an internal focus, leading to point *C*, or *punctuation* (i.e., selection of macro organizational and institutional model in the global community process and transition to a rule-based regime system) of the global complex system process as a whole. As pointed out earlier, decision making (and thus the process of agency) does not take place in an isolated environment but rather in a strongly contextual one. Agency affects not only the environment in which it unfolds, but is also formed by it. Thus, it is important not only to focus on the agents (on a multitude of levels) but also to identify the contextual environment in which this agency takes place.

After having discussed these general assumptions, we now turn to the theoretical foundations of the model put forward here.

EWP Framework

The model we develop in this book is based on the empirical and methodological contributions made by Modelski and Thompson (1996; see also Thompson, 2000a). This allows us to gain the advantage of the insights of a long-term empirical study without the need to replicate their work rather complementing it theoretically as well as empirically. Regarding the study of the relationship between innovation, systemic change, and the emergence of successive waves of different long cycles.

The aim of the EWP framework is to provide a way to look at the "big picture" of the development of the human species, yielding a periodization of world history as a phased evolution of the world system. It also aims to serve as a way of ordering the growth of the world economy, of world politics, and of the accretion of a world community, allowing for the past millennium a finer-grained depiction of structural change and the global level, with an explicit role for agents of change, leading sectors, and world powers.

The four mechanisms driving the evolutionary globalization process and constituting a social learning algorithm are

- variety creation (very broadly: cultural process);
- cooperation or segregation (social process);
- selection (political process); and
- preservation and transmission (economic process).

As such a synthesis has to be an ordered one, all world system processes have a time-structure that allows for successive optimizations of these mechanisms in a formal-logical *learning sequence* (following the numbered sequence above). World system processes in this view, then, are seen as nested and synchronized (i.e., coevolving) four-phased temporal learning experiments driven by common evolutionary logic inherent in all these processes.

The main foci of the EWP framework lie on:

- the identification of the broad context of world system change;
- the eras of world system history, which reflect the conventional periodization of the development of the human community;
- world social, political, and economic change (represented as a sequence of major institutional changes of particular subsystems of the world system); and

- global change in the modern era (identified as organizational change driven by the emergence of and changing world power leadership as well as the leading sectors of the global economy).

Modelski and Thompson's leadership long-cycle approach (Modelski, 1978; 1987a; 1987b; Modelski and Thompson, 1988; 1996; Thompson, 1990; 2000a; Rasler and Thompson, 1989; 1994) assumes a significant relationship between these various subsystems (cultural, political, economic, social) and aims to identify—and empirically test—the long cycles of economic and political systems. Modelski and Thompson assume that the change of socioeconomic paradigms (and political and economic leadership) is a continuous and interconnected process. Thus, we would expect to find not only disruptive but also continuing elements in those changing paradigms.

Technology plays an important role in the development of these interconnected processes, as they mark a path-dependency, limiting the possibility space available to the actors (on all levels). These path-dependencies can be crucial for explaining the rise and fall of successive system leaders and their impact on the functioning of the world's political economy:

> Viewed horizontally, the technological mainsprings of each system leader seem as if they were orphans without mother or father. Viewed longitudinally, we can trace their roots across multiple K-waves and periods of economic leads. The longitudinal view should not detract from the revolutionary transformations in technology that have occurred. Discontinuities are definitely there, but so are ample elements of continuity. (Thompson, 2000a, 210–11)

Those technological styles (or paradigms, see also the earlier discussion on neo-Schumpeterian approaches) last a certain amount of time until a new form of economic organization better placed to help the actors adapt to a changed environment replaces them. Rather than focusing on the analysis of whether certain sociopolitical systems follow a certain growth and decline pattern (as for example Dark does in his work), Modelski and Thompson build their analysis on existing neo-Schumpeterian evolutionary frameworks of analysis but broaden existing approaches, mainly based in economics, to include a wider set of factors and broader and more long-term oriented world-historic perspective.

From a leadership long-cycle perspective we can identify a continuous cycle of a process of emerging leadership of a single unit of an expanding and increasingly globalizing world system, followed by its decline and simultaneous rise of a set of challengers. After a clash between the declining and rising units (i.e., subsystems), the new system rises to establish its leadership role within the entire system, establishing a new way in which the overall system is composed and changes to some degree its parts interact with each other. Their analysis is based in large parts on the following assumptions (Modelski and Thompson, 1996; see also Thompson, 2000a).

Assumption: Leading Sectors. As in every modern economy, growth in the different sectors varies and some sectors show extraordinary growth due to transformations caused by innovations in those sections of the economy. Rostow (1978) has noted two basic types of technological innovations: (1) small, incremental improvements to prevailing practices; or (2) major, often radical technological breakthroughs, which are most likely to create leading sectors. These sectors lead the rest of the economy with their high growth, spillover effects and high profits. Investment in those areas grows, costs go down, and new markets are developed.

Assumption: The Clustering of Leading Sectors. The next assumption presumes that the arrival of leading sectors appears in clusters of related innovations, or in mutations on older ways of doing things. Some of those mutations emerge as selections by firms as the result of doing things in a very different or revolutionary new way, which quickly evolve as the new standard. This new technology is used as a new means of transportation for important commodities and often combined with the development of new industries and other types of economic activities. The average lifecycle of leading sectors is about two generations or fifty years in duration (Yakovets, 1994).

Assumption: Lead Economies. Just as leading sectors drive and shape the entirety of economies, so do lead economies shape the world economy. These lead economies are the center of the clustering of innovations and new technology. For a finite time, those leading economies can profit from their monopoly rents that come with their pioneering economic activities. However, as other economies eventually are able to catch up (through imitation, diffusion, and increased competition), and while the innovations of the lead economy become the new economic paradigm, those innovation rents begin to decrease. Therefore, the status of the economic leadership of states is dependent on the ability of the leader to keep ahead of the competition and continue to innovate and dominate the markets or even create new ones.

Assumption: Hierarchy and Mobility on the Technological Gradient. The role of innovations is especially important in regard to a state's role (exemplified in its economy) in the world system. The more a state is able to concentrate innovations in its territory or sphere of influence the more likely it is to become the leading economy of the world economy and the higher it can be placed on the world economy's technological gradient (see Galbraith, 1989) and thus the world system. Just as in a domestic economy, some states have managed to find themselves production niches closely following the leading economies engaged in relatively sophisticated production on a fairly narrow scale, yet others tend to end with lower quality technology. It is important, though, to note the mobility up and down the gradient. Every domestic economy is driven by competition. In the same manner, the possible development of lower ranking economies upward the (technological) gradient accelerates the development of the world economy. This makes it unlikely, that a lead economy will infinitely keep its leading role.

Assumption: The Historical Sequence of Lead Economies. Modelski and Thompson (1996) identify a few countries that over the past 1,000 years have almost monopolized inventions and innovation for a certain length of time, whereas other economies can be found further down the technological gradient. The ascendant and descendent of those lead economies in the world economic system are captured in K-waves of innovation (see earlier discussion) and long cycles, periods of variable political and military leadership reflecting the rise and later decline of a single world power over a time-period of approximately 100 years. Long cycles, as previously discussed in much detail, are

> instances of structural change because they are processes that in recent centuries have periodically rearranged the structure of global political arrangements and given rise to the phenomenon of world powers. (Modelski and Thompson, 1996, 7)

Long cycles are marked by the following sequence: the development of certain revolutionary inventions (such as the creation of new trade routes or the steam engine) leading to a number of key innovations, which tend to be clustered, both geographically and in time. These innovations in turn give rise to the development of leading sectors, enabling states to develop the leading system (i.e., as most visibly manifested in respective national economies) in the economic sphere of the world system (i.e., the world economy). The more an actor is able to concentrate innovations in its territory or sphere of influence the more likely it is to become the leading economy of the world economy and the higher it can be placed on the world economy's technological gradient (see Galbraith, 1989). The most successful actors in the modern system have turned out to be states (see previous discussion, also Spruyt, 1994). The development of leading sectors also enables actors (i.e., in our case most often states) to monopolize this sector for a given time and enjoy extraordinary monopolist rents. This, in turn, enables them to establish and confirm their military predominance.

Modelski and Thompson identify nine sequentially related sets of innovation-based leadership between 930 and 1973 CE: two Chinese (Northern and Southern Sung), two Italian (Genoese and Venetian), one Portuguese, one Dutch, two British (Britain I and II) and, so far, one American (see table 2.1).

Table 2.1 shows the hypothesized relationship between the long-cycle sequence of world powers, K-waves, and the leading sectors of those K-waves. To reiterate, K-waves represent the process of structural change in the global economy. Unlike the Schumpeterian business cycles, the K-waves in this context center not on prices or macroeconomic quantities, but on leading commercial and industrial sectors on a global scale, in the economies originating them (Modelski and Thompson, 1996, 9). Each of the long cycles or world power episodes is tied to a specific pair of K-waves. As each K-wave lasts about fifty–sixty years (see discussion above), each leadership long cycles lasts around 100 years. This relationship is also graphically captured in figure 2.1.

The second column of table 2.1 shows the global lead industries of each respective K-wave. For example, the domination of Baltic and Atlantic trade routes (in K11) turned out to be the leading driving force behind the Dutch economy and its basis to rise to global leadership (LC6). The first K-wave of each long-cycle pair stretches the first two phases of every long cycle (agenda setting and coalition building). The second K-wave covers the last two long-cycle phases (macrodecision and execution).

A holistic framework such as the EWP matrix requires necessarily a world historical context from the very start of the analysis. Several such accounts of world history exist.[6] McNeill's (1991) early contribution

Table 2.1 Hypothesized Relationship between Learning Long Cycle, K-waves, Global Lead Industries, and Network Phases (All Years CE)

Learning Long Cycle, K-wave	Global Lead Industries	Predicted Takeoff	Predicted High-growth
LC1 North Sung			
K1	Printing and paper industry	930–960	960–990
K2	National market, Champa rice, iron casting, paper currency	990–1030	1030–1060
LC2 South Sung			
K3	Administration reform	1060–1090	1090–1120
K4	Maritime trade, navigation (compass)	1120–1160	1160–1190
Commercial Maritime Network System/External			
LC3 Genoa			
K5	Champagne fairs	1190–1220	1220–1250
K6	Black Sea/Atlantic trade	1250–1280	1280–1300
LC4 Venice			
K7	Galley fleets	1300–1320	1320–1355
K8	Pepper	1355–1385	1385–1420
LC5 Portuguese			
K9	Guinea gold	1430–1460	1460–1494
K10	Indian pepper	1492–1516	1516–1540
LC6 Dutch			
K11	Baltic and Atlantic trades	1540–1560	1560–1580
K12	Eastern trades	1580–1609	1609–1640
LC7 Britain I			
K13	Amerasian trade (esp. sugar)	1640–1660	1660–1688
K14	Amerasian trade	1688–1713	1713–1740

Continued

Table 2.1 Continued

Learning Long Cycle, K-wave	Global Lead Industries	Predicted Takeoff	Predicted High-growth
Industrial production System/Internal			
LC8 Britain II			
K15	Cotton, iron	1740–1763	1763–1792
K16	Railroads, steam	1792–1815	1815–1850
LC9 United States I			
K17	Steel, chemicals, electric power	1850–1873	1873–1914
K18	Motor vehicles, aviation, electronics	1914–1945	1945–1973
Digital Commercial Network System/External			
LC10 United States II			
K19	ICT, Biotechnology	1973–2000	2000–2030
K20	Networking, (?)	2030–?	?–?

Source: Adapted from Thompson (2000a, 11) and own additions.

can be regarded as a standard specification of epochal divisions over the past several millennia, conforming under the familiar headings of ancient, classical, and modern.[7] In this account, the political organization of the world system has now passed through three stages (see table 2.2). Whereas in the first stage, starting well before 3000 BCE, the Middle East epitomized the center of world development, the second stage featured no such dominant center but was rather characterized by what McNeill terms "cultural balance" in which "each of the four major civilizations developed more or less freely along its own lines" (McNeill, 1991, 253). The third stage–here the 1500 CE periodization represents a wide consensus in the literature–witnesses the emergence of a new dominant theater with the rise of western dominant influence on the development of the global world system (see table 2.2).

McNeill's periodization has not gone unchallenged.[8] We refer here to two competing influential periodizations, as provided by Wallerstein (1974) and more recently Buzan and Little (2000) and compare them to Modelski's periodization of phases of the world system process

Table 2.2 Phases of World System Evolution, McNeill, Wallerstein, Buzan and Little, and Modelski

Conventional Designations	World Historical Eras, Categories and Dates (McNeill) Period	World Historical Eras, Categories and Dates (Wallerstein) Period	World Historical Eras, Categories and Dates (Buzan and Little) Period	Phases of World Systems Process (Modelski) Period
	Precivilization 60000–3500 BCE	Minisystems 60000–6000 BCE	Pre-international systems 60000–3500 BCE	
Ancient	Civilizations (interlinked since 1700 BCE) Middle Eastern dominance 3500–500 BCE	World empires 6000–1500 CE	Interlinked, multiple international systems 3500 BCE–1500 CE	Learning-infrastructural 3400–1200 BCE
Classical	Eurasian cultural balance 500 BCE–1500 CE	—	—	Community-building 1200 BCE–930 CE
Modern	Global civilization Western dominance 1500 CE–worldwide cosmopolitanism	World Economy 1500 CE–global market	Global, single international system 1500–1989 CE (?)	Collective (species-wide) organization 930–3000 CE
Postmodern			Postmodern two-worlds international system 1989 CE–(?)	Stabilization 3000–5000 CE

Sources: McNeill (2005), Wallerstein (1974), Buzan and Little (2000), Modelski (2000).

(see table 2.2). In contrast to McNeill, Wallerstein (1974; 1989) views the ancient world as characterized by autonomous and self-sufficient *minisystems* formed by hunter-gatherer bands. With the rise of agriculture, however, seen by Wallerstein as one of the most important developments in world history, these systems become absorbed into more developed economic systems of largely autonomous world empires that dominated the globe until the emergence of a "true" world economy, starting its rise in 1500 CE.

Buzan and Little (2000) mark 60000–40000 BCE as the beginning of pre–international systems with the emergence of long-distance exchange networks among hunter-gatherer bands, with sedentary, hierarchical units, displaying some signs of characteristic *international* behavior, beginning to emerge between 10000–6000 BCE. For Buzan and Little, the year 3500 BCE marks the erosion and absorption of pre–international systems and the emergence of durable, state-like units, and economic and full international systems, such as the rise of empires and international economic systems linking international systems in the Middle East and South Asia around 2000 BCE, and the emergence of an Eurasian economic international system around 500 BCE. Buzan and Little also identify 1500 CE as the starting date for the emergence of a new dominant unit, the modern state, a leap in interaction with ocean-going sailing ships leading to the making of nearly global international system by the linkage of Eurasia and the Americas (and, more arguably, the beginnings of capitalism and industrialism). Whereas McNeill (1991, 806–7) in his account only hints somewhat vaguely at the long-term vision of a possible fourth stage through the establishment of "a world-wide cosmopolitanism," Buzan and Little see the (possible) establishment of a "postmodern" era, in which the defining features of the international system are determined more by economic processes than military-political ones, starting in 1989 CE.

Modelski (2000, 33) argues, that the launching of the world system as a major institutional complex for the human species should be regarded as an "epochal innovation." He proposes that the world system has now nearly passed through three (out of four) evolutionary phases (see table 2.3):

- the learning-infrastructural phase (laying down the cultural base for the entire process > cultural possibility space);
- the community-building phase (foundational for enterprises of large-scale cooperation > social structure of cooperation);

- the collective organization phase (selection of worldwide organization > political collective selection);
- the consolidation phase (marking the reinforcement and replication of the system), the last epoch in this process, emerges only far in the future (possibly around 3000 CE) and to some degree corresponds with the idea of a *postmodern* phase as found as well in McNeill's as well as Buzan and Little's approach.

The first phase (see table 2.3) creates the possibility space for building the world system, and does so by drawing upon the resources developed in the preceding era (i.e., the advancements in the gradual emergence of

Table 2.3 Extended Evolutionary World Politics Model of Process of Globalization, 930–2080 CE

Starting (~Year)	Global System Process	Global Community Process	Global Political Evolution (Long Cycles)	Global Economic Evolution	Network Structure
930	preconditions	*Experiments* Reforming	*Eurasian Transition* North Sung South Sung	*Sung Breakthrough*	buildup
1190		Republican	Genoa Venice	*Commercial/ Nautical Revolution*	external
1430	global nucleus	Calvinist	*Atlantic Europe* Portugal Dutch Republic	*Oceanic Trade*	external
1640		Liberal	Britain I Britain II	*Industrial Takeoff*	transition internal
1850	global organization	*Democracy* Democratic groundwork	*Atlantic-Pacific* United States	*Information* K17 Electric, steel K18 Electronics *Digital* K19 Informational industries K20 Digital Network (?)	internal transition external external (?)
2080					

Source: Adapted from Modelski (2000) with own additions.

agriculture). This possibility space is created by means of city-building, which, gradually spreading, exemplify the major nodes in a system of interconnected (and partly preexisting) networks of intercontinental proportions. Cities, in this view, are the *hardware*, whereas the invention of writing (i.e., recording and storing information, as well as organizing social life both to the past and to the future) provides the *software* of the infrastructure of world system learning (see e.g., Hobart and Schiffman, 1998).

Developing on the basis of this learning-infrastructural foundation, the next phase of the world system goes on to community-building on a scale beyond tribe and city, innovating the structures of wider cooperation (i.e., system-exchanges) implicit in the world system. Modelski argues that such cooperation is fostered during this phase to a large degree by religion, forming the basis for solidarity and cooperation, enhancing education and communication, large-scale political organization, and long-distance trade.

Given this possibility space, competitive pressures of several kinds (e.g., economic competition, political conflict, ideological confrontation, scholarly debates) select the organizational forms with the best fit for the merging complexities of the world system, setting up the stage for the next and third phase of organizational selection. Here, the collective management of human affairs becomes the operative problem at both the newly developed national, as well as the equally new global levels.

Eventually, such collective organization (the phase the world system is currently still undergoing) finally gives way to adaptation (i.e., stabilization comprising an adaptive adjustment to the macrosystem environment), eventually preparing the stage for another process of evolutionary developments.

According to this pattern, a world system is indeed a long-term process, not created overnight, nor even a millennium. Rather, it is an epochal learning project for an entire species, the human race, that takes up a typical evolutionary pattern: after a slow start, gathering up a core of cooperation, and after some trials and errors, reaching the possibility of a punctuation at the selection phase of this process. This selection stage of collective (species-wide) organization has been underway for the past millennium, starting approximately a 1,000 years ago with the emergence of the first long cycle of a *modern* (in Modelski's terminology "fine-structured") world system emerging in China. It marks therefore the beginning of the globalization process as understood in this study.

It is during this period that the above-discussed organizational revolution starts to produce the prominent forms of collective (species-wide) action dominating our modern globalized world: nation-states, armies and navies, corporate business entities, universities as well as other NGOs and intergovernmental organizations, and so on. In other words, the growing network of global institutions all giving substance to what we perceive to be today's global system (Modelski, 2000, 36).

The Global Complex System Matrix

We base our study on the empirical analysis of the development of the modern era system (i.e., the current global organization phase in the world system process) of Modelski and Thompson (1996). The model developed here extends their focus, taking into account the dynamic processes of the evolutionary drive of the world system process understood as a complex global system (as discussed above) and the different dynamics as they unfold in the various stages of its development and their corresponding network structures.

As argued earlier, the world system, especially in its more developed form beginning with the collective organization phase, is formed not only by political, but also economic, social, and cultural (i.e., learning) dynamic structures driven by the process of evolutionary logic as outlined earlier. Globalization (i.e., the global complex system process) thus understood constitutes a set of coevolving processes:

- global economic evolution (of trading systems and world markets);
- global political evolution (of nation-state systems, world power competitions, and international organizations);
- democratization (i.e., the formation of a potential democratic community[9]); and
- the creation of a world public opinion[10] (through media and learning processes).

What is inherent to these processes is the evolutionary logic that drives them on all levels, from the individual/group to the global system process as a whole (see previous discussion). As a result of this evolutionary logic the ultimate agents of these processes are individuals and organizations sponsoring and advancing innovation that results in the strengthening of the global layers of interactions. Assuming these structures to be evolutionary they consequently must be identified as nested in nature, but proceeding on different time scales, we consequently must identify them as nested, coevolving structures (see Modelski, 2000, 37–43). Thus, to understand the development of globalization, we need to trace the coevolution of all these structures over time. The EWP matrix (based on the EWP framework discussed in the previous section) offers a particularly effective framework to do so.

The EWP matrix, summarized in table 2.4, enables us to analytically separate the overall process or world system evolution into four distinct, but interrelated, evolutionary processes whose temporal dimensions stand to each other in a relations of 1:2:4:8, each in turn composed of four phases. The seemingly perplexing regularity of this sequence can is the result of the generation-based agency we discussed earlier. The process of human innovation, processes of trial and error, adaptation, and institutionalization ultimately form the basis of the evolutionary logic of all sequences, both micro and macro.

The evolutionary world economic process, which establishes the major modes of organization of production and exchange in agriculture, mining, industry, and other economic activities, unfolds over a period of approximately 1,000 years (separated into four phases driven by the evolutionary logic discussed earlier). During this process, periods of productive development and surge of new technologies (enabling new *technological styles*), such as bronze or iron, alternate with others that expand networks of interchange, pioneering new trade routes, and thus enabling the broader disperse of innovations. A major shift (in terms of the general mode of organization) has taken place during the emergence of the modern era with a shift from a command economy toward a market structure, slowly covering the entire globe.

This process is nested in the process in what Modelski terms the active zone process, defined as the spatial locus of innovation the world system, representing the political process driving the world system evolution, and unfolding over a period of roughly two thousand years (again separated into four phases). As innovations (and their diffusion) are at the heart of social and cultural innovation, (subsystem-) environments that foster the generation of variety (or greater possibility space) become the active zones of the world system. The political structures of these active zones are characterized by zones of autonomous entities, such as state systems, and intermediate political networks (rather than by empires, that tend to attract the attention of historians). So far, we can distinguish three such periods, focusing upon a broad geopolitical zone (Middle East, Eurasia, Oceanic zones) that shows regional movement in each of

Table 2.4 Evolutionary World Politics Matrix, Modern Era, 930–2230 CE

Agenda Setting (Global Problems) PERIODS	Coalition Building	Macrodecision (Major Warfare/ Global War)	Execution After 1500 CE: World Power Next Challenger	Long Cycle
A. Eurasian Transition (preconditions)				
930 information	960 Song founded	990 war with Liao	1020 Northern Sung	LC1
1060 integration	1090 reform parties	1120 war with China	1060 Southern Sung	LC2
1190 world empire (?)	1220 Mongol confederacy	1250 Mongols conquer China	1280 Genoa Mongol Empire	LC3
1300 trade	1320 shipping links	1350 Genoa, Mongols routed	1380 Venice Timur	LC4
B. Atlantic Europe (global nucleus)				
1430 discovery	1460 Burgundy-Habsburg connection	1494 wars of Italy and Indian Ocean	1516 Portugal *Spain*	LC5
1540 integration	1560 Calvinist International	1580 Dutch-Spanish wars	1609 Dutch Republic *France*	LC6
1640 political framework	1660 Anglo-Dutch alliance	1688 war of Grand Alliance	1714 Britain I *France*	LC7
1740 industrial revolution	1760 trading community (global organization)	1792 Revolutionary/ Napoleonic wars	1815 Britain II *Germany*	LC8
C. Atlantic-Pacific				
1850 knowledge revolution	1878 Anglo-American special relationship	1914 World Wars I and II	1945 United States I *China (?) India (?)*	LC9

Continued

Table 2.4   Continued

Agenda Setting (Global Problems) PERIODS	Coalition Building	Macrodecision (Major Warfare/ Global War)	Execution After 1500 CE: World Power Next Challenger	Long Cycle
1973 integration	2000 democratic transition	2026	2050 United States II (?)	LC10
2080 political framework	2110	2140	2170 China (?), India (?)	LC11
2200 digital network (?)	2230	2260	2300	LC12

Source: Based on Modelski (2001), Modelski and Thompson (1996), Thompson (2000a), and own additions.

Notes: All years CE. LC (number) denotes long cycle of global politics.

its (four) phases, lasting approximately 500 years, and reflected in standard eras of world history accounts (see table 2.4).

   The political process is again nested in a process of world socialization, lasting about one millennium, and representing major phases of concentration of metropolitan power and the formation of (often) dependent hinterlands, that from time to time organize themselves to effect a system leveling (or dependency reversal). This process reflects the enormous and persistent tensions that the pressures for innovation (as a consequence of the various coevolutionary processes) and the demands for equality (the operative condition of every human community) produce. So far, we can identify two such periods, here noted as a crude structured world dominated by empires of major civilizations and characterized by attacks on this dominance in order to share in (or at times replace it completely), and a fine-structured world, resulting in a more complex reaction-counteraction process of the center/hinterland tension. In this environment, the tension fosters more complex forms of mutation, for example in organizational structures, enabling and encouraging more forms of cooperative arrangements, as for example demonstrated in Spruyt's analysis of the evolution of the state system. All these processes are imbedded in the macro world system process, providing the overall (and fundamentally cultural) context in which the other processes take place.

   From this follows that the phase of the global world system process that comes closest to the most common perception of globalization (i.e., the idea of an interdependent single world) has begun to develop around 930 CE, developing the preconditions (global system process) through variation generation and experiments during the buildup of a global community (global community process). This process is driven by the dynamics of the nested political and economic processes, decreasing the possibility space during each phase and moving the globalization process forward through the trial-and-error process that is part of the evolutionary drive logic and the punctuations that mark the transition to a rule-based regime, that marks a selection of the fittest organizational and institutional setting (i.e., the setting that provides the best adaptive strategy and the highest degree of information processing efficacy).

Reform movements in Sung China (ca. 1100 CE), and republican experiments in the city-states of Northern Italy (ca. 1300 CE) are such variations and trials, leading to the creation of a global nucleus (see table 2.4) in the clustering of various forms of republican organization and a liberal-maritime alliance. These in turn provided the basis of a future democratic community starting in the nineteenth century (see table 2.4). The economic process nested within this political variation creation (and their coevolution) has been examined in great detail in Modelski and Thompson (1996, 37–43). The methodological and conceptual tools developed in this application of the EWP matrix mark the basis of the model employed and further developed here.

It is important to keep in mind that all these nested sequences of coevolving process constitute subsystems in their own right—not independent of the larger global complex system (macro-) process, but self-contained to a certain degree. They all, however, follow the same evolutionary logic and thus can be understood as part of the larger (global) complex system as well as complex subsystems in their own right.

Figure 2.3 graphically summarizes our model of the modern era globalization process based on the previously discussed assumptions. In our model (following the schematic representation in figures 2.1 and 2.2), the global complex system process reaches the *edge of chaos* (i.e., hypercoherence) during the industrial takeoff phase (roughly around the time from 1740–1970 CE with the center in 1850 CE), resulting in the end of the experimental phase in the global community process and starting with the democratic phase as its selected fittest global social system (see tables 2.3 and 2.4). The relationship and interdependence between the level of system complexity, network structure, and global community process development (and its nested, coevolving global political and economic processes) is most visibly reflected in this instance of systemic collapse and renewal. The punctuation of the

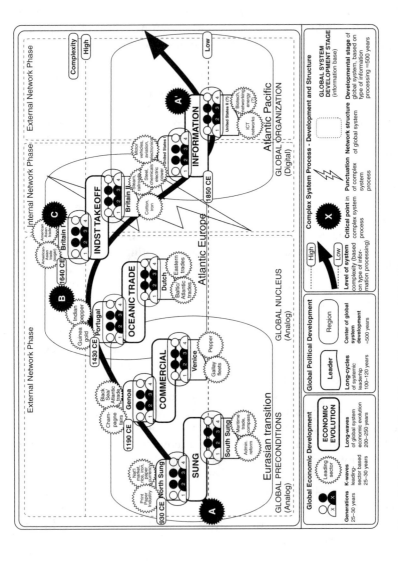

Figure 2.3 Complex Global System Development Matrix

Source: Leadership long-cycle schema based on Modelski and Thompson, 1996.

system is graphically represented by the lightning-flash symbol in the center of the internal network phase. During this punctuation, the network structure changes from an external structure to an internal one (starting around the middle of the eighteenth century with the close of the oceanic trade phase), manifesting the selected organizational and institutional structures, until a new phase of evolutionary dynamic sets in the late twentieth century during the information phase (see tables 2.3 and 2.4 and figure 2.3).

The outer (rounded) bold box marks the boundaries of the start of the global complex system process (the *modern era* in the EWP matrix), starting around 930 CE (see for timing tables 2.2 and 2.3), and thus ultimately the globalization process as it is understood here. Nested within this process, the fine-lined, left-and-right-rounded boxes mark the global political process as it unfolded so far (Eurasian transition, Atlantic Europe, Atlantic Pacific). In its most inner core, the bold-lined boxes represent the global economic process elements (Sung, Commercial, Oceanic trade, Industrial takeoff, Information, Digital) that form the long-waves of socioeconomic adaptation strategies (i.e., economic evolution). This inner core, as discussed earlier, is itself driven by the trial-and-error learning experiments that are part of the K-wave-based lead-economy and leading sector dynamic.

The arrow forming a wave in the inside of the global system process indicates the level of complexity of the global system developmental process. The top and bottom dotted lines, labeled high and low indicate the level of complexity. Graphically representing the complex system development as laid out in our model, the level of complexity starts out relatively low and rises steadily until it reaches the edge of chaos (i.e., hypercoherence, point *B*) and eventually begins its decline phase (point *C*). The dotted boxes mark the respective network structures of the global complex system process (i.e., the modern era in the EWP matrix). During the rise of the level of complexity (i.e., during the time of a complex regime, compare figure 2.2), the system is characterized by external network structures. Beginning with the reach of a hypercoherent state (the *edge of chaos*, switching to periodic behavior and a rule-based regime), the global system development is marked by internal network structures for the duration of the decline of complexity and the switch back to a complex regime (at the *edge of order*). This point also marks the return to external network structures as the main structural component of the global system.

On the basis of the theoretical model graphically represented in figure 2.2, figure 2.3 reflects the development of the empirically traced relationship between the coevolution of the economic, political process of globalization based on the EWP framework (see table 2.3, describing the leading sectors of each economic K-wave and the lead economies of each political long cycle and long-wave of global world system leadership in the larger context of the development of the global system as a complex system.

The roots of the three main network systems in existence so far can be found in the evolutionary trials (as part of the evolutionary development of variety creation) during the two Chinese-dominated periods emerging roughly in 900 CE. Especially the Southern Sung period during the eleventh and twelfth century provides many elements that are similar to those present in the following maritime network system. Given their lineage and the larger evolutionary pattern of development, however, it is analytically more sensible to regard them as evolutionary trials rather than part of the first external network system.

Network Structures

The empirical observation of the network structure of the complex systems becomes a crucial element of any global system study based on the concept developed here. But how might we identify the types and changes of structure? How do we tell a *complex regime* from a *rule-based* one? The network structure is best identified in the observation of the inner core of the nested global system process, the process of global economic evolution. It is here, where the level of agency and the interaction between the system elements remains most visible and where the evolutionary drive propelling the process (as discussed above) is easiest to dissect. We therefore turn our attention now to these two nested processes.[11]

Both, Arrighi (1994; see also Arrighi et al., 1999) and Modelski and Thompson (1996) emphasize the critical division between territorially driven and (commercial) capitalist power structures. Where Modelski and Thompson argue for the continuation of this divide, Arrighi argues that Britain was able to fuse both structures, while during the following U.S. leadership a slight diffusion back toward a more capitalist orientation took place. Shifting the focus on the structure of networks can combine both perspectives and the division between socioeconomic interaction modes dominated by internal or external networks rather than a focus on capitalism and territorialism.

The difference between the leading sectors in the maritime commercial (or digital commercial) and the industrial systems is, as

Sen (1984) points out, the dual strategic significance for military self-sufficiency and national economic independence held to provide the rationale for the desire to acquire this group of industries. Great powers in this system try to establish internal rather than external networks, in order to, as Rosecrance puts it, "excel in all economic functions, from mining and agriculture to production and distribution" (Rosecrance, 1999, 6).

This emphasis on self-sufficiency and national economic independence characterizing the industrial environment stands in stark contrast to the necessities of an external network– and service-based environment as found in the maritime commercial and the digital commercial systems. Of course, this does not imply that trade dies away or renders unimportant. Far from it, trade remains an important factor in rivalries amongst nation states. It is, however, not the central basis of the leading sectors as in the maritime trade network system. The actors have at this stage established a wide set of *rules of engagement* that help them to cope with the environmental pressures and established those rules in norms and institutions.

This distinction is compatible with both, Modelski and Thompson's and Arrighi's model, especially in regard to Arrighi's discussion of the newly emerging systemic mode. Thus, along the lines of socioeconomic interaction modes, we can identify four distinct phases in the evolution of the global complex system:

- a mixed territorial/maritime phase of evolutionary exploration (Sung China);
- a maritime commercial phase (Genoa, Venice, Portugal, Dutch, Britain I);
- an industrial phase (Britain II, United States I); and
- the emerging digital commercial phase (United States II).

All four phases can be divided into two metasystems (as a result of leading sectors and the different socioeconomic interaction modes). Systemic leadership is either characterized by the dominance of internal (territorial; industrial) or their external (maritime commercial; digital commercial) network structure.

The *commercial maritime system* is in large part characterized by its emphasis on external networks of production and other value-adding processes (including division of labor) and the importance of flows within the world economic system. The leading sectors in this phase are predominately service- or flow-oriented. In Modelski and Thompson's

(1996) account these leading sectors includes the Champagne fairs and Genoan Atlantic trade and trade in the Black Sea during long-cycle three (under Genoan leadership), Romanian (Black Sea) and Levantine galley fleets during long-cycle four (Venice), the control over Guinean gold and Indian pepper (Portugal), Baltic, Atlantic, and later Asian trade control of the Dutch, and Amerasian trade control of the British during long-cycles five, six, and seven respectively.[12]

The *industrial system*, by contrast, has its main center located in internal production networks. The leading sectors in this mode are commonly associated with our understanding of *industrialization*—Britain's dominance of cotton and iron production, and later railroads and steam during the eighth long-cycle, followed by the American leadership in steel, chemicals, electric power, motor vehicles, aviation, and electronics during the ninth long-cycle in Modelski and Thompson's count.

This study is mainly concerned with the argument that we are currently witnessing the rise of a new broader socioeconomic interaction mode, here referred to as the digital commercial system owing to its strong resemblance of the earlier maritime commercial mode, especially in terms of its strong emphasis on external networks in the world economy. This system, however, denotes a new, unique interaction mode as a result of its inclusion of digital information as a new commodity and its much more sophisticated integration of production networks.

So far, we have witnessed one occurrence of systemic leadership and systemic transition (as understood in our model), where the existing leader (Britain) was aiming to maintain and strengthen its leadership and are currently experiencing a similar transition. It is this co-occurrence of systemic leadership and systemic transition that allows for the development of what we term the *Phoenix cycle* of renewed systemic leadership, discussed in greater detail in the following section.

Economic and Political Leadership Transitions

One of the main characteristics of systemic leadership transitions in most treatments of the subject is the seeming inability of the existing leader to establish a similar leadership position in a newly emerging and structurally different commercial and organizational arrangement. This shift in the geographical and political location of power has been explained as the outcome of the leader's experience of success in the current setting, creating an entrenched institutional setting (in a broader sense) that proves adaptive in defending its turf but less so in fostering the rise of new leading sectors. Our previous discussion of the process of generational learning and institutionalization that occurs within a long cycle (i.e., a complex sub-subsystem of the larger complex global system) that leads first to the establishment of systemic leadership and ultimately its demise (see figure 2.1) has captured this process in detail. However, the case of Britain's continued leadership over an extended period of time (and separate long cycles) has shown that this is not always the case.

In divergent but broadly compatible forms acknowledged by both, Arrighi (1994, Chapter 1), and Modelski and Thompson (1996, 71–72), we have witnessed a phenomenon we term the *Phoenix cycle* (for a more extensive discussion, see Rennstich, 2004). In instances where the systemic chaos is not only driven by the regular process of systemic leadership crisis and breakdown, but also coincides with a systemic crisis (and eventual breakdown), the existing leader can defend its systemic leadership position in the transforming global complex system. This shift is triggered by a change in the major socioeconomic interaction mode of the system, leading to a system metastructure shift. Only if the *parallel* development of a new cluster of innovations and the rise of new leading sectors can occur *within* its domain, the existing leader is able to extend its leadership position (see figure 2.4). So far only one such instance occurred, namely Britain's ability to defend her leadership position during the eighteenth and nineteenth century.

The process leading to the development of a systemic chaos as depicted in figure 2.4 is normally driven by the clustering of innovations outside the leader's realm (both in a geographical and technological sense), paired with the technological diffusion of core leading sectors technologies (again in a broader sense) and the emergence of new leading sectors. This triggers the centralization of new systemic capabilities in one or two newly new centers, eventually causing the rise of a challenger (or challengers) to the existing systemic leader.

Figure 2.4 graphically summarizes the impact of the transition from an internal to an external network structure (or vice versa) is important not only in terms of the change in the general structure of the new commercial and organizational arrangement but also for the location of the new global leadership.

As shown by a number of authors from various research traditions,[13] past success often entails the very ingredients for future demise. Whereas continuous innovation still takes place within the existing leader, adaptation to a newly emerging, changed environment (as a result of the rise

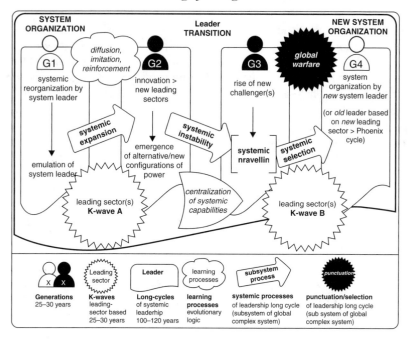

Figure 2.4   System Leadership Transition

of new leading sectors elsewhere) proves very hard for a society that can (and usually does) become locked into economic practices and institutions that in the past proved so successful. Powerful vested interests resist change, especially in circumstances when a nation is so powerful as to institutionalize its commercial and organizational arrangement on a global level, a change dire needed however to maintain its leadership. Gilpin (1996, 34) thus concludes that "a national system of political economy most 'fit' and efficient in one era of technology and market demand is very likely to be 'unfit' in a succeeding age of new technologies and new demands."

The cyclical emergence of new commercial and organizational arrangements as shown by Modelski and Thompson, Freeman, and others entails such an environmental change. Thus, system leadership transitions usually involve the shift from one leader to another due to what Boswell (1999, 265) calls the "advantage of backwardness." If we view the emergence of new commercial and organizational arrangements as a largely endogenous process, its emergence also causes an environmental shift that can be understood as an exogenous factor as well. However, the response of the existing leader to this change is largely driven by endogenous factors again.

The same can be said for the change from one socioeconomic interaction mode to another, setting off the transition from an internal network structure system to an external network–structured one (and vice versa). It is the set of leading sectors (an endogenous process) that causes (over time) the change of the systemic structure and thus a change of the meaning of *fitness* in the evolutionary selection process. The shift from one socioeconomic interaction mode to another, then, is also both an endogenous but to some degree also an exogenous process.

As pointed out earlier, we have witnessed in the past that under certain circumstances the old systemic leader is capable of maintaining its leadership position. Instead of withering away, these leaders are able to renew themselves, like a phoenix arising from the ashes of its declining old leadership position. Several reasons account for this phenomenon.

Unhindered Rise of a Second Center of Systemic Capability

One of the main obstacles for the existing systemic leader, as discussed earlier, is the entrenchment of its own success. The institutionalization of its successful strategies creates powerful incentives to "remain on course." These institutions prove not only to be *sticky* (in the sense that they outlast their original intent and aim to preserve the existing rather than adapt to change) but also defensive. New ways of doing things are thus less likely to emerge where such entrenched resistance exists, a phenomenon we can observe both on the micro- (e.g., individuals and firms) and macrolevel (e.g., states).

A crucial factor we have to take into account is the kind of global problems (as identified by Modelski and Thompson, 1996) the actors are trying to address. In a systemic environment that is driven by the same socioeconomic mode, these *problematiques* will be more closely connected than in a situation in which the power strategy is based on two different capitalistic modes. It is important to keep in mind that the two network systems (internal or external) are reflective of different power strategies. The rise of a new commercial and organizational arrangement reflective of a different network environment provides less of a threat to the existing entrenched order and thus will be met with less resistance.

We know that the emergence of new leading sectors is a path-dependent process. Leading sectors of a new network environment are products of a different path than that of the existing commercial and organizational arrangement (despite their coexistence and often to some degree parallel historical trajectories). Originating in different power-logics, they can be quite complimentary in their development as for example Nef (1934) has demonstrated so eloquently. For Nef (1934, 22)

> the commercial revolution ... had a continuous influence reaching back to the Reformation upon industrial technology and the scale of mining and manufacturing. But so, in turn, the progress of industry had continuously stimulated in a variety of ways the progress of commerce. The former was quite as "revolutionary" as the latter, and quite as directly responsible for the Industrial Revolution.

This compatibility or even complimentary character is to a large degree the result of not only the difference in power strategies but also the difference in commercial strategies. External network arrangements tend to be service-oriented (in today's economic language) whereas internal network systems tend to be production-focused (see also earlier discussion on the difference between internal and network systems above). Thus, in the same manner as the commercial supremacy of Britain helped her to build up her industrial strength, the U.S. informational technologies and digital networking capabilities are based upon the strength of her earlier strengths in an internal network environment (i.e., microelectronics, mass production, aerospace technologies, and semiconductor production). As a result, the parallel development of two centers of systemic capabilities (one rooted in the external network power logic, the other in the internal network power) is not only possible but also complimentary and self-reinforcing.

Outward versus Inward Investment Flows

Another argument regularly put forward for the likely rise of a new hegemon is the notion of capital searching for new and better opportunities (i.e., higher returns as a result of new monopoly rents). For reasons laid out above, these opportunities tend to arise outside of the institutionalized setting of the existing leader. This process usually leads to the flow of capital from the existing leader to the rising new one. However, in the case of a systemic network structure shift and thus the possible development of dual centers within the same "containers of power" (Giddens, 1987), these capital flows can (as in the case of Britain during its transition from a external network to an internal network power logic) remain internal and simply shift from one center to another but within the realms of the existing leader.

We are witnessing a similar process currently in the case of the United States where not only internal flows are switching from an internal network power logic to opportunities arising in the emerging external network power logic driven enterprises but also external flows are significant for the rise of this new commercial and organizational arrangement. This does not only take place in the form of venture capital financing, but also to a much larger degree in a shift from established institutions of capital distribution to newer forms. Put differently, in the case of a combined hegemonic and systemic breakdown, the old hegemonic leader reemerges out of the ashes of its crumbling old commercial and organizational arrangement fed by the internal flows of its monetary capital (as well as that from others) and as a result is able to develop dual centers of systemic capability. The current codevelopment of dual financial centers within the United States may serve as an example of the continuation of this process.

Advantage of Old Leadership Position
Thus, instead of a disadvantage, the declining leader can use its existing institutional setting and capabilities not only to defend its predominance of the current commercial and organizational arrangement. At the same time it can facilitate these capabilities to its advantage by channeling the increasingly liquid capital flows not outside, but rather to the parallel developing new center of systemic capability. The ashes of its hegemonic decline prove to be fruitful in nurturing the rising new center. This does not prevent the rise of challengers. And it does not preclude the further unraveling of the existing order leading to a hegemonic breakdown. However, the unique circumstances of a combined systemic and hegemonic transition provide the old leader with a significant head start in the development of its capabilities in the newly emerging system for reasons laid out above.

In the following chapters, we shall argue in greater detail the impact of the system network structure on the nested economic and political processes, contrasting the three main phases laid out in our model, the commercial maritime network phase (external), the industrial production phase (internal), and the emerging digital commercial network phase, with a main focus on the last. In the following section, we will discuss the argument that the impact of the transition from an internal to an external network structure (or vice versa) is important not only in terms of the change in the general structure of the new commercial and organizational arrangement but also for the location of the new global leadership.

Following our model, we would expect a return to an external network structure, first visible in the global economic evolution process, in the currently evolving new phase. The nineteenth K-wave, then, should be characterized in its leading sectors by this external network structure just as earlier K-waves developing in such a context did before. As the remainder of this study will show, this is indeed the case.

Network Trajectories—Previous Enterprise Systems

With a focus on the development of leading sectors as part of our model of the development of the global complex system, we can identify three distinct network systems so far:

- the commercial maritime system;
- the industrial production system; and
- the emerging new digital commercial system.

As we have argued earlier, both, the commercial maritime and the digital commercial system are characterized by their emphasis on external network relations, whereas the industrial production phase (as an outgrow of the punctuation of the global complex system process in our model) is primarily reinforcing existing organizational and institutional patterns through internal networks. A great deal of literature (discussed previously) has shed light on the organizational and institutional as well as the agency patterns in the previous two systems and needs only a brief reflection in this context. Before we go on to discuss the newly emerging digital commercial system, we briefly review the organizational structures of leading sectors in the economic global system process as it has evolved so far.

External Network Systems: Commercial Maritime System

As laid out in our model (see figure 2.2), we have argued that globalization as we experience it today has emerged roughly around 900 CE with the rise of complex and diversified organizations, including nation-states (Spruyt, 1994), as well as more complex business enterprises

(Moore and Lewis, 1999) and the formation of networks of organization at the global level. As Modelski and Thompson (1996, 145) have argued, these organizations could not have taken place without significant innovation in the fields of information processing (e.g., printing; oceanic communication), military technology (e.g., gunpowder weapons), and economic innovations (e.g., media of exchange).

Sung China is widely regarded as the geographic space where this inception (or emergence of *preconditions* in our model) has occurred (e.g., Reischauer et al., 1960; Elvin, 1973; McNeill, 1982; Jones, 1988; Gernet, 1996; Modelski and Thompson, 1996). Sung China's four consecutive K-waves (see table 2.1) and their accompanying leading sectors provided the basis of the emergence of the commercial maritime system, the first instance of an expanding, global commercial system characterized by its reliance on external network structures.

Asia, however, was not to be the center of the development of the emerging commercial maritime system. Although Asia remained a crucial and integral part of the emerging commercial maritime system, it was due to the dynamics of leading sectors developing in Europe that the system fully evolved (for a discussion on the dynamics behind this development, see Modelski and Thompson, 1996, Chapter 9).[14]

The commercial maritime system (or in other words a pattern of interregional and oceanic trade, focused upon the institutions of the world market) has evolved in several steps so far. Emerging from the Venetian and Genoese trade network systems, over the Dutch commercial network, to the British trading system, each long-wave (of coevolving two economic K-waves and one political leadership cycle) in the Modelski and Thompson (1996) sense, has witnessed an increase in complexity and geographical widening of the system as a whole.[15]

Genoese and Venetian Trade Network System

By the tenth to eleventh century, after medieval Europe emerged from its *dark ages*, European development and population growth was expanding again, and with it demand for luxury goods (such as spices and silk) and the ability to pay for them (Lopez, 1987). Trade, or as Bernard (1976, 274) put it, "links with the outside world more over, the very essence of commerce" was to provide the dynamics behind Europe's progress. Similar to the earlier bursts of innovation in Sung China (see table 2.1), this pattern repeated itself, however, now centered on the Genoese and later Venetian trading operations. Thus, the ultimate focus of leading sector trade for the European subsystem was the reordering of the flow of high value goods from Asia to Europe.

Whereas Genoa led in the development and expansion of the commercial space, namely the development of the Champagne fairs as a major trading platforms for the trade-network nodes, shifting later to an emphasis on the Black Sea trade, Venetian maritime advancements manifested and institutionalized this system, developing into a dominating commercial network node in the expanding world trade system (see Modelski and Thompson, 1996, Chapter 10).

Portuguese Trading Network System

In a further widening of the maritime-based network (over the less efficient land-based networks), the Portuguese were able to eliminate a layer in the distribution of goods, establishing a presence on the coast of West Africa, gaining direct access to the sources of gold in the interior. This turned out to be a crucial innovation in a century when all of Europe was suffering from a shortage of precious metal, creating in its turn a new leading sector.

Even more important was the further expansion of the maritime network (opened by the voyage of Vasco da Gama, 1497–1499) into a truly oceanic trading network. Not only did it link the rich and complex maritime trade of Asia with the Atlantic, enabling a (relatively short-lived) monopoly over the extremely lucrative spice trade (pepper in particular) and thus in its wake a creation of a new leading sector, but also did it initiate the movement of the hub of European intercontinental trade away from the Mediterranean to the Atlantic (see Modelski and Thompson, 1996, Chapter 6).

Dutch and British Network Systems

As Curtin (1984, 179) has pointed out, maritime trade, in particular, has constituted the leading sector of commercial growth in the world economy, perhaps as early as the ninth century, but certainly between the fifteenth and nineteenth centuries. The emergence of The Netherlands' trading supremacy was founded on its strong role in intra- and intercontinental trade. It rooted in its success in the transportation of bulky, low-priced commodities (e.g., grain, herring, salt, and timber) to and from the Baltic region. This enabled early Dutch specialization in inexpensive but numerous freight-carrying ships and the development of an efficient shipbuilding industry.

As a consequence, the Dutch were able to move into, and in the end control, the richer trades of Europe and the world namely with the capturing of the Eastern trade routes after 1580 (Israel, 1989). Together with its function as a distribution center of Spanish-American silver to the Northern European area (including Germany, and the British Isles, see Braudel, 1972), The Netherlands developed into the central node of the world trading network, both in terms of trading activity and finance.

Again we witness the now familiar pattern of the establishment of a superior network infrastructure, followed by an extension of this advantage in the advancement of superior organizational capital accumulating[16] and enterprise structures. The development of cheap yet reliable freight-carrying ships such as the *fluyt* and the buildup of an efficient shipbuilding industry clearly fit our description of technological innovations that enable the creation of extraordinary growth and the evolvement of a new leading sector. Only through the clustering of various innovations in sixteenth-century Netherlands were the Dutch able to create their expertise and advantage in transportation necessary for the generation of their trade routes and shipping dominance. It is thus in seventeenth-century Netherlands where we can find the first and most successful example of a worldwide corporate business organization, the Dutch joint-stock chartered companies.

A prime example of the manifestation of this organizational form was the Dutch East Indies Company, or in its original name, the Verenigde Oost-Indische Compagnie (VOC), established in 1602 (for a discussion of the VOC as an institutional innovation, see Steensgaard, 1982; see also Steensgaard, 1974; 1981; see also Meilink-Roelofsz, 1986).[17] Together with the West-Indische Compagnie (WIC), founded in 1621, the Dutch not only dominated important parts of the Eastern trades, but also pioneered the Atlantic triangular trade, linking European manufacturing communities, with slave-procuring communities of Africa, and plantation communities of the Americas (Emmer, 1981; Unger, 1982; Postma, 1990).[18]

This predominant position as a center node of the worldwide trade network was successfully contested by England, after its trade had went a substantial transformation (Richardson, 1987, esp. Chapters 4–5). As Scammell (1989, 232) notes, the major commercial focus for England after 1650 was largely on oceanic expansion, "with the impetus coming from a surge in Asian and American imports and the simultaneous growth of a lively market in the Americas (North, South, and Caribbean) for domestic exports and reexports."

Another crucial factor became the advancement of production techniques, transforming former luxury goods into mass consumed goods by substantially lowering their price of production and thus increasing availability to a larger market (Mintz, 1985; see also Davis, 1954). Thus, Britain was able to extend the Dutch trading network, not only in size but, maybe even more importantly, in depth (i.e., vertical integration/ control of production), accompanied by the increasing importance of London as the major financial node of world capital.

Transition to Internal Network System

It was during Britain's expansion of the trade network, that increasingly advanced production technologies became a crucial factor in the advancement of the system (Pomeranz and Topik, 1999, Chapter 7; Davis, 1954). The new production techniques affected the operating scale and sophistication of the British economy as a whole in regards to the development of critical organizational and institutional advancements as well as availability of capital. This led the transition from a focus on a (externally oriented) commercial network node to a focus on internal network nodes advancing production on a relatively large scale, what is now widely known as the *industrial revolution*. This transition can best be viewed in the structural change of textile manufacturing under British organization.[19]

In the seventeenth and eighteenth century, production factories set up by companies such as the English East India Company on the (Eastern) outer realms of the British (and more generally, European) controlled network of the world economy spanned entire continents and included a sophisticated system of financing and what in today's terms would be referred to as outsourcing of production to external, independent contractors. In the latter half of the eighteenth and nineteenth century, this production system was replaced by factories organized around individual firms in the center of a less externally oriented, but more vertically integrated world economy with its center in Britain.[20]

Starting out in the beginning of the seventeenth century by concentrating on Surat and Bantam, it had by the 1680s moved on to Madras and Coromandel, and, by the end of the century, began to expand its operations in Bengal, Bihar, and Orissa, centralizing as much as it could of the Indian supply of piece goods through its use of the *dadni* (i.e., contract) system (see e.g., Sinha, 1953; also Sinha, 1956, esp. Chapter 2; Chaudhuri, 1978, Chapters. 11–12; Raychaudhuri, 1982; Barr, 1991).[21] The networks of procurement and supervision set up by the English far surpassed in volume and density those of their predecessors and competitors, characterized by a simultaneous commercial and territorial expansion (Arrighi et al., 1999, 108).

This marked a significant change from a preference of control over trading nodes to a preference for greater control of the production of key commodities, which involved necessarily greater territorial control as well. Thus, following a practice introduced in Bengal in the 1750s, the *dadni* system, which relied to a great degree on outsourcing the production to contracting partners, was replaced by an agency system. Under this new system, each of the company's factories integrated (i.e., *insourced*) production in specialized centers, so-called arangs (Raychaudhuri, 1982, 282).

The resulting higher level of centralized integration foreshadowed the transition from an external network–based production structure to an internal one. By the end of the eighteenth century, the regime of factories abroad was "an outdated and disintegrating regime... a regime in crisis" out of which a "new regime of factories at home" emerged, "which, by the 1830s, had effectively supplanted the regime of factories abroad" (Barr, 1991, 82). This new regime was characterized by the concentration of production and major reorganization of labor and other factors of production, in new spatial arrangements, and with an increasing emphasis on mechanization of production.[22] Thus, as Cameron (1989, 196) points out,

> the industrial superiority Great Britain had achieved by the first quarter of the nineteenth century rested on technological advances in two major industries, cotton textiles and iron manufacturing, supported by an extensive use if coal as an industrial fuel and by the growing use of the steam engine as a source of mechanical power.

This is reflected in the kind of leadings sectors dominating the sixteenth K-wave in the count of the complex global system framework. Network infrastructure now concentrated primarily on internal networks, that is network under direct territorial (rather than the more open maritime) control of states, such as canals and railway networks (Buzan and Little, 2000, 281–84).

Internal Network Systems:
Industrial Production Systems

As laid out in our complex global system model (see figure 2.3), several processes culminated around the punctuation (i.e., "catastrophic change") of the global system process in 1850 CE, within roughly a 200-plus year window. This punctuation acted as a global selection process, not only on the global community process level, with selection of democratic states as the predominant form in the international system, but also the transition on the global political evolution level, with a transition from the Atlantic European to the Atlantic-Pacific region as the main theater of development.

In addition, on the global economic evolution level, we can witness the transition from the industrial takeoff phase to an "information" based phase (discussed in greater detail further on). As argued earlier, this punctuation and macroselection phase is characterized by its predominance of internal network structures in the global system, with important implications for the development of the most-inner nested global economic evolution process, as reflected in the change in leading sectors.

With the increasing move of governments to internalize economic activity, reflecting a shift from a strictly *capitalist logic of power* to a more *territorialist logic* (see Arrighi, 1994, Chapter 1), the emphasis of major powers, and those aspiring to such a position, shifted from an aim to be move from being the "trade-store of the world" to the "workshop of the world." Global network extension now comprised territorial rather than maritime coverage, combining the two and creating in turn an ever more complex global system.

To be sure, the distinction between the two systems remains often blurred, especially in the case of Britain's two long cycles of leadership in the global system development. Our point is not to argue for the replacement of external networks and their commercial structure by internal networks, but rather a shift in significance of one over the other in terms of its importance for the evolutionary logic driving the systems development.

The United States, with its geographic advantages, vast natural resources, and ready supply of labor, was emerging in the middle of the nineteenth century as the most successful challenger to British industrial predominance (Pomeranz and Topik, 1999, 237–38). The *American System of Manufacturing*, a label provided by their British competitors, was based on a system of interchangeability of parts and provided the basis for America's success in mass-production industrialization, later termed *Fordism*. Developed at the Springfield Armory in Springfield, Massachusetts in the early 1800s, the system of interchangeability of parts marked a crucial innovation in the production process (Hounshell, 1984; see also Rosenberg, 1976; Smith, 1977).

Again we witness the same pattern of innovation surge, leading to the development of new leading sectors, creating a U.S. lead in steel production, chemicals, and electricity and later motor-vehicle production, creation of an aviation industry, and dominance in electronics and mass production of consumer goods (see table 2.1). Also, during the twentieth century we can witness yet another shift of the center of the main worldwide capital center, this time to other side of the Atlantic, centered in New York City. The U.S. leadership resulted in a never-before experienced level of integration and internalization, a phenomenon widely studied so we do not need to reiterate it here in greater length.[23]

Conclusion

As we have shown earlier, the variety creation (i.e., cultural) and cooperation/segregation (i.e., social) processes are very long-term (macro) processes, whereas the selection (i.e., political) and especially preservation/transmission (i.e., economic) processes as the nested inner drivers of globalization are in comparison more short-term in duration. In order to provide more empirical foundation and to test the global complex framework developed here, we focus our study on these two processes, without losing the larger context in which they operate and unfold out of sight. Although Modelski and Thompson as well as others have provided detailed accounts of the historical unfolding of the two coevolving inner-core processes of economic and political global evolution, few such studies exist that focus on the very recent development of these processes (Berry, 1991; Hall and Preston, 1988; Freeman and Louçã, 2001).

In the following chapters, we shall provide an analysis of the continued development of the evolutionary global system process. Applying the complex global system framework and focusing on the development of the new technological style, here identified as the informational network (iNet) economy, we trace the shift from an internal to an external network structure and the implications of these processes for the coevolving political process (in terms of global leadership transition and major power rivalry development). The focus of this study will be on the two inner cores of these nested processes (i.e., the ones moving the fastest), the preservation and transmission (economic) and selection (political) processes.

The following chapter provides a brief discussion of past leading sectors and implications of their emergence and development for the currently unfolding new leading sectors, and focuses on the continuation of K-waves in the global world system, the timing of the growth spurts, and continued national clustering of leading sector development.

CHAPTER THREE
─────────────────────

Drivers of Global Change—Leading Sectors of the Informational Network Economy

In the previous chapter, we have laid out a framework that allows us to analyze globalization (i.e., the global complex system process) as a set of nested and synchronized (i.e., coevolving) four-phased temporal learning experiments. Given the time frames in which these processes unfold, the focus of our analysis that aims to answer the question if this process is indeed continuing or not, has to be on the two inner cores of the global system development: At its very center, the global complex system framework places (1) the global economic evolution process (of trading systems and world markets). This process is cyclically related to (2) the global political evolution process (of nation-state systems, world power competitions, and international organizations). The complex global system framework proposes the following evolutionary logic of globalization, constituting a *social learning algorithm*:

1. variety creation (very broadly: cultural process);
2. cooperation or segregation (social process);
3. selection (political process); and
4. preservation and transmission (economic process).

The previous chapter has examined the historical unfolding of the global complex system so far. The question approached here is whether we can apply a long-cycle model to current developments or whether they are merely phenomena of the past. In other words, do long cycles continue to exist in a digitally networked, highly globalized world economy?

As noted earlier, we expect technological styles to be limited in duration, as innovations and learning enable alternative and fitter styles to emerge elsewhere. Following our model, the timing of the most recent long cycle would imply that we are currently in such a transitional phase. Table 2.1 list this observed and expected sequence, graphically represented in figure 2.4, which show that we would expect the development of a new cyclical phase at around 1970[1] with a predicted high-growth period of the successful actors in this new economic environment to emerge around 2000.

A good model should not only be able to construct long cycles in hindsight but also to match with predicted developments utilizing empirical evidence. Modelski and Thompson (1996, esp. Chapter 11) have done this successfully with past long cycles and opened the discussion about the emerging nineteenth K-wave. Here we shall present further empirical evidence that support the efficacy of the EWP model.

As laid out in the previous chapter, our model provides a strong theoretical basis for the prediction of a continuation of the global system development process beyond the industrialization phase, into our current day and possibly also the foreseeable future. To do so, we now present in the following section growth data for the first phase of the hypothesized newly emerging technological style and long-cycle process (from around 1970 to 2000) of now-established leading sector technologies that match past patterns of the developmental long cycle. In doing so, we should also be able to locate the geographic distribution of leading sector development.

The empirical evidence presented here lends further support to our model and allows us to identify the United States as the emerging new (and old) leading great power in the global system. Thus, the newly developing leading sectors do not only follow in their developmental pattern that of previous leading sectors. They are also located, as was the case in Britain, in the territory of the existing global system leader, as we would expect from our Phoenix cycle hypothesis.

Transition to an External Network System:
The Rise of a Digital Commercial System

With the increasingly apparent demise and unraveling of the Fordist model of the dominance of internal networks beginning the 1970s, the punctuation of the global system seemed to have given birth to a new phase of extending external network dominance. This holds true not only on the macro or world-systemic level but also on less aggregated levels as well. As Best (2001) has demonstrated in his study of production systems this process has entailed a move "from a closed network to a business model organized around the leadership and design dynamic internally and open systems externally" (Best, 2001, 54).

Whereas the Japanese manufacturing mastery in the 1970s and 1980s of internal network management through a closed network model of production provided the basis of increasing share over existing leading sector production, the parallel development, mainly in the high-tech regions of the United States, created a new *open systems business model* (Best, 2001, Chapter 3). A business policy of *focus on network* facilitated the implementation and diffusion of the principle of systems integration not only in the organization of technology but maybe even more importantly in the business organization as well (Best, 2001, Chapter 4; see also Miles et al., 1997). This created the decentralized environment for the emergence of new innovative clusters that allowed for the crucial diffusion characteristic of all previous new leading sector developments.

Initially these external networks remained mainly within the boundaries of national economies, with networking emerging as a means of coordination enhancing the resource creation activities of enterprises (Richardson, 1972). Later on, however, these networks increasingly extended across national borders and regions (Miles et al., 1997). Fostered by the rise of digital communication interfaces—most visibly so in the various forms of the Internet—lowering significantly the cost of access and creation of open systems and the availability of standardized and truly global logistical solutions, a multitude of cost-efficient organizational open systems have replaced previously closed systems or open national systems.

As Dicken (1999; see also Dicken, 2003) argues, in effect, the global economy is made up of a variety of complex intraorganizational and interorganizational networks intersecting with geographical networks structured particularly around linked agglomerations or clusters of activities. This emerging external network–based system is the focus of our study and will be explored on the institutional and organizational level in the following section.

Previous authors have focused on the close relationship between the expansion of transportation infrastructures and the expansion of industrial economies (e.g., Berry, 1991; Hall and Preston, 1988). Even a superficial study of this linkage makes it obvious, that the close relationship between communication and transportation networks thus makes it necessary to study the development of communication systems and their impact as well. Some authors, such as Hall and Preston (1988, 187) have argued, that the information infrastructure may be just as important as the infrastructure of physical transport or even more so.

In the following section we shall identify in greater detail the institutional and organizational characteristics of this newly emerging external network–based global system. What differentiates it from the previous external network system is its digital nature with implications for its scale—both horizontally (i.e., geographic diffusion) as well as vertically (i.e., connected units)—and its impact on the creation of new leading sectors.

Network Trajectories

Complexity is the management of information. As previously discussed in the context of complex systems, the pace of the most inner process in the global complex system process, and thus the duration of the K-wave, is determined by two biological control parameters: the cognitive (i.e., *collective* learning rate), driving the rate of exchanging and processing information at the microlevel, and the generational (see previous discussion), that constrains the rate of transfer of *knowledge* (i.e., information integrated into a context) between successive generations at the macrolevel (Devezas and Modelski, 2003, 834–35).

Information and knowledge are two separate but intertwined concepts and the centrality of both in the new digital external network system requires a closer look at the historical development of their organization and development. A classic definition of information (from a mathematic and scientific viewpoint) refers to the reduction of uncertainty in a communication system (Shannon, 1948). It thus includes any pattern of energy or matter we can find in nature as a container of information.

As pointed out, knowledge, does not simply equal information, but rather refers to "ideas and facts that human mind has internalized and understood," (Headrick, 2000, 4) often acquired and assembled in a complex fashion, a complexity that makes its nearly impossible to simulate in a mechanical fashion (i.e., artificial intelligence). It is, in other words, information embedded into a larger socioeconomic, cultural, and political context. As societies grow more complex and the amount of accumulated knowledge rises, the need for information handling becomes an important determinate of successful organization and mastery of this complexity.

Rather than aiming to identify a starting point for a *knowledge society* that necessarily will be somewhat arbitrary it seems more useful in respect to the framework employed in this work to view the entire development of humankind as the development of a knowledge society. This, as our framework suggests, has not been a linear progress, however, but rather a process marked by periods of sharp accelerations in the amount of information that people had access to and in the creation of information systems to deal with it (ibid., 8).

To understand the evolution of the new digital network it is thus necessary to have an understanding of the forms of information systems that mark its development. Headrick (ibid., 4–5) defines information systems as the "methods and techniques by which people organize and manage information, rather than the content of the information itself." Information systems in this understanding are supplements of the mental functions of thought, memory, and speech and thus the technologies of knowledge.

Headrick uses five dimensions on which to categorize information systems, namely information (1) gathering; (2) classification; (3) transformation; (4) storage; and (5) communication. Employing these dimensions, he identifies the rise of a new information system, driven as the previous information systems by the combination of information-demand, -supply, and—organization, emerging in the period 1700–1850. This new information system ultimately provided the basis for the digital informational system that is now emerging as the main central nervous system of the global system. Rather than the result of new (mechanical) technological tools, Headrick (ibid., 217) argues that it was a cultural change driven by social, economic, and political upheavals and transformations.

Similarly, Hobart and Schiffman (1998) argue for a dynamic interplay between technology and culture, shaping and being shaped by it, resulting in three distinctive information ages: classical, modern, and contemporary. Like Headrick, they place the roots of the contemporary information system in the cultural (combined with the technological) developments in the eighteenth and nineteenth century.

Whereas Headrick, as a historian, focuses more on the past evolution of the new information system, Hobart and Schiffman extend their analysis to identify in addition the rise of a distinct new information system based on its digital character.[2] In this system, they argue, information no longer acts as a universal, abstract model of the world, either classifying or analytical, but rather has become a world unto itself, in which abstract symbols can be assigned arbitrarily to any objects and procedures whatsoever. As an important precursor, the rise of relational mathematics in the modern age realized the information potential of number and organized it in a broad-reaching, reductionist hierarchy, digital information has elicited the information potential of purely abstract symbols, fabricating a realm of pure technique apart any foundation in knowledge (ibid., Chapter 8).

The notion of a special emphasis on communication systems and its impact on political as well as economic organization has earlier been highlighted by Innis (1950). He also argues that "the subject of communications . . . occupies a crucial position in the organization and administration of government and in turn of empires and western civilization" (ibid., 3). Innis differentiates between *Type 1* (i.e., durable—heavy and very portable—communications media [e.g., stone, clay, and parchment] allowing cultures to control time) and *Type 2* (i.e., ephemeral—light and easily portable—communications systems [e.g., papyrus and paper] allowing cultures to control space) cultural archetypes. Innis notes that none of these cultures are exclusive.

Durable and ephemeral communications media frequently coexist, especially so in more complex societies. However, excessive concentration on one type of communications media usually elicits competition from the other. Similar to the argument developed in a more broader context of networks here (and not just limited to communication systems), Innis (ibid., 216) argues, that a crucial element of the interaction between "cultures" (i.e., different social groups that have embedded information as knowledge in different contexts, as our generational model would suggest) is their adoption and use of different communication systems to control space. In other words, Innis's focus on communication systems as a determinant for political and economic organization analyzes the same phenomenon authors such as Mackinder (1904; 1981), Fox (1991), Tilly (1989), Rosecrance (1986; 1999), and Hugill (1999) have studied from a more sociopolitical organizational perspective.

What unites these authors is their perspective that control over space differs with the types of politicoeconomic organization employed (roughly a division between *trading* and *territorial* states), an argument of course further explored here in terms of the relationship between control over space and the network-structure of the global system. Especially Rosecrance's (1999) latest extension of his argument as well as Hugill's (1999) study of the relationship between communication systems and geopolitics bear great importance on the study undertaken here.

Taking Innis's analysis a step further, Hugill (1999) in his study of the relationship between communication systems, geopolitics, and the global system, also emphasizes the "two-way flows of information that predominate as mechanisms of military [i.e., political] and economic control" (ibid., 4). He argues, that the geopolitical interests from trading states (in the framework of this work, states that exert their power mainly in external networks) and territorial (i.e., internal network–based states) differ in terms of the military and communications systems they employ. Whereas trading states have an interest in exerting weak control over long distances, territorial states wish to exert strong control over short distances (ibid., 7). The former thus tend to invest in long-range military and communications systems, in other words they aim to establish external networks of control.

Hugill's extensive study of the evolution of mainly four crucial communications technologies (i.e., telegraphy, telephony, radio, and radar) starting at 1844 (our noted point of punctuation of the global system and ultimately the birth-point of the newly emerging external network system) demonstrates, how especially long-range radio and the digital (i.e., programmable) computer, both evolved from Type 1 communication technologies into Type 2 and thus have become enablers of external network establishment and control. The pattern of existing technology being transformed in innovative spurts and clusters again proves the breeding ground for the emergence of a new long cycle of global system development. As noted earlier, however, a crucial difference to the former cycle is that it marks the return of the global system to a complex regime, based on external network structures.

Analyzing the historical trajectories of modern day information systems from an organizational perspective and with a focus on the information transmission dimension, Spar (2001) provides a study connecting the ventures of Portuguese explorers of the fifteenth century (in our framework starting during long-cycle five (LC5), see table 2.1) to the development of the telegraph and radio in the middle of the nineteenth century, and the advent of satellite television and the Internet in the twentieth century. She identifies a common dynamic in the development of new information systems, with bursts of innovation at the beginning, creating new commercial opportunities, creating a gap between economic, social, and technological activity and political control, with economic and technological development driving political advancement of the system. Spar argues that communication (or in Headrick's framework *transmission*-) technology deserves special attention, "for communication is the sinew of both commerce and politics, the channel through which information—and thus power—flows" (ibid., 9).

From a more technological perspective, Hall and Preston (1988) make a similar argument that the origins of the newly emerging system must be traced back to the transformations in communication system technologies beginning roughly in the around the middle of the nineteenth century, with the invention of the electrical telegraph (1830s) as well as the telephone and the typewriter and the phonograph (1875–1890). These new inventions marked the emergence of what the authors call *New Information Technology* industries, embracing the technologies (i.e., mechanical, electrical, electromechanical, electronic) that record, transmit, process, and distribute information (ibid., 5). This, of course, is congruent with our own framework and consistent with the argument of a punctuation of the global system development around this period, resulting in a connected, yet new and distinct external network system based on the digital central nervous system.

Network Economics

In his study of network industries, Shy (2001) argues it is necessary to view network markets as unique and distinct markets. What characterizes (and distinguishes) these markets are (1) complementarity, compatibility, and standards; (2) consumption externalities; (3) switching costs and lock-in; and (4) significant economies of scale in production. Goods and services that are part of network markets should thus be viewed as *systems of complements* rather than individual products (e.g., computer hardware and digital software or Digital Versatile Disc (DVD) players and DVDs). One is relatively useless without the other; the real use of the services or items only comes into effect within a system.

This raises the need for compatibility (e.g., software running on certain hardware platforms, cable connections featuring compatible designs) and thus raises the issue of common standards and the need for coordination. In other words, questions of coordination and standards become crucial in network markets. These standards in turn unlock the unique features of network externalities, which can profoundly affect market behavior of firms and individuals. Once users of these systems have invested into their use (by obtaining certain technology, licensing contracts, training and learning, etc.), they experience so-called *lock-ins* because switching costs (from one system to another) can be relatively high (e.g., reinvestments of the above lock-in factors, as well as additional search costs and loyalty costs).

Switching costs affect price competition in two opposing ways. First, in the case of already locked-in customers, firms may raise prices knowing that consumers will not switch unless the price difference exceeds the switching costs to an alternative system. Second, in case of consumers not yet locked-into one system, systems-providers/sellers will compete fiercely (e.g., through discounts, free trials, free complimentary products and services, etc.) in order to attract customers and create a *critical mass* of installed bases of consumers (i.e., customers locked in the providers/sellers system).

In economic terms, the combination of often very high fixed sunk costs with almost negligible marginal costs implies that the average cost function declines sharply with the number of items sold. Once a critical mass is obtained, network markets can be extremely profitable (e.g., Microsoft's system software, Windows, enables a profit margin of over 80 percent for the firm). Since all successful networks rely on a critical mass to develop their network externalities (i.e., when the value of a good depends on the number of other people who use it) and thus raise the value of the offered system, the establishment of standards and their control becomes a clear determinant of commercial success.

The convergence between organizational requirements and technological change has established networking as the fundamental form of competition in the now truly globalized economy (Ernst, 1994; Hatzichronoglou, 1996). Those networks also act as gatekeepers. Barriers to entry into the most advanced industries (such as electronics or biotechnology) have skyrocketed, making it extremely difficult for challengers to enter the market by themselves. It even hampers, best demonstrated in the case of biotechnology, the ability of large corporations to open up new product lines or to innovate their own processes in accordance with the pace of technological change.

Cooperation and networking offer the only possibility to share costs and risks, as well as to keep up with constantly renewed information. Inside the networks, new possibilities are abundant. Outside the networks, survival is increasingly difficult (Castells, 1996, 171). Under the conditions of fast technological change, networks, not firms, have become the actual operating unit (Kelly, 1999; Davis and Meyer, 1998; Borrus and Zysman, 1997a). However, firms continue to be the main organizational framework for the operating units. As Peter Drucker points out, it is the form of the corporational organizational structure that changes, not the role of the corporation as the organizational structure:

The command-and-control organization that first emerged in the 1870s might be compared to an organism held together by its shell.

The corporation that is now emerging is being designed around a skeleton: information, both the corporation's new integrating system and its articulation.... The new approach defines a business as the organization that adds value and creates wealth. (Drucker, 1995, 63)

The role of the network, or what Castells calls the networking logic (Castells, 1996), therefore substantially changes the character of the global economic environment. Whereas traditional rules of competitive strategy focus on competitors, suppliers, and customers, companies selling complementary components (*complementors*) in the iNet economy become equally important (Shapiro and Varian, 1999, 10).

Cross-national production networks permit firms to weave together the constituent elements of the value-chain into competitively effective new production systems, while facilitating diverse points of innovation and in turn have turned large segments of complex manufacturing into a commodity available in the market (Borrus and Zysman, 1997b). Taken together with the above discussed merging of all networks into one supranetwork: the Internet (Johnson, 1999; Borzo, 1999), this global digital network and its infrastructure enable the culmination of many different markets, both on a horizontal and vertical scale, which in the past had been separate entities, into one exchange-space. In sum, we see the development of network enterprises, which in turn constitute the iNet economy.

Protocols and Standards

As noted earlier, in markets driven by network economies, standards and protocols reign supreme. The transition from an internal network system to an external network based one is not only reflected in the structure of economic organization, but also in the kinds of networks themselves. Borrus and Zysman (1997a) distinguish between *provider-supplied networks* and *user-driven networks*. Provider-supplied networks are defined and controlled by the network company which provides a set of service or possibilities to its customers. User-driven networks are at least in part defined and controlled by the user who designs them to fulfill specific functions. These user-driven networks generate a competitive market for the systems enabling these networks and often constitute what Christensen (1997) describes as *disruptive technologies* (i.e., technologies, that are based on previous technologies, but establish a new lineage and force users into a new network thus understood).

In this respect, provider-supplied networks (for example the telegraph or initially also phone networks) were the natural extension of network industries based on an internal networking logic. The control over the network and its systems was regarded essential for its control. By contrast, user-driven networks are much more attuned to an external networking logic, since they allow for competing systems relying on a set of standards that allow and enable end-to-end interoperability of the corporate communications infrastructure. Suppliers in such an environment rely on *open-but-owned* systems: open at the interface to permit interconnection of systems from other vendors, but owned to reap a return from innovation. In short, users demanded highly functional and interoperable systems (Borrus and Zysman, 1997b).

The by now classic example of this transition from dominance of system providers controlling the entire or large parts of the value-chain to dominance of standard setters in the disintegrated value chain is the rise of the *Wintel* standard accompanying the personal computer (PC) revolution (see Borrus and Zysman, 1997b; 1997a; see also Kim and Hart, 2002). Rather than controlling the production of entire systems, as was traditionally the case in the information processing industry, IBM's personal computer strategy encouraged the provision of alternative system (i.e., IBM-compatible PCs) provision to ensure a faster growth of the overall platform.

This allowed the main critical component providers—Intel for the hardware and Microsoft for the software—over time to set the standards that enabled the interoperability of the various system component providers (i.e., hardware and software providers competing against the Apple system). As Kim and Hart (2002) argue, Wintelism does not just apply to the specific case of the PC industry but in fact represent a new form of industrial governance originating in the computer industry, but now applicable to all information industries (see also Martin, 2002; and Shapiro and Varian, 1999, esp. Chapter 9). A crucial factor allowing firms to wage (and win) a war of standards is control over intellectual property rights and patents, or put differently, an advantage in its *intellectual capital.*

Intellectual Capital

The concept of intellectual capital[3] is neither new as a concept, nor as a phenomenon. It has existed since the beginning of human economic activity: early agricultural activity, knowledge of shipping routes, tacit knowledge of production processes groomed and protected in the form of guilds (and what we would term today the *brand name* of the Fuggers banking family) are just a few examples. What places intellectual capital into such a central role in the new digital commercial system are the impact of the transition to an external network–based system and the digital character of these networks on intangibles. Not surprisingly, intellectual property rights (IPRs) "have moved from an arcane area of legal analysis and a policy backwater to the forefront of global economic policymaking" (Maskus, 2000, 1).[4]

Since the mid-1950s, it has become apparent that the accumulation of physical capital by itself could not explain why some countries performed better than others, or even why growth rates differ between industrial countries. Many other factors could affect growth, development and productivity of a firm or a country (Ducharme, 1998, 3). Early empirical work by Kendrick and his collaborators (1976) and Denison (1967) has shown that a large proportion of productivity improvement could not be explained by just the inputs of capital and labor, but also by residual factors such as investment in health, education and skill, research and development and more generally in the acquisition and transmission of know-how. More recently, empirical studies in various OECD (Organisation for Economic Co-operation and Development) countries have shown that investment in these complementary assets has outgrown that related to the gross formation of fixed capital (Ducharme, 1998).

Intellectual capital comes in many forms: often cited examples include (1) brand value[5] and (2) research and development (R&D).[6] In economies based on the global digital commercial system, both brand-value and the innovational advantage enabled through R&D, become central and highly valuable assets (see e.g., Lev, 2001; Shapiro and Varian, 1999; Stewart, 1997). For each of them exist well-established measurements.[7] Intellectual capital, however, goes beyond these well-studied assets.

As Lev (2001) argues, there are three major nexi of intangibles, mainly distinguished by their relation to the generator of the assets: (1) discovery; (2) organizational practices; and (3) human resources. Not only are intangible assets created out of a combination of these factors. Often they are also embedded in physical assets (technology embedded in products) and in the human resource (the tacit knowledge of employees). However, the fact that this creates considerable problems in respect to measurement and accountability in the value–creation process should not lead to the conclusion that these are residual factors. Similar to state-granted monopolies in the earlier maritime commercial system (e.g., in the form of management of trade or protected production techniques), intellectual capital in the digital commercial system provides essential components of leading sector advantage and creation. Life science and biotechnology patents (including not only processes, but also biological components such as genes) as well as intellectual property in the form of music, film, and other artistic creations are but two examples.

It is important to note a vital difference between tangible assets on the one hand, and intangible assets on the other.[8] Physical, human, and financial assets (i.e., tangible assets) are rival assets. Alternative uses compete for the services of these assets. For example, a machine or employee assigned to a certain task cannot be assigned to a second task simultaneously. Physical, human, and financial assets are thus rival or scarce assets characterized by positive opportunity costs (the costs attached to the opportunity of using the asset elsewhere forgone). The same does not hold true for intangible assets.

Intangible assets are, in general, nonrival, that is a given deployment does not preclude them from the usefulness of the asset in other deployments. Beyond the initial original investment, this results in negligible opportunity costs. What generally characterizes intangible assets is that they often require large fixed costs and minimal or sometimes zero marginal (incremental) costs. The classic example is the production of software: the costs of the initial development (or *first copy*) of a software program can be immense, while the costs of producing copies of the software are close to zero, regardless of scale.

As Grossman and Helpman (1994) point out, knowledge investments (i.e., intangible assets) are cumulative as opposed to machinery and equipment (i.e., tangible asset) investments, which are deteriorating in value and often constitute of simple replacement investments. Thus, intangibles often exhibit increasing returns to scale. Given the attributes of the above discussed digital network economies, these effects put not only a premium on intellectual capital but places it in fact at the center of leading sector development and thus eventually into the center of the majority of economic activity.

Digital information networks enable a leverage of intangible assets on a level that renders the past impact of intangibles minuscule. To a large degree this is the result of the organizational changes made possible by digital networks (discussed in detail in chapter 2) as well as the change from information as a means of production to a good in itself (either in digital form, as for example Wal-Mart's use of point-of-sale data, or through its manipulation, as in the case of biotechnology).

Current IPRs have their precursor in trading and commercial monopolies in earlier maritime commercial network based systems. States granted a commercial right often including areas outside of its immediate control (i.e., sovereign domain). These rights were also encompassed the same dimension current IPR systems involve, namely the (1) standards enacted to establish a creator's rights to exclude others from the economic value of the commercial rights granted; (2) the limitations imposed on those rights for purposes of domestic economic and social policy; and (3) the enforcement of the rights granted.

These standards manifested themselves as important factors for conducting business, as well illustrated in the success of the Champagne Fairs during the thirteenth century. The trading monopolies illustrate well the limitations and problems of enforcement of those rights. At times states assisted the commercial agents with the enforcement of these rights (or at least allowed them to do so on their own), as for example with the various East India trading companies, but often enforcement proved to be a difficult task then as much as it is today.

IPRs thus are closely associated with a global system based on external network systems. The recent rise in the importance of IPRs reflects the growing centrality of intellectual property in a digital commercial network economy. Numerous regional trade agreements such as the North American Free Trade Agreement (NAFTA) and bilateral accords between the European Union and countries in the Middle East and North Africa have protection of intellectual property at their core. Maybe more importantly, on the multilateral level the Agreement on Trade-related Aspects of Intellectual Property Rights (TRIPs) as a founding component of the World Trade Organization (WTO) has elevated the recognition and enforcement of IPRs to the level of inviolable international commitment (Maskus, 2000, 1).[9]

As Maskus (2000, Chapter 3) points out, to understand the sources of pressure for change in global protection of IPRs it is necessary to understand the dependence of newly emerging leading sectors on various forms of IPRs. We can thus identify (1) the patent complex (mainly in the life sciences, i.e., pharmaceuticals, biotechnology, and plant varieties), and (2) the copyrights and trademark complex (consisting of recorded entertainment, software, Internet transmissions, and branding and quality inputs).[10] Innovative firms in all industrial sectors seek patents and their protection. They are especially important, however, for capturing returns to basic inventions in invention in pharmaceuticals, agricultural and industrial chemicals, and biotechnology, that is, the life sciences complex. These sectors are characterized by high R&D costs while simultaneously facing considerable appropriability problems, wearing their commercial secrets "on their face," as Reichman (1994) puts it.

The second complex, consisting of copyright issues, concerns the protection of original artistic and literary expression in a multitude of media (e.g., print, audio/video, live performances fixed in some medium, derivate products and services, broadcasts, software, video games, electronic databases, integrated networks, transmission over the Internet, etc.). What unites the seemingly distinct economic sectors of recorded entertainment, software, and electronic commerce is their reliance on IT (information technology) and their digital form. In addition, the value of brands and quality inputs has also risen to levels that require extensive IPR protection to justify the inputs into the creation and preservation of these values.

Our model marks the punctuation of the global system around the mid nineteenth century as the starting point of the economic information phase of the global system process. Accordingly, the negotiations of the Paris Convention (1883) covering various industrial property rights and the Berne Convention (1886) mark—consistent with our model—the first significant international activity regarding IPRs with implications for today's intellectual property regime. The extension of these early IPR standards in the form of the TRIPs agreement (mainly as a result of pressure from the United States and to some degree also the European Union) provided global copyright protection for computer programs, electronic transmissions, broadcasts, and phonograms, requires countries to prevent the use of integrated circuits that infringe protected designs, advances the protection of trade secrets, and commits countries to take action against copyright and trademark piracy, even where this activity is economically significant and an important employer. As Maskus (2000, Chapters 4 and 5) demonstrates empirically, this development leads to the strengthening of the new digital external network based system and results accordingly in an increase of commercial flows (in the form of trade of technical inputs, FDI, and licensing).

Role of Monopolies

Critics may argue that the digital nature of leading sectors in the new K-wave imply incompatibility with the existing leadership long cycle paradigm. The development of a leading economy based on first-mover advantage in leading sectors requires the ability to establish (quasi-) monopolies and their associated rents. The following question there-fore arises: will the K-waves become shorter and leadership cycle dy-namics slowly dissolve as technological change emerges in increasing speed so that monopolization over a sufficient time period becomes impossible? Furthermore, the argument could be raised that technology and high-technology production have become increasingly multina-tionalized, making it increasingly more difficult for one world power to monopolize leading sectors.

Indeed, this is not the case. Monopolies do not only continue to exist in the iNet economy but are in fact one of its main characteristics (see e.g., Shapiro and Varian, 1999; Kelly, 1999). As Shapiro and Varian (1999, 173) point out, the informational economy "is populated by temporary monopolies." Whereas monopolies in former industrial K-waves were characterized by the economic environment of econo-mies of scale, the iNet economy is driven by economics of networks that foster the development of large monopolies in the form of stan-dards and protocols (Brynjolfsson and Kahin, 2000; Shapiro and Varian, 1999; Kelly, 1999; Gates, 1999).

Monopolies have changed their character in the iNet economy, be-cause of what economists call *positive feedback effects*. Positive feedback is characterized by its dynamic. After an initial threshold or *critical mass* is reached, it reinforces initial success with exponential further growth and destroys competition in the same manner (Shapiro and Varian, 1999, 176–78). In other words, the development of monopolies still follows an S-curve shaped model. As in previous K-waves, these mo-nopolies (not in the strictest form but rather understood as market dominator) follow a similar life-cycle pattern and are characterized by an early phase of low, slow growth (usually paired with the coexistence of a multitude of competitors or other, similar actors), then strong growth, which eventually plateaus out (maturity) and then an extended period of decline in relative terms (not necessarily absolute terms), with the rise of new competitors and loss of market share, etc.

The example of America Online (AOL) serves as a well-observed demonstration of this process (e.g., Swisher, 1998; Wilkinson, 2001; Burgelman and Meza, 2000). Early in its existence, America Online was by no means the only player in the emerging business of computer network access provision. However, after AOL managed to reach the necessary critical mass to draw on positive feedback effects, its growth followed the typical S-shaped pattern of exponential growth, allowing the company to overcome the significant competition from firms such as Prodigy and CompuServe. This enabled AOL later in its lifecycle to withstand challenges even from well-placed (and well-funded) competitors such as Microsoft. Now facing the decline phase in the life cycle process, and severe challenges on many fronts, AOL nonetheless remains the most important single network provider to date.

Whereas it is true that technological monopolies seem to be somewhat shorter in duration than monopolies in previous K-waves, the ability of challengers to replace early starters and their monopolistic position proves equally difficult in the iNet economy as in previous times: the history of Microsoft, America Online, and others provide ample evidence. In sum, monopolies as a result of major innovations and innovative clustering, although different in nature, continue to exist.

Capital

The previous discussion brings up the need to pay special attention to the role of capital in these processes. The term has many meanings: the way it used here entails both, capital assets allocated to the economic actors as well as the enterprise assets those actors can offer in return. The form in which enterprises can obtain capital is also connected to the previously discusses properties. The molecularization trend coupled with a stronger emphasis on entrepreneurial behavior of all nodes in the value-network also changes the optimal structure of capital allocation and distribution. Greater entrepreneurial behavior entails greater risk. This implies that the old form of capital distribution—banks loaning capital assets as debt and receiving interest in return—is not the optimal form of capital asset distribution in the iNet economy. Although stock exchanges and private investors have of course existed for a long time, only in recent times have we seen the development of what Kelly calls the "equity culture" (Kelly, 1999, 157).

With easier access to information and through the digitalization of information networks, technology has accelerated the change from making loans to making investments. Despite the rise of a few enormously large and globally active banks, increasing amounts of wealth are now held in equity, and not in debt, to a point where over 50 percent of U.S. households own stocks, with the bulk of stocks controlled by pension funds. Even if companies rely on debt to raise capital, they are able to do so directly from investors (in the form of so-called *junk-bonds*). The falling costs and increasing ease of transactions disperse the ownership of those investments wider than ever before history. This is not only reflected in the expansion of ownership of shares in middle class U.S. households, but also in the phenomenon of so-called *micro-loans* in developing countries. Both of these developments are linked increasingly to the growth of digital networks (Economist, 1999). In addition, the growing importance of venture capital and other private forms of capital has developed this form of capital allocation into a sizeable alternative to other markets of financial capital. We also see a change in the form of compensation of (knowledge) workers, where stock options are exchanged for the knowledge workers offer as their asset.

The form of capital (or assets) of the value-creating agents is also changing. Intangible assets have taken a center stage in the iNet economy. Value creating agents offer intellectual, human, and structural capital (Davis and Meyer, 1998, 198). The intellectual (or "brain") capital (Stewart, 1997) of organizations (or individuals) includes items such as copyrights, patents, and brand-value (von Krogh et al., 2000; Quinn, 1992). Human capital includes not only the knowledge of agents, but also their *social capital* (i.e., relationships with customers or experts). Structural capital describes the "experience and expertise of organizations embedded in processes, policies, and systems" (Davis and Meyer, 1998, 198; see also Stewart, 1997). Davis and Meyer (1998, 161–63) even suggest that individual agents will take advantage of securities markets in order to raise capital they need to finance their investments (i.e., education). We see the first examples of this development in the entertainment business (artists securitizing their future work) and sports (athletes securitizing future proceeds from marketing contracts).

In general, markets can be seen as matchmakers of buyers and sellers.[11] Prices in financial markets may be set roughly through two different types of mechanisms: (1) quotes of prices at which registered dealers in securities are willing to buy and trade. This is the underlying principle of price finding at Nasdaq. In other words, the Nasdaq provides a *quote-driven* system of electronically (or rather digitally) linked competing market makers. Alternatively, prices may be identified by (2) price matching of bid and ask offers. This is the price mechanism employed at the NYSE, also referred to as an *order-driven* market. In the case of the NYSE this involves, as noted earlier, an order-driven system with physical trading and monopoly market makers (or specialists) who have to follow certain rules and provide liquidity.

We currently witness the parallel importance of the declining old capitalist mode (industrial > internal network structure) financial center, the New York Stock Exchange (NYSE), with its roots in the *space-of-place* power logic, but at the same time the rise and development of new capitalist mode (digital commercial > external network) financial network center, characterized by its roots in a *space-of-flows* power logic, namely the Nasdaq. Although its origins can be traced back to May 17, 1792, when twenty-four brokers subscribed to the *original brokers' agreement*, forming the first organized stock market in New York, the NYSE was institutionalized in 1817 under the name *New York Stock & Exchange Board* which was changed in 1863 to its current-day name *New York Stock Exchange*.

Replacing London as the world's largest financial center, New York and its NYSE have become by far the world's largest equity market, two and a half times the size of the next market in Japan (followed closely by London). The members (i.e., owners) of the NYSE are closely connected to the rise of the commercial and organizational arrangement that lead to the rise of the U.S. leadership in the world system. And the NYSE remains a highly influential capital market for United States (and increasingly international) enterprises. The NYSE's physical floor provides the basis for its main characteristic in trader–market terms: Membership on the NYSE is strictly limited and relatively expensive. As a result, traders wishing to buy or sell a specific security must contract with a member (or *commission broker*) to represent them as an agent on the trading floor.[12]

Thus, membership itself becomes a commodity that may be used, sold, or leased by the member. It is important to note, however, that the exchange does not maintain a monopoly on trading in listed securities. With the rise of, first, voice communication,[13] and, later, increasingly electronic and digital communication networks starting in around the 1970s, mainly large insurance groups, investment and pension funds, and banks have engaged in *over the counter* (OTC) transactions (see below).[14] This has allowed them to bypass the NYSE and other established major trading floors and also allowed smaller and independent exchanges to develop and flourish. The NYSE remains, however, by far the most successful trading-floor based market place for equities in the world.

New York, however, has also been home to the parallel development of the world's dominating electronic marketplace in the form of the National Association of Securities Dealers Automated Quotations System (Nasdaq). Brought online in 1971, it automated the work of an informal dealer network handling off-exchange trading in unlisted stocks commonly referred to as the *over the -counter* (OTC) market.[15]

Nasdaq's traders are dealers who make markets (i.e., trade out of their own securities inventories). They buy and/or sell (i.e., *make a two-sided market*) by quoting a price they would pay a prospective seller (i.e., a *bid*) or a price they would charge a prospective buyer (i.e., an *ask*). Rather than relying on the public as market participants, market makers trade with each other from their own inventories. In contrast to the NYSE, a *double-auction market*, the Nasdaq market is a *negotiated market*. Rather than relying on a combination of internal and external markets, Nasdaq may have multiple market makers and allows the direct negotiations between sellers and buyers. Whereas the NYSE assigns the specialist to make markets based on offers in the order flow, Nasdaq features a centralized computer database. This database makes the firm quotations initiated by Nasdaq market makers (not by traders placing orders) visible immediately to everyone in the system. Traders, who are interested in buying or selling shares, must either be dealers, who can trade directly with other dealers, or must hire a Nasdaq dealer as an agent.

Nasdaq has since firmly established its dominance of the capital-side of the emerging digital network system. This is of course consistent with the time frame provided by our model of the emergence of a digital commercial external network system. As the world's largest electronic stock market, Nasdaq is not limited to one central trading location. Rather, trading is executed through Nasdaq's sophisticated computer and telecommunications network, which transmits real-time quote and trade data to more than 1.3 million users in 83 countries. Nasdaq's *open architecture* market structure allows a virtually unlimited number of participants to trade in a company's stock and is the result of an actively pursued spread of its hubs in other established markets. In 1994, Nasdaq surpassed the NYSE in annual share volume and despite the decline in trade and volume after the dot-com bubble burst in 2001 remains a powerful market with the potential to make floor-based markets such as the NYSE obsolete in the not too distant future.

The New Leading Sectors
of the Global System

A leading sector is (not just initially) not necessarily very large in comparison to other economic sectors. What is of interest is whether the sector's *impact on growth* tends to be disproportionate in its early stages of development. Although the establishment of a new economic sector will initially require much greater shares of investment resources than its early output would seem to justify, the expected long-term returns provide incentives for investors to make the necessary resources available. As the sector continues to exploit its particular contribution to efficiency and productivity, its linkage to overall economic growth should stabilize (Thompson, 1990, 211). In sum, we are looking for initial high growth and disproportional contribution to general growth and productivity. Can we already describe the character of the new K-wave? What are the major innovations of this new K-wave? What are its leading sectors? In addition, if so many actors seem to be aware of the importance of these new leading sectors, why is it possible that some nations still have the ability to develop a lead in those sectors over other nations? Is it still possible in such an environment to monopolize leading sectors?

Early on, a number of authors have argued for *telecommunications* (e.g., Mensch, 1979; Freeman, 1987a; Modelski and Thompson, 1996; Goldstein, 1988; Lipsey, 1999; Bornschier and Chase-Dunn, 1999), *information technology* (e.g., Tinbergen, 1983; van Duijn, 1983; Bruckmann, 1987; Hall, 1985; Yakovets, 1987; Freeman, 1987a; Modelski and Thompson, 1996; Goldstein, 1988; Thompson, 1990; Lipsey, 1999; Bornschier and Chase-Dunn, 1999), but also *biotechnologies* (e.g., Ray, 1983; Bruckmann, 1987; Yakovets, 1987; Goldstein, 1988; Thompson, 1990; Lipsey, 1999; Bornschier and Chase-Dunn, 1999) to be singled out as critical new sectors.

Most authors in one way or another stress the importance of information and communication technology (ICT) as a new leading sector. Most of the authors focus more on the hardware side of ICT (microprocessors, electronic components). Others include the software aspect (including a new sector made possible only by recent developments in ICT, biotechnology).

As in earlier leading sectors, we can trace the development of ICTs through various K-waves. Hall and Preston (1988) show how information technology emerged through the last four K-waves, beginning with the development of the telegraph in the 1830s. Standage (1998) traces the modern-time Internet back to the mid-1800s with the development of a telegraph network.

However, simply identifying ICT industries as a key sector is not sufficient. Many countries (and certainly all the likely candidates for systemic leadership) now realize the strategic importance of ICT and try to develop their industry accordingly. What is crucial is the emergence of an appropriate socioeconomic complex. This combination of the creation of economic innovation and fostering sociopolitical institutions form the nucleus of a new technological style. As a result, these complexes also foster the development of an early head start in emerging leading sector development.

Focusing on the analytical level of states, the superiority of past nations appears (apart from certain key necessary, but not sufficient elements, such as population size, geographical features, etc., for every potential leading state) in no ways mere fate or some sort of "destiny." Instead, states in the past obtained leadership positions through the establishment of a supportive and enabling institutional environment for other agents (individuals, firms, etc.). Through a combination of private and public institutions can under certain circumstances foster the innovational *milieu* that leads to the typical clustering of economic and sociopolitical innovations, which in turn can lead to the development of new leading sectors and ultimately the development of a new technological style.

The development of a leading economy based on these leading sectors formed the foundation of political and economic leadership in the world economy. As Landes (1999, Chapter 15) points out, Britain's success during its industrial revolution has been well observed by other states at the time. However, nowhere were these improvements so widespread and effective as in Britain, in large part a result of her formal and informal institutions. Britain featured the "right" set of institutions to "invent" a new socioeconomic paradigm of doing things better and more efficiently. This enabled her to set new standards that others had to follow. In other words, Britain was able to set the standards of a new technological style. This also holds true for the development of leading sectors in K-wave nineteen (K19). As Kitschelt (1991, 454) argues

> familiar macro-variables, such as the timing of industrialization and the preexisting political economic institutions, are still useful in explaining the trajectories within which industrial sector portfolios are chosen and instituted. In other words, national conditions constrain the learning process of new industrial capabilities and governance structures. . . . The choice of technology, in turn, must be "endogenized" and explained in part as a consequence of institutional capabilities and constraints.

If our aim is to match the predicted development of a new long cycle with the actual development of the world economy, it is necessary to mark the recent changes in the global technoeconomic paradigm that have occurred.

Networking and ICT

We can already identify the evolution of what might be termed the informational Network, or iNet economy. The core technologies of this new technological style are information and communication technologies (ICT) enabling new forms of *networking* (i.e., collaborative value creation) and sociopolitical interaction.

Table 3.1 summarizes the size and growth in ICT of some of the most important world economies. The data range from 1980 to 2000 and measure the share of the entire nonresidential gross fixed capital investment that was spent in the respective national economies on ICT equipment. The table shows an early and clear focus on ICT investment in the United States emerging on a broad base after many initial innovations of the 1960s and 1970s (such as the microprocessor and PCs) had matured into basic investment goods in the 1980s. The only other country investing more that ten percent of its nonresidential gross fixed capital formation in the form of ICT goods at this point were the Netherlands, that early on emerged as the center ICT cluster within the EU zone.

Amongst the states with overall potential for systemic leadership, the United States builds on its early lead of a share of 15 percent in 1980, to nearly a third of all of capital investment being spent on ICT equipment at the end of the (potential) K-wave emerging in the 1970s. The United States extended its investment in this area during the critical period of 1990, investing nearly 23 percent in this field, compared with only 10.8 percent in Japan, 13.2 percent in Germany, traditionally an ambitious competitor in this field, and only 8.5 percent in France, again a country with high ambitions to emerge as a leading technology producer and thus to be expected also a large investor into ICT equipment. The EU average in 2000 still remained about half of the percentage of investment in the United States, with 16.9 and 31.4 percent respectively. The countries emerging as strong investors of ICT equipment are among the familiar group identified earlier, with Finland (29.4 percent), Sweden (21.6 percent), but also the UK seriously investing in information and telecommunication technology, largely as a result of their mobile technology clusters. Australia, and to some degree the UK, on the other hand now boast advanced PC-based networks tying

Table 3.1 ICT Equipment* Investment in OECD countries, Percentage of Nonresidential Gross Fixed Capital Formation, Total Economy, 1980–2000

Country	1980	1990	2000
Spain	5.6	11.9	10.1
Portugal	6.1	10.6	11.4
Belgium	—	—	12.0
Austria	7.1	10.0	12.8
France	6.1	8.5	13.1
Ireland	4.6	8.3	14.6
Greece	3.9	9.3	15.7
Japan	7.0	10.8	16.0
Italy	8.0	14.2	16.7
EU(MP)	6.9	12.3	16.9
Denmark	6.4	11.1	19.1
Germany(MP)	7.7	13.9	19.2
Netherlands	11.2	15.5	20.9
Canada	9.1	13.2	21.4
Sweden	5.0	9.7	21.6
United Kingdom	5.6	13.8	22.0
Australia	7.3	13.9	22.5
Finland	7.8	12.7	29.4
United States(MP)	15.2	22.5	31.4

Source: OECD data, estimates based on national accounts, data underlying Colecchia et al. (2002).

Notes: * ICT equipment is defined here as computer and office equipment and communication equipment; software includes both purchased and own account software. Software investment in Japan is likely to be underestimated, owing to methodological differences.

(MP) Indicates (potential) major power status (as measured by accepted standards in the International Relations literature) and thus potential for systemic leadership in the global complex system.

their economies into the global commercial digital network as a result of their increased focus on this technology and increased investment since the 1990s.

Table 3.2 provides a closer look at the development of the contribution of IT equipment to the growth in capital equipment implied in the earlier data in the country that in our survey so far has emerged as the clear leader in information and communication technology worldwide, the United States. Whereas capital equipment spending has risen to 16.5 percent in 1998 (from 10.5 in 1993), the contribution to this rise from

Table 3.2 Contribution of IT Equipment to Growth in Capital Equipment, United States, Percentage, 1993–1998

	1993	1994	1995	1996	1997	1998
Change in real spending for capital equipment	10.5	11.0	11.5	10.9	12.1	16.5
Contribution of real spending for IT equipment	3.5	3.8	6.9	6.9	6.8	9.6
Contribution of real spending for all other types of capital equipment	7.0	7.2	4.6	4.0	5.3	6.9
Contribution of IT investment spending to change in real capital equipment spending (rounded)	33.0	35.0	60.0	63.0	56.0	58.0

Source: Adapted from Henry (1999, 23).

Note: IT equipment is defined as investment in information processing– (and related) equipment. Capital equipment is defined as investment in durable equipment by producers.

IT equipment spending has risen almost threefold from 3.5 in 1993 to 9.3 in 1998, with contributions to the growth in equipment spending has stayed relatively stable during this period and clearly below ten percent. The contribution of IT to the change in real capital equipment spending in the United States has risen from a third in 1993 to over half of total capital equipment investment spending.

This trend is very well illustrated in figure 3.1, which charts the share of information technology investment as part of all equipment investment in the United States, from the early emergence of these technologies in the 1960s to nearly the end of a potential K-wave around 2000. The graph follows the typical S-curve shape we would expect for a leading sector investment development (here measured as a share of equipment investment). From an initial, slow-growth start, the share of investment in ICT equipment starts to switch into high-growth around the start of our expected K-wave (approximately 1970) with a trend to slow in its growth at the end of the K-wave. Although not reflected in the available data plotted here in this graph, the data in table 3.2, which measures not the overall share, but the contribution to the growth of equipment spending, reflect the trend toward a flattening even before

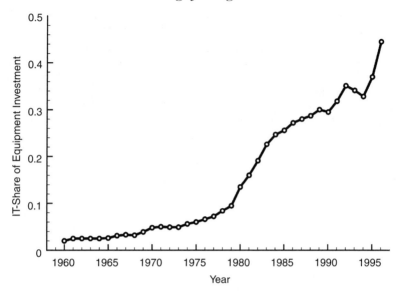

Figure 3.1   IT-share (%) of Equipment Investment, United States, 1960–1996
Source: Margherio et al. (1998, Figure 6).

the high of the Internet investment bubble at the end of the 1990s. The bursting of this Internet investment bubble in 2001, another typical occurrence as part of development of investment in leading sectors, has further helped to slow the rate of growth, although the overall share remains very high.

As we have argued earlier, the first K-wave (as part of a long cycle of sociopolitical dominance) require the long-cycle leader to dominate in the critical infrastructure-technologies that provide the basis not only of the important high profits during the first K-wave, but more importantly also provide the basis of the continued success during the following period as the basis of the technologies and leading sectors that become critical for success during the second K-wave. For the hypothesized development of an information-bases long cycle as proposed here, these technologies would involve critical components of the information-processing, such as semiconductors.

We therefore focus now our empirical observation on this critical technology. Figure 3.2 reflects the typical development of a leading sector growth pattern (S-shaped growth, with slow beginning, exponential growth in the middle, and a flattening out in the final part). Over the course of our proposed first K-wave (from roughly the beginning of the

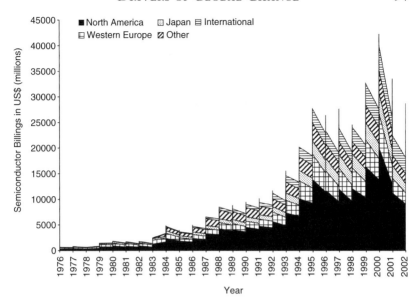

Figure 3.2   Semiconductor Sales ($ million), 1976–2002

Source: Semiconductor Industry Association (http://www.sia-online.org, accessed February 3, 2003).

1970s to the end of the 1990s) figure 3.2 graphs the worldwide sale of semiconductors (in millions of U.S. dollars). For the purposes of our discussion here, we have listed grouped together North American sales in the black, bold line that graphs the exponential trend-line. The dark-grey line represents the sales from Western Europe, the lighter-grey line the sales from Japan over the period from 1976 to 2002. The United States emerges early on as a key supplier of this critical good for the development of ICT equipment and is able to establish and further expand its dominance in this technology until the end of the K-wave the sales flatten out on a high level (as expected).

What characterizes the current technological revolution that enables the basis of innovative clustering of this developing new K-wave (K19 in our count, see table 2.1) is not so much the centrality of knowledge and information, but the application of such knowledge and information to knowledge generation and information processing/communication devices, in a cumulative feedback loop between innovation and the use of innovation (see Castells, 1996; Hall and Preston, 1988; Saxby, 1990). Whereas the leading sectors of earlier external network dominated K-waves, first the Baltic and Atlantic trade routes and later the Eastern trades, were dominantly maritime, the leading sector of this period are increasingly turning into *digital commercial trade routes*.

The Internet serves as a trade route in the sense that the new commodity of the possibly newly emerging, digital-information-based long-wave at the beginning of a new complex regime (see figure 2.3) is transported along its lines. However, information itself is not the only commodity. E-commerce, or the electronically enabled retailing of software, digital books, digital services (e.g., online-brokering and e-banking), and digital outsourcing (e.g., data-processing) are now common phenomena. It is reasonable to add the growing number of Web-enabled transactions (*e-business*) of nondigital items and services, both business-to-business (B-to-B) and consumer-to-business (C-to-B), to this count. In sum, the Internet as infrastructure and enabler of networking already constitutes a significant global digital trade route and is increasingly developing into the central interchange circuit not only for commercial exchange but also for almost any other form of human interrelations.

The Internet

From its root as a U.S. defense network over its role as an international *virtual college* of scientific and academic researchers to the globally expanding World Wide Web (WWW), the history of the Internet has been one of exponential growth in both number of users and number of hosts connected to the network (Hudson, 1998; Zakon, 2006). In the late 1960s, the Advanced Research Projects Administration (ARPA), a branch of the U.S. Defense Department, developed the ARPAnet as a computer network linking universities and high-tech defense department contractors. Access to the ARPAnet was generally limited to computer scientists and other technical users. Its aim was to create a digital network that was capable of being flexible enough to reestablish itself in case of damage to one of its linkages (i.e., an attack by the USSR).[16]

In essence, the Internet is a "network of networks" (Berners-Lee and Fischetti, 1999, 18). Its most important feature is a set of standardized protocols (i.e., *conventions* by which computers exchange data, sliced into little *packets*, over various kinds of carriers). Central to the success of the Internet was the development of two main protocols governing this process: IP (Internet Protocol) and TCP (Transmission Control Protocol). Other protocols, such as the Hypertext Markup Language (HTML) or the domain name system governed by the Internet Assigned Number Authority (IANA) have proven equally important.

In just eight years, the NSFNET Backbone had grown from six nodes with 56 kbps (normal modem-based access speed-rate) links to 21 nodes with multiple 45 Mbps links (broadband speed-rate). The Internet grew to over 50,000 networks on all seven continents, with approximately 29,000 networks in the United States (Leiner et al., 2003). By 1990, the ARPANET itself was finally decommissioned. However, after $200 million from 1986 to 1995 in U.S. funding for the NSFNET program, TCP/IP had supplanted or marginalized most other wide-area computer network protocols worldwide, and IP was well on its way to becoming the most important bearer service for the global information infrastructure (Leiner et al., 1998). Although still heavily dominated by the United States in terms of numbers of both users and hosts, the Internet is now widely accessible in all industrialized countries and in major cities of most developing countries.

It is important to note, however, the central position (not only in geographical terms) the United States takes within this new digital network. As a result of the emergence of the Internet as a global common standard of the digital network, the United States still maintains its central role of this global network. By the early 1990s, the United States not only possessed the most developed computer networks in the world, but also—due to the result of the telecommunications and later dot.com boom in this period—was left with the most widely dispersed digital infrastructure, making it a priority for other countries to focus on links to the United States rather than on links between themselves and thus reinforcing the centrality of the United States in the digital hierarchy. Cukier (1999) for example notes, that it is often cheaper for national service providers to lease high-capacity Internet connections (from U.S. companies) from any European capital to the United States than from one capital to another within the continent (and thus through European providers).

As Townsend (2001b) demonstrates, whereas every region and nearly every country is now tied into the digital network in the form of a direct Internet connection to the United States, direct connections between other countries are less common. This is especially visible in the connection structure between different major regions, such as Europe and Asia, where direct connections are almost nonexistent. As a result, the United States still serves as a central switching facility for interregional data traffic and thus as a the central node of the digital external network system.

In his study of the development of the modern international telecommunication network, Barnett (2001) also finds evidence for a network he describes as one large interconnected group of nations arrayed along a center-to-periphery dimension. His findings indicate, that

> as the world moves into the information age, the international telecommunications network has become more dense, more centralized, and more highly integrated. The fact that the network is becoming more centralized during this period [from 1978 to 1996] indicates that an increasing amount of information is flowing through the core countries rather than being exchanged directly among the more peripheral nations. (Barnett, 2001, 1649)

Also important in the larger context of the historical global complex system development is the reemergence of major cities as important nodes of the external network development. During the transition from an internal network-based system to an external-based one, so called *global cities* acted mainly as sites (or network nodes) where transnational flows of goods, capital, and people were tied into national and regional economies (Sassen, 1997; see also Sassen, 1991). In other words, they tied the internal network structured economies to the global system.

As newer studies (Zook, 2000; 2001; Townsend, 2001b; 2001a) focusing on digital communication networks (and thus primarily Internet-based) have shown, many large, dense metropolitan clusters of Internet activity exist outside the archetypical global cities of New York, London, and Tokyo.[17] Evidence thus exists to demonstrate that new telecommunications networks reflect a more complex system of inter-urban information flows than implied by earlier works centering on the global city hypothesis, connecting a wider range of cities in a more complex way (Townsend, 2001a; 2001b).[18]

This renewed focus on a *centers and hinterlands* structure of the global system as well as the geographic centrality of the United States for the functioning (and control) makes it clear that despite its increasingly digital nature the global system is still very much a geopolitical one in the traditional sense of the meaning. Far from creating a sphere of "space- and placelessness" (e.g., Cairncross, 2001; Benedikt, 1991), the new external network based system despite its transformative dynamics does not render the spatial logic of existing modernist societies obsolete.

As Kitchin (1998; see also Dodge and Kitchin, 2001, Chapter 2; Mattelart, 2000) argues, geography continues to matter as an organizing principle and as a constituent of social relations. It cannot be entirely eliminated because of the interaction of the virtual space with the world beyond ICT networks and cyberspace, which only in combination constitute the external networks on which the global world system is based. Thus, it is more useful to distinguish spatial logic—as both Castells (1996) and Rosecrance (1999) point out—between the *space of flows* and *space of places.* As Morley and Robins (1995, 116) put it:

> If we have emphasized processes of delocalization, associated especially with the development of new information and communications networks, this should not be seen as an absolute tendency. The particularly of place and culture can never be done away with, can never be transcended. Globalization is, in fact, also associated with new dynamics of re-localization. It is about the achievement of a new global-local nexus, about new and intricate relations between global space and local space. Globalization is like a jigsaw puzzle: it is a matter of inserting a multiplicity of localities into the overall picture of a new global system.

For students of world history and the *longue durée* in the Braudelian tradition this story is all too familiar. Braudel (1992a) identified so called *world cities* (i.e., single cities dominating the world economy in which they operate), notably Venice, Antwerp, Genoa, Amsterdam, as crucial drivers of modern social change in Europe. Later replaced by the sequence of what Lee and Pelizzon (1991) have termed *hegemonic cities,* or rather economic centers of hegemonic states, these centers have experienced a three-phased development from adaptation to later integration (or nationalization), followed by the demise of this new focus on territoriality and the return of a network of central nodes of a global commercial, social, and cultural (and thus political) network (Taylor, 1995). Again, this development fits within our proposed model of a punctuation of the global system during the industrialization phase (with its focus on global internal networks and thus a stronger emphasis on territoriality) setting the stage for the emergence of a new, external network–based system with a renewed emphasis on world or rather global cities as its central nodes.

Shapiro and Varian (1999) argue that the main pillar of what is here referred to as the iNet economy is not a fundamental shift in the nature or even magnitude of the information itself but rather advances in information technology and infrastructure. The crucial difference to prior paradigms is the dramatic increase in the ability to manipulate information (Shapiro and Varian, 1999, 8–9). The changes that lead to the increased networking described above are rooted in the information technology infrastructure but also reinforce its development.

Increases in capacity, speed and digitalization, have provided possibilities to integrate graphics, text, video and sound (including voice) in applications, while the integration of computing and communication technologies has created possibilities of accessing and using interactively services and applications. Increasing bandwidth and speeds now permit transport integration and unprecedented flexibility and performance in network use as infrastructure to economic activities. The trend toward large numbers of highly sophisticated devices increasingly relying upon a network also constitutes a discontinuous transformation in the demands being placed upon the network infrastructure in terms of both the transmission volumes and the new pattern of use it will have to support (Borrus and Bar, 1993).

Rapid innovations in communication and computing technologies have reduced dramatically the per-unit costs of switching and transmitting information on networks. On transcontinental routes investment costs per voice path have declined from $6000 in 1989 to $1000 and on domestic markets the price of ISDN connection which provides two digital access lines is approaching, in some countries, the price of access for residential customers to the public switched telecommunication network (OECD, 1997, 12). In addition, developments in data compression techniques, and high capacity storage technologies complement these other developments. Convergence is taking place between technologies, infrastructures and at the content, service and application levels (OECD, 1997, 12). As Andrew Grove, the chairman of Intel, describes it, information technology producing industries will soon be seen just as "the Web infrastructure industry" (quoted in Lohr and Markoff, 1999; see also Greenstein, 2000).

The exponential growth in the number of Internet participants is remarkable. Figure 3.3 demonstrates this growth graphically. Starting from a population of under 16 million in 1995, termed as the beginning of the popular or public opening of the Internet in the form of the WWW, it has continued its extraordinary growth throughout the last decade, now counting nearly 600 million users worldwide, and connecting nearly ten percent of the world's population. This growth remains unhindered and continues its exponential path thus far.

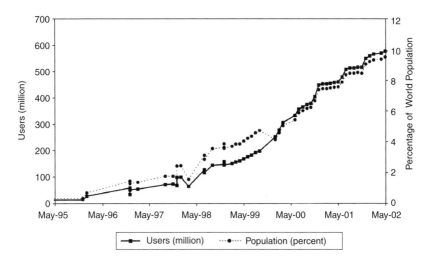

Figure 3.3 Internet Growth, Users and Share of World Population, 1995–2002
Source: http://www.nua.com, accessed December 14, 2002.

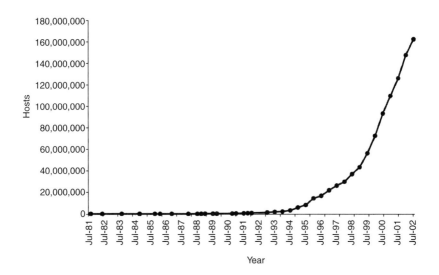

Figure 3.4 Internet Host Survey Count, 1981–2002
Source: Internet Software Consortium (http://www.isc.org/index.pl?/ops/ds/, accessed September 11, 2007).

Already, IP-based traffic exceeds voice traffic in several big markets, including the United States and Great Britain. IP traffic is rising at around 1,000 percent a year compared to PSTN (public switched telephone network) growth of under 10 percent (FT Information Technology Survey, 1999). Figure 3.4 portrays the growth of the core of the digital network, the Internet. Measuring the nodes constituting the Internet from 1981 on, the figure demonstrates the exponential growth of the Internet not from a user perspective but rather from the inside of the network. The release of the Internet into the public realm between 1994 and 1995, and also partially as a result of the creation of the WWW and additions to the network in terms of new standards (the so-called hypertext protocol and other W3 standards), the Internet not

Table 3.3   Number of Internet Hosts (gTLDs Adjusted[1]) and Web Sites, per 1,000 Inhabitants, July 1997–July 2001

	1997	Difference 2001	Actual 2001	OECD Share (Percent)[2]	Web Sites per 1,000 Inhabitants[3]
Turkey	0.26	3.37	3.63	0.00	0.3
Mexico	0.21	4.46	4.66	0.00	0.2
Slovak Republic	n/a	7.66	7.66	0.00	n/a
Korea	2.14	8.92	11.07	0.00	0.7
Poland	2.04	12.19	14.23	0.00	2.0
Portugal	3.11	10.71	13.82	0.00	1.7
Greece	2.77	14.59	17.37	0.00	1.2
Czech Republic	4.44	12.33	16.77	0.00	5.3
Hungary	3.18	16.02	19.20	0.00	2.7
Spain	4.01	22.17	26.17	0.01	3.0
France	5.26	21.94	27.20	0.01	4.3
Italy	3.68	36.76	40.44	0.02	6.1
Ireland	12.97	21.63	34.60	0.00	3.3
Japan	8.40	39.79	48.19	0.05	1.6
Germany [MP]	10.27	40.05	50.33	0.04	22.0
EU [MP]	12.25	40.79	53.04	0.18	12.7
Belgium	7.93	51.77	59.70	0.01	6.0
United Kingdom	15.66	54.05	69.71	0.04	24.2
Austria	7.23	76.89	84.12	0.01	10.8
Switzerland	20.68	53.41	74.09	0.00	16.9

Continued

Table 3.3   Continued

	1997	Difference 2001	Actual 2001	OECD Share (Percent)[2]	Web Sites per 1,000 Inhabitants[3]
OECD	20.33	80.28	100.60	1.00	17.5
Australia	30.91	60.17	91.08	0.02	9.4
Denmark	26.02	72.51	98.53	0.00	21.0
New Zealand	29.78	76.39	106.17	0.00	10.6
Netherlands	21.86	96.94	118.81	0.02	17.2
Norway	40.93	89.34	130.27	0.01	30.4
Sweden	35.00	142.02	177.02	0.01	19.3
Canada	30.41	152.66	183.07	0.05	24.7
Iceland	40.24	139.51	179.74	0.00	18.5
Finland	68.07	115.20	183.28	0.01	7.2
United States [(MP)]	56.51	218.75	275.26	0.67	46.5

Source: OECD, Information Technology Outlook 2002, calculations based on Netsizer (www. netsizer.com).

Notes: (MP) Indicates (potential) major power status (as measured by accepted standards in the international relations literature) and thus potential for systemic leadership in the global complex system.

[1] Global top-level domains (gTLDs) are distributed to the country of location.
[2] July 2001.
[3] July 2000.

only continued to double in growth every year but in fact increased its growth rate even further.

Table 3.3 breaks down the distribution of number of Internet hosts and web sites by individual countries. It also highlights the geographical differences in the dynamic unfolding of the growth of the Internet over the critical period between 1997 and 2001. Despite the enormous growth rates in some selected Northern European, namely the Scandinavian, countries, Northern America has not only continued to dominate the making up of the inner core of the Internet but also extended its dominance. Even if taken together, the European Union countries are the home of 18 percent of all Internet hosts and web sites. The vast majority of these sites and servers remain located in the United States (67 percent).

These numbers, however, widely underestimate the number of people connected to the global digital network, since it only takes into account users of the Internet that access it through PCs and leaves out the large number of users accessing the global digital network through other, mostly wireless, devices, such as mobile phones or other personal digital devices. The high overall number of Internet nodes and continued growth present in the relatively small Scandinavian and Benelux countries also indicates the need to look beyond the PC-based infrastructure of the Internet. It is in these countries that we can witness the marriage of the two main arteries of the global digital network: the digital communication networks, mainly in its mobile variant, and the digital data networks.[19]

Traditionally the geographic area featuring the most innovative clusters of mobile communication technology (see e.g., Steinbock, 2001), these countries, together with Japan, have been on the forefront of integration of mobile technology and thus its existing networks into the more general digital backbone, the PC-based Internet (Economist, 2002a; 2002b; Andrews, 1999; WuDunn, 1999). However, U.S.-based companies are catching up fast in this arena as well (The Economist Technology Quarterly, 2002). It is thus necessary to present here additional data reflecting the full composition of the global digital network.

Table 3.4 provides a broad overview over the development of global communication networks in the last decade of the (potential) new K-wave (where we would expect a major growth-rate).[20] Whereas the total market (measured in market revenue) has nearly tripled over this period, the distribution of growth is uneven. Telephone revenue increased from $331 billion in 1991 to $509 billion in 2001 (with international connections contributing a relatively modest contribution, rising from $37 billion in 1991 to $60 billion in 2001, a figure that has remained relatively stable since the late 1990s), but the real growth lays elsewhere. Mobile phone provision created revenues of only $19 billion worldwide in 1991. By 2001, mobile phones created revenues of more than $300 billion. Similarly, the increasing importance of data connections providing the backbone of the digital communication network in the form of digital data connections is reflected in the quadrupling of revenues from $53 billion in 1991 to over $200 billion a decade later.

Digital Mobile Communication Network

Existing ICT studies on the emergence of a *digital nervous center* (in the context of this study the digital external network structure) focus mainly on the information technology (IT) and the long-distance components of the communications network. The main focus is thus

Table 3.4 Key Global Telecom Indicators for the World Telecommunication Service Sector, 1991–2001, US$ billions (Adjusted for Inflation)

US$ Billions	1991	1992	1993	1994	1995	1996	1997	1998	1999	2000	2001	2002	2003	2004
Telecom market revenue (current prices and exchange rates)														
Services	403	448	470	517	596	672	712	767	843	920	968	1,039	1,126	n/a
Equipment	120	132	135	158	183	213	234	248	269	290	264	275	300	n/a
Total	522	580	606	675	778	885	946	1015	1,112	1,210	1,232	1,314	1,426	n/a
Telecom services revenue breakdown (current prices and exchange rates)														
Telephone[1]	331	350	359	386	428	444	437	456	476	477	479	478	475	552
International[2]	37	43	46	47	53	53	54	56	58	60	56	52	48	32
Mobile	19	26	35	50	78	114	142	172	218	278	317	364	414	454
Other[3]	53	72	77	81	89	114	133	139	155	165	180	195	210	210
Telecom services capital expenditure (current prices and exchange rates)														
Total[4]	124	131	135	139	158	170	176	177	186	198	201	205	215	190
Other statistics														
Main telephone lines (millions)	546	574	606	645	691	741	795	849	907	986	1,053	1,086	1,140	1,207

Continued

Table 3.4 Continued

US$ Billions	1991	1992	1993	1994	1995	1996	1997	1998	1999	2000	2001	2002	2003	2004
Mobile cellular subscribers (millions)	16	23	34	56	91	145	215	318	490	740	955	1,166	1,414	1,758
International telephone traffic minutes (billions)[5]	38	43	49	57	63	71	79	89	100	118	127	131	142	145
Personal computers (millions)	130	150	170	190	230	260	320	370	430	500	550	615	650	775
Internet users (millions)	4.4	7.0	10	21	40	74	117	183	277	399	502	619	724	863

Source: Adapted from International Telecommunication Union 2006 (http://www.itu.int/ITU-D/ict/statistics/at_glance/KeyTelecom99.html). Reproduced with the kind permission of ITU.

Notes: All expenditure data in billions of current US$ converted by annual average exchange rates. Country fiscal year data aggregated to obtain calendar year estimates. N/a indicates data are not available.

[1] Revenue from installation, subscription, and local, trunk, and international call charges for fixed telephone service.
[2] Retail revenue.
[3] Including leased circuits, data communications, telex, telegraph, and other telecom-related revenue.
[4] Note that the data of the growing number of new market entrants are not always reflected in national statistics.
[5] From 1994 including traffic between countries of former Soviet Union.

an IT-centered distributional one: Server technology providing digital nodes of distribution, the software architecture of the digital network "root" (Mueller, 2002), and the use of PC technology to access the network (both from a hardware and software angle). From a communications perspective, the focus is mainly on the long-distance network infrastructure (i.e., transatlantic submarine glass fiber and other high-capacity communication cables) providing the backbone of the network, Internet Service Provider (ISP) issues regarding broadband and phone-based access to the network, pricing and availability of capacity and switching technology.[21] To some degree, this is a reflection of the dominant structure of the digital network in North America, the birthplace of many of its leading technologies and innovations. This view, however, ignores other vital parts of the global digital commercial network structure. Notably wireless or mobile technology provides a means of access to the network in many areas outside of the United States and increasingly also within it.

Particularly in Europe and Asia, the distribution of highly advanced mobile handsets allowing sophisticated access to digital communication networks has enabled users usage of the global digital commercial network that stretches beyond their mere use as wireless phones. A core technology is the so-called Short Message Service (SMS), widely popular in Europe and Asia.[22] Its use contrasts with the dominant form of communication on the Internet, the usage of email or its sister technology, Instant Messaging.

With the integration of SMS and Internet services, this technology has become an important means of access to the digital global commercial network outside of North America, the only area where PC distribution still outweighs the distribution of mobile or cell phones. Several factors have combined to raise the profile of SMS. These include technological developments, Internet expansion, the changing profile of mobile users due to prepaid cards,[23] rapidly increasing applications for electronic commerce and the fact that the service appears to be superseding paging as mobile penetration rates increase (Paltridge, 2000, 63).

Most mobile operators (initially mostly outside of the United States, but since the mid 2000s increasingly also there as well) are offering an increasing range of services related to electronic commerce and other commercial activities, including mobile banking. SMS is also being increasingly used for some electronic commerce applications. These include payments, job dispatch, remote point of sale, remote monitoring

(e.g. monitoring vending machines), and similar tasks (Simon, 2000).
Mobile workers can send messages to their office (e.g. "task #abc
complete—en-route to next customer"), whereas offices can send information to mobile workers such as for pick up and delivery addresses
(Paltridge, 2000, 64). A good example of the integrative character of
this technology is its ability to bridge existing digital technologies and
make them accessible in a unique way. For example,

> The Short Message Service is ideal for sending Global Positioning
> System (GPS) position information such as longitude, latitude,
> bearing and altitude. GPS information is typically about 60 char-
> acters in length, leaving room for other information such as the
> vehicle registration details, average speed from the tachometer and
> so on to be transmitted as part of the same short message. Because
> the position updates are automatically generated, mobile network
> operators find that vehicle positioning applications are amongst
> the leading generators of short messages. (Simon, 2000)

But SMS technology bridges not only various communication and information technologies. It also allows for a cost- and time-efficient
integration of other components of the external network system, such
as expatriate workforces in the global economy. Diamond (2002)
describes, how SMS and mobile-based technology enables the roughly
ten percent of expatriate Philippine workforce to combine their two
separate lives:

> Today, the sprawling Philippine population is held together with
> the newest forms of groupware. Foreign workers rely on a variety
> of Web services for not only staying in touch with their home-
> towns...but also creating communities in their new locales...
> Moreover, the country's residents send and receive more cell phone
> text messages than citizens of any other nation...Morillo's story is
> quintessentially Philippine. His mother is employed as a fabric
> cutter on the Persian Gulf island of Bahrain. "When I run out of
> food," he explains, pulling a Nokia phone from his pocket, "I send
> my mother a text message telling her I need money for bread." His
> mom deposits dinars in a Bahrain bank, and a few days later
> Morillo ambles over to an ATM and withdraws pesos. Filipinos
> like Morillo send more than 100 million such missives daily. Each
> 160-character message costs 1 peso (2 U.S. cents) within the
> Philippines and 10 pesos internationally, making this possibly the

cheapest place on earth to get hooked on texting. And it's only the calling party who pays. A typical cell phone costs the equivalent of $50; most people buy prepaid cards that, for $6, cover the cost of 300 domestic messages. I MISS YOU; SEND MONEY; DO YOUR HOMEWORK—it's how OFWs [a widely used acronym for overseas Filipino workers] and their families remain families. Rosaria Reyes, the Filipina domestic helper killed by a suicide bombing in Israel last year, transmitted a message to her son the night before her death: Go to sleep already. MATULOG KA NA. (Diamond, 2002)

With the increasing sophistication of the mobile-based technology the *poor man's email*, SMS, has become the interface of choice for access to the digital commercial system for many users outside of the United States and increasingly there as well. Now firmly integrated into other existing technologies of the digital nervous central system, this technology has allowed the essential integration of the hinterlands into the major center network. A digital divide is certainly a reality in terms of level of integration, both in width and depth. It is, however, by now a divide that is being bridged by new forms of digital technologies of different levels of sophistication, creating together a truly global (in terms of its geographic reach) digital external network system (see Franda, 2002a; Franda, 2002b; 2002b; Scott, 1998; International Telecommunication Union (ITU), 2006; 2007).

The change in the structure of the setup of the global digital network is mirrored in the changes in distribution of access nodes to the network. Table 3.4 lists some of the most important elements of this change. Whereas the number of main (i.e., land-based) telephone lines only doubled during the 1990s, a clear shift toward mobile phones as an at least equally important means of access to the global digital network has occurred during this time period. From a base of a mere 16 million users, the number of subscribers of mobile phone services has now surpassed the number of land-based line subscribers. This is an especially important development given the widespread use of access to the global digital network (outside of the United States) through mobile digital devices (see discussion earlier in this chapter). It also complements the rise of the other means of access to the global digital network dominating in Northern America; from a base of 130 million PCs installed in 1991 worldwide, the number of installed PCs has risen to 550 million.

Table 3.5 Mobile Subscribers in OECD Countries, 1990–1999

Country	1990	1991	1992	1993	1994	1995	1996	1997	1998	1999
Australia*	184,943	291,459	440,103	682,000	1,096,836	1,920,341	3,882,097	4,748,477	5,858,000	6,426,000
Austria	73,698	115,402	172,453	221,450	278,749	383,535	598,804	1,164,270	2,242,800	3,122,850
Belgium	42,880	51,420	61,460	67,771	126,944	235,000	478,172	974,494	1,748,000	2,186,500
Canada	583,000	786,000	1,022,754	1,332,982	1,865,779	2,589,780	3,420,318	4,206,992	5,320,000	6,000,000
Czech Republic	0	1,242	4,651	11,151	27,357	45,725	200,315	521,469	965,500	1,288,854
Denmark	148,220	175,943	211,063	357,589	503,500	822,370	1,316,592	1,444,016	1,760,000	2,291,700
Finland	225,983	283,051	354,221	459,074	675,565	1,039,126	1,502,003	2,162,574	2,946,948	3,123,410
France	283,200	375,000	436,700	467,000	803,000	1,439,900	2,440,139	5,754,539	11,210,000	14,218,400
Germany	272,609	532,251	974,890	1,768,000	2,466,400	3,733,000	5,782,200	8,175,500	13,925,000	17,400,000
Greece	0	0	0	28,000	154,000	550,000	700,000	900,000	2,057,000	2,804,860
Hungary	2,645	8,477	23,292	45,712	142,000	261,000	473,000	705,000	1,073,000	1,278,500
Iceland	10,010	12,889	15,251	17,409	21,845	30,883	46,302	65,746	106,000	145,310
Ireland	25,000	32,000	44,000	57,065	81,666	132,183	290,000	510,747	946,000	970,000
Italy	266,000	568,000	783,000	1,206,975	2,239,700	3,925,400	6,413,412	11,733,904	20,480,000	24,500,000
Japan	868,078	1,378,108	1,712,545	2,131,367	4,331,369	10,204,023	20,876,820	38,253,000	47,308,000	49,702,000
South Korea	80,005	166,198	271,868	471,784	960,258	1,641,293	3,180,989	6,895,477	13,982,919	20,500,000

Luxembourg	824	1,130	1,139	5,082	12,895	26,868	45,000	67,208	94,000	164,000
Mexico	63,900	160,900	312,600	386,100	571,800	688,513	1,021,900	1,740,814	3,349,475	4,935,560
Netherlands	79,000	115,000	166,000	216,000	321,000	537,012	1,016,000	1,688,550	3,347,000	5,018,915
New Zealand*	54,100	72,300	100,200	143,800	186,000	328,311	422,800	606,200	710,000	789,900
Norway	196,828	227,733	280,000	368,100	582,500	980,300	1,261,445	1,676,763	2,121,000	2,387,520
Poland	0	0	2,195	15,699	38,942	75,000	216,900	812,000	1,928,000	3,070,502
Portugal	6,500	12,600	37,262	101,231	173,508	340,845	663,651	1,506,958	3,075,000	3,752,327
Spain	54,700	108,451	180,296	257,261	411,930	928,955	2,997,212	4,330,282	7,051,000	10,809,000
Sweden	461,200	568,200	652,000	785,000	1,381,000	2,008,000	2,492,000	3,169,000	4,109,000	4,414,000
Switzerland	125,047	174,557	215,061	259,200	328,300	446,000	662,700	1,044,400	1,672,300	2,240,000
Turkey	31,809	47,828	61,395	84,187	175,471	436,549	806,339	1,609,808	3,506,100	5,585,700
United Kingdom	1,114,000	1,260,000	1,507,000	2,215,820	3,940,000	5,670,000	6,817,000	8,344,000	14,874,000	16,795,000
United States	5,283,055	7,557,148	11,032,753	14,712,000	22,550,000	31,400,000	44,042,992	55,312,293	69,209,321	76,859,770
OECD	10,537,234	15,083,287	21,076,152	28,874,809	46,448,314	72,819,912	114,067,102	170,124,481	273,497,363	292,780,578

Source: OECD. Made available at http://www.oecd.org/sti/ICTindicators. (accessed Jan 13, 2001).

Note: * Australian series is for June and New Zealand for March.

Table 3.6 Mobile Subscribers, Worldwide, 1995–2001

Country	Cellular Mobile Subscribers					
	('000)		CAGR (percent)	Per 100 Inhabitants	Percent Digital	As percent of Total Telephone Subscribers
	1995	2001	1995–2001	1995–2001	2001	2001
Algeria	4.7	100.0	66.5	0.32	100.0	5.1
Angola	2.0	86.5	87.4	0.64		52.0
Benin	1.1	125.0	121.8	1.94	100.0	67.8
Botswana	—	278.0		16.54	100.0	64.9
Burkina Faso	—	75.0		0.64	82.7	56.6
Burundi	0.6	20.0	81.3	0.29	100.0	50.0
Cameroon	2.8	310.0	119.1	2.04	100.0	75.3
Cape Verde	—	31.5		7.21	100.0	33.6
Central African Rep.	—	11.0	151.0	0.29		52.4
Chad	—	22.0		0.29	90.9	66.7
Congo	—	150.0		4.82		87.2
Côte d'Ivoire	—	728.5		4.46	100.0	71.3
D. R. Congo	8.5	150.0	61.4	0.29		88.2
Djibouti	—	3.0		0.47		23.2
Egypt	7.4	2,793.8	169.0	4.33	100.0	29.5
Equatorial Guinea	—	15.0		3.19		68.5
Ethiopia	—	27.5		0.04	100.0	8.8
Gabon	4.0	258.1	100.3	20.45	99.2	87.4
Gambia	1.4	55.1	83.5	4.12		61.1
Ghana	6.2	193.8	77.5	0.93	25.5	44.5
Guinea	0.9	55.7	97.1	0.69		68.6
Guinea-Bissau	—					
Kenya	2.3	600.0	153.2	1.92	99.9	64.8
Lesotho	—	33.0		1.53	100.0	59.8
Libya	—	50.0		0.90	100.0	7.6
Madagascar	1.3	147.5	120.0	0.90		71.6
Malawi	0.4	55.7	129.4	0.54	100.0	50.7
Mali	—	45.3		0.39		47.6
Mauritania (1)	—	7.1		0.27	27.3	
Mauritius	11.7	300.0	71.6	25.17	66.7	49.4
Mayotte	—					
Morocco	29.5	4,771.7	133.4	15.68	100.0	80.0

Continued

Table 3.6 Continued

Country	Cellular Mobile Subscribers					
	('000)		CAGR (percent)	Per 100 Inhabitants	Percent Digital	As percent of Total Telephone Subscribers
	1995	2001	1995–2001	1995–2001	2001	2001
Mozambique	—	169.9		0.84	100.0	65.5
Namibia	3.5	100.0	74.8	5.59	100.0	46.0
Niger	—	1.8		0.02		7.9
Nigeria	13.0	500.0	83.7	0.43		48.1
Rwanda	—	65.0		0.82	100.0	75.1
S. Tomé & Principe	—					
Senegal	0.1	390.8	283.9	4.04	100.0	62.2
Seychelles	0.1	44.1	209.7	53.87	100.0	67.4
Sierra Leone	—	26.9		0.55		54.2
South Africa	535.0	11,029.7	65.6	25.19	100.0	69.1
Sudan	—	105.0		0.33	100.0	18.8
Swaziland	—	66.0		6.47	100.0	67.3
Tanzania	3.5	427.0	122.7	1.19	100.0	74.2
Togo	—	95.0		2.04	100.0	66.4
Tunisia	3.2	389.2	122.8	4.01		26.9
Uganda	1.7	322.7	138.6	1.43	100.0	83.5
Zambia	1.5	121.2	106.9	1.14	97.6	58.6
Zimbabwe	—	328.7		2.41	100.0	56.4
Total: Africa	*646.40*	*25,683.0*	*84.7*	*3.22*	*92.6*	*55.1*
Antigua & Barbuda		25.0		32.29		40.2
Argentina	340.7	6,974.9	65.4	19.26		46.2
Aruba	1.7	53.0	77.1	50.00		58.8
Bahamas	4.1	60.6	56.6	19.66		32.9
Barbados	4.6	53.1	50.3	19.62		29.2
Belize	1.5	39.2	71.3	16.05		52.6
Bermuda	6.3	13.3	13.2	20.64		19.2
Bolivia	10.0	744.0	105.1	8.99		59.1
Brazil	1,285.5	28,745.8	67.8	16.73		43.4
Canada	2,589.8	10,858.3	27.0	36.19		34.9
Chile	197.3	5,271.6	72.9	34.23		59.5
Colombia	274.6	3,265.3	51.1	7.63	100.0	30.9

Continued

Table 3.6 Continued

Country	Cellular Mobile Subscribers					
	('000)		CAGR (percent)	Per 100 Inhabitants	Percent Digital	As percent of Total Telephone Subscribers
	1995	2001	1995–2001	1995–2001	2001	2001
Costa Rica	18.8	311.3	59.7	7.57	100.0	24.8
Cuba	1.9	8.1	26.9	0.07		1.4
Dominica (1)		1.2		1.56		5.0
Dominican Rep.	56.0	1,270.1	68.3	14.65	65.5	57.1
Ecuador	54.4	859.2	58.4	6.67	60.0	39.1
El Salvador	13.5	800.0	97.5	12.50		57.2
Grenada	0.4	6.4	58.8	6.41		16.4
Guadeloupe		292.5		63.59		58.8
Guatemala	30.0	1,134.0	83.2	9.70		60.0
Guyana	1.2	75.3	98.2	8.66		48.5
Haiti		91.5		1.11		53.4
Honduras		237.6		3.61		43.4
Jamaica	45.1	700.0	57.9	26.94		57.7
Martinique		286.1		71.53	100.0	62.5
Mexico	688.5	21,757.0	77.8	21.68		61.2
Nicaragua	4.4	156.0	81.3	2.99	100.0	49.6
Panama		600.0		20.70	100.0	58.3
Paraguay	15.8	1,150.0	104.3	20.40	100.0	79.9
Peru	73.5	1,545.0	66.1	5.92		43.3
Puerto Rico	287.0	1,211.1	27.1	30.65		47.7
St. Kitts and Nevis (1)		1.2		3.12		5.2
St. Vincent (1)	0.2	2.4	61.5	2.08		8.7
Suriname	1.7	87.0	92.9	19.77	100.0	52.9
Trinidad & Tobago	6.4	256.1	85.2	19.70		45.1
United States	33,785.7	128,374.5	24.9	45.08	84.9	40.3
Uruguay	39.9	520.0	53.4	15.47		35.4
Venezuela	403.8	6,489.9	58.9	26.35		70.7
Virgin Islands (US) (1)		35.0		28.90		33.9
Total: Americas	*40244.30*	*224,362.6*	*33.2*	*26.7*	*51.8*	*42.1*

Continued

Table 3.6 Continued

Country	Cellular Mobile Subscribers					
	('000)		CAGR (percent)	Per 100 Inhabitants	Percent Digital	As percent of Total Telephone Subscribers
	1995	2001	1995–2001	1995–2001	2001	2001
Armenia		24.2		0.64	100.0	4.4
Azerbaijan	6.0	621.0	116.7	7.98	91.8	41.8
Bahrain	27.6	299.6	48.8	42.49	100.0	63.3
Bangladesh	2.5	520.0	143.4	0.40	80.8	47.9
Brunei Darussalam	35.9	137.0	25.0	40.90	100.0	60.8
Cambodia	14.1	223.5	58.5	1.66	96.7	87.0
China	3,629.0	144,820.0	84.9	11.03	100.0	44.5
Georgia	0.1	295.0	254.0	5.39		25.4
Hongkong, China	798.4	5,776.4	39.1	85.90	100.0	59.7
India	76.7	6,431.5	109.2	0.63	100.0	14.3
Indonesia	210.6	6,520.9	77.2	3.12	98.0	47.5
Iran (I.R.)	15.9	2,087.4	125.4	3.23	100.0	16.1
Israel	445.5	5,260.0	50.9	80.82		62.9
Japan	11,712.1	74,819.2	36.2	58.78	100.0	49.6
Jordan	12.4	866.0	102.9	16.71	100.0	56.7
Kazakhstan	4.6	582.0	124.1	3.62		24.1
Korea (Rep.)	1,641.3	29,045.6	61.4	62.08	100.0	56.1
Kuwait	117.6	877.9	39.8	44.54	100.0	65.0
Kyrgyzstan		27.0		0.54		6.5
Lao P.D.R.	1.5	29.5	63.6	0.55	100.0	36.0
Lebanon (1)	743.0	44.0	120.00	21.3	100	52.2
Macao, China	35.9	194.5	32.5	43.41	80.1	52.4
Malaysia	1,005.1	7,477.0	39.7	31.42	95.6	61.6
Maldives		18.9		6.89	100.0	41.0
Mongolia		195.0		8.12	99.7	61.1
Myanmar	2.8	13.8	30.7	0.03	98.1	4.5
Nepal		17.3		0.08	100.0	5.5
Oman	8.1	324.5	85.2	12.37		58.0
Pakistan	41.0	812.0	64.5	0.56	65.3	19.4
Palestine	20.0	300.0	57.0	9.06		53.9
Philippines	493.9	11,700.0	69.5	14.96	90.6	77.9
Qatar	18.5	178.8	46.0	29.31	99.5	51.6
Saudi Arabia	16.0	2,528.6	132.5	11.33	100.0	43.9

Continued

Table 3.6 Continued

Country	Cellular Mobile Subscribers					
	('000)		CAGR (percent)	Per 100 Inhabitants	Percent Digital	As percent of Total Telephone Subscribers
	1995	2001	1995–2001	1995–2001	2001	2001
Singapore	306.0	2,991.6	46.2	72.41	100.0	60.6
Sri Lanka	51.3	667.7	53.4	3.56	75.1	44.6
Syria		200.0		1.20	100.0	10.5
Taiwan, China	772.2	21,706.4	74.4	96.88	100.0	62.8
Tajikistan		1.6		0.03		0.7
Thailand	1,297.8	7,550.0	34.1	12.33	81.2	55.5
Turkmenistan (1)		9.5		0.2		2.5
United Arab Emirates	129.0	1,909.3	56.7	61.59	100.0	64.5
Uzbekistan	3.7	62.8	60.1	0.25		3.6
Viet Nam	23.5	1,251.2	94.0	1.54	99.3	29.1
Yemen	8.3	152.0	62.5	0.80	78.9	26.4
Total: Asia	*23727.9*	*33,9570.2*	*56.6*	*9.42*	*96.9*	*46.2*
Albania		350.0		8.82	100.0	63.9
Andorra (1)	23.5	52.8	2.80	30.2	100	40.8
Austria	383.5	6,565.9	60.5	80.66	99.6	63.3
Belarus	5.9	138.0	69.1	1.35	85.9	4.6
Belgium	235.3	7,690.0	78.8	74.59	39.9	60.0
Bosnia		233.3		5.74	100.0	34.1
Bulgaria	20.9	1,550.0	104.9	19.12		34.7
Croatia	33.7	1,755.0	93.3	37.70		50.8
Cyprus	44.5	314.4	38.5	45.59	99.9	42.0
Czech Republic	48.9	6,947.2	128.4	67.49	99.3	64.3
Denmark	822.3	3,960.2	30.0	73.79	99.5	50.6
Estonia	30.5	651.2	66.6	45.54	100.0	56.4
Finland	1,039.1	4,044.0	25.4	77.84	102.3	58.7
France	1,302.5	35,922.3	73.8	60.53	100.0	51.4
Germany	3,725.0	56,245.0	57.2	68.23	100.0	51.8
Greece	273.0	7,962.0	75.4	75.14	100.0	58.7
Greenland	2.1	16.7	41.9	29.86		39.0
Guernsey	2.4	31.5	54.1	50.22	100.0	36.5
Hungary	265.0	4,968.0	63.0	49.81	99.1	57.1
Iceland	30.9	235.4	40.3	82.02		55.3
Ireland	158.0	2,800.0	61.5	72.94		60.1
Italy	3,923.0	48,698.0	52.2	83.94		64.0

Continued

Table 3.6 Continued

Country	Cellular Mobile Subscribers					
	('000)		CAGR (percent)	Per 100 Inhabitants	Percent Digital	As percent of Total Telephone Subscribers
	1995	2001	1995–2001	1995–2001	2001	2001
Jersey	4.4	61.4	55.4	70.44	100.0	45.4
Latvia	15.0	656.8	87.7	27.94	99.1	47.5
Lithuania	14.8	932.0	99.5	25.32		44.7
Luxembourg	26.8	432.4	58.9	96.73	80.9	55.5
Malta	10.8	138.8	53.1	35.40	172.5	40.0
Moldova		210.0	396.6	4.78	14.8	23.7
Netherlands	539.0	12,352.0	68.5	76.70	100.0	55.3
Norway	981.3	3,737.0	25.0	82.53	98.7	53.4
Poland	75.0	10,050.0	126.2	26.02	93.2	46.9
Portugal	340.8	7,977.5	69.1	77.43	95.4	64.5
Romania	9.1	3,860.0	174.3	17.24	43.2	48.4
Russia	88.5	5,560.0	99.4	3.79	82.0	13.5
Slovak Republic	12.3	2,147.3	136.4	39.74	99.4	58.0
Slovenia	27.3	1,515.7	95.3	75.98	41.0	65.5
Spain	945.0	26,494.2	74.3	65.53		60.3
Sweden	2,008.0	7,042.0	23.3	79.03	98.0	51.7
Switzerland	447.2	5,226.0	50.6	72.38	100.0	50.2
TFYR Macedonia		223.3		10.92	100.0	29.3
Turkey	437.1	20,000.0	89.1	30.18	97.7	51.4
Ukraine	14.0	2,224.6	132.7	4.42		17.3
United Kingdom	5,735.8	46,282.0	41.6	77.04	100.0	56.7
Yugoslavia		1,997.8		18.71	11.7	45.0
Total: Europe	*24102.2*	*350,251.7*	*56.2*	*43.75*	*72.3*	*51.9*
Australia	2,242.0	11,169.0	30.7	57.61	100.0	52.6
Fiji	2.2	80.9	82.4	9.86	100.0	46.7
French Polynesia	1.1	67.3	97.0	28.46	100.0	56.1
Guam	5.0	32.6	36.8	20.74		29.0
Kiribati		0.5		0.58		12.1
Marshall Islands	0.3	0.5	10.8	0.70		10.5
Micronesia						
New Caledonia	0.8	67.9	108.6	30.97	100.0	57.3
New Zealand	365.0	2,288.0	35.8	59.88	77.9	55.7

Continued

Table 3.6 Continued

Country	Cellular Mobile Subscribers					
	('000)		CAGR (percent)	Per 100 Inhabitants	Percent Digital	As percent of Total Telephone Subscribers
	1995	2001	1995–2001	1995–2001	2001	2001
Northern Marianas (1)	3.0	20.1	1.20	5.7		12.5
Papua New Guinea		10.7		0.20		14.7
Samoa		3.2		1.78		21.7
Solomon Islands (1)	1.2	38.0	0.20	0.3		13.0
Tonga	0.3	0.2	3.9	0.24	100.0	2.1
Vanuatu	0.1	0.3	19.4	0.17		4.9
Total: Oceania	*2,621.0*	*13779.20*	*31.8*	*44.04*	*95.9*	*52.7*
Total: World	*90,695.20*	*954,262.4*	*48.0*	*15.69*	*77.1*	*47.6*

Source: International Telecommunication Union (ITU Statistical Annex, 2002). Reproduced with the kind permission of ITU.

Note: (1) Data from 2000.

Table 3.5 breaks down the growth of the mobile digital comm-unication networks from 1990 to 1999 in OECD countries, whereas table 3.6 traces the growth of mobile networks from 1995 to 2001 worldwide. Given its large population size, it is not surprising to see the United States not only starting out on the highest base and thus the most mature (analog) cellular network with over 5 million subscribers in 1990. This number has reached nearly 77 million in 1999. Though starting from a much lower base, Western European countries such as Germany, France, Italy, and Spain have managed to develop signifi-cant, technologically advanced and digital-based mobile communica-tion networks with subscriber rates ranging from over 10 million in Spain in 1999, more than doubling this number in only two years to a subscriber base of more than 26 million. Germany has seen even more growth in this period, from over 17 million subscribers in 1999 to over 56 million in 2001. In Italy, the first Western European country where the number of mobile subscribers have surpassed those of land-based communication lines, 24 million mobile subscribers in 1999 have dou-bled to 49 million in 2001.

Among the advanced economies and political major powers, the United States (largely as a result of its size) emerges as the leading nation, featuring the second largest mobile user base in the world, with over 128 million subscribers. In comparison to larger Western European countries such as France, Great Britain, or Germany, but also smaller countries such as the Netherlands, Ireland, Denmark, Norway, and Finland, with a average penetration rate of around three quarters of the population (in 2001), its penetration rate of 45 percent in 2001 demonstrates the higher reliance on other means of access to the global digital network, mainly in the form of PCs. The United States remains the only developed country with a higher rate of PC than mobile user-penetration. It should be noted, however, that this trend is changing fast, with digital mobile networks expanding rapidly in the United States since 2001.

Japan, Taiwan, and especially South Korea take on a special role in the bridging of the PC-based and mobile-based access to the global digital network, being leaders, both in terms of technological sophistication but also installed bases, in both technologies. Table 3.6 captures the enormous development of digital mobile communication networks in those two countries. From a base of roughly 868,000 mobile subscribers in Japan, and only 80,000 in South Korea, both countries emerged as clear leaders of sophisticated digital mobile networks in Asia (as well as in the world) as early as 1995, when both countries had developed networks with subscription rates reaching over ten million and over 1.6 million, respectively.

By 1999 these numbers had further expanded (see table 3.5 and 3.6). Japan boasted one of the largest digital mobile networks in the world, with an installed base of nearly 50 million in 1999 and 75 million in 2001, followed by South Korea, which has developed subscriber base of over 20 million users in 1999 and 29 million in 2001. In addition, South Korea boasts one of the most sophisticated installed base of broadband Internet access and the highest relative user penetration in any larger population economy (see table 3.7). Similarly, Taiwan with its special role as a key electronic equipment provider in the area of PC and mobile communication manufacturing has established from a base of 772,000 in 1995 a quasi ubiquitous, fully digital and advanced mobile distribution of 22 million subscribers or 97 percent of the population (see table 3.6).

Table 3.6 extends the survey of mobile subscriber growth to include the development of the global mobile network on a worldwide scale, now connecting nearly a sixth of the world population with close to a

Table 3.7 Broadband Penetration, Subscribers per 100 Inhabitants, 2002–2006

Rank	Country	2002	Rank	Country	2004	Rank	Country	2006
1	Singapore	24.4	1	Iceland	24.6	1	Iceland	34.5
2	Iceland	20.1	2	Singapore	24.4	2	New Zealand	31.2
3	Denmark	14.5	3	Finland	20.5	3	Finland	29.4
4	South Korea	12.3	4	Denmark	17.9	4	Singapore	24.4
5	Sweden	10.7	5	Faroe Islands	17.2	5	Canada	24.3
6	Norway	10.2	6	South Korea	16.4	6	Norway	23.2
7	Canada	9.1	7	New Zealand	16.0	7	South Korea	23.0
8	Belgium	7.9	8	Norway	16.0	8	Denmark	21.6
9	United States	7.5	9	Canada	15.6	9	United Kingdom	19.8
10	New Zealand	6.6	10	Sweden	15.4	10	Sweden	19.6
11	Finland	6.2	11	Belgium	11.3	11	Australia	18.2
12	Netherlands	5.8	12	United States	10.8	12	Luxembourg	17.5
13	Ireland	5.7	13	United Kingdom	10.5	13	Faroe Islands	16.9
14	Austria	4.6	14	Ireland	10.5	14	United States	16.6
15	Japan	3.8	15	Netherlands	10.0	15	Switzerland	16.4
16	Estonia	3.5	16	Switzerland	8.6	16	UAE	15.5
17	Germany	3.0	17	Austria	8.3	17	Netherlands	14.5
18	Switzerland	3.0	18	Estonia	8.1	18	Belgium	14.4
19	France	2.9	19	France	7.6	19	Japan	13.0
20	United Kingdom	2.8	20	Japan	7.4	20	Ireland	12.8
21	Spain	2.2	21	Italy	6.9	21	Croatia	12.3
22	Portugal	2.0	22	Germany	6.9	22	France	12.2
23	Australia	1.8	23	Hungary	6.4	23	Germany	12.2
24	Latvia	1.7	24	Luxembourg	6.3	24	Italy	12.2
25	Italy	1.6	25	Australia	5.9	25	Hungary	12.1
26	Israel	1.3	26	Latvia	5.4	26	Israel	11.4
27	Cyprus	1.2	27	UAE	5.2	27	Austria	11.4
28	Hungary	1.1	28	Czech Republic	5.0	28	Spain	10.9
29	Luxembourg	1.0	29	Israel	4.8	29	Slovenia	10.6
30	Brazil	0.9	30	Portugal	4.8	30	Kuwait	10.2

Source: Figureseeq, a database covering seventy-four countries belonging to Teleconomy Group (www. teleconomy.com).

Notes: Raw data is drawn from national statistical bodies and international organizations and processed by Teleconomy. Forecast data are the results of tailored econometric models run for each country. Net Figures managing consultant: qmars.safikhani@teleconomy.com.

billion subscribers. It is noticeable, that especially among developing nations currently not endowed with an extensive telecommunication network the mobile network is largely completely digital (and thus relatively advanced and able to tie in with existing digital global network telecommunication and especially data networks). In addition, these networks provide many less developed countries with a relatively cost-efficient way to supplement and in some case actually build national telecommunication networks that allow a tie-in into existing global digital network structures. For example, nearly all the mobile networks in Africa are based on digital technology, whereas Europe still features many areas with analog legacy systems and as a whole features only 72 percent digital networks of all mobile networks (see for example Belgium, which despite its high mobile penetration rate of three-quarters of all its inhabitants, still relies largely on nondigital technology). These networks, however, are rapidly being replaced with digital infrastructure as well (see esp. the latest ITU surveys on this subject, International Telecommunication Union (ITU), 2006; International Telecommunication Union (ITU), 2007).

Table 3.6 also reveals the increasing importance of mobile communication and data networks in China, already the largest mobile subscriber market in the world, featuring nearly 145 million subscribers (in 2001). Maybe even more important, the Chinese mobile market is still characterized by its rapid growth. The compound average growth rate (CAGR) between 1995 and 2001, despite the relative large base of nearly four million subscribers in 1995, was an astonishing 85 percent and shows no sign of slowing down. This contrasts sharply with India, the second largest state in the world after China in terms of population, which featured a total of 6.4 million subscribers in 2001. In contrast to China, India relies much more on PC technology for its connection into the global digital network, featuring the fastest growing computer service industry worldwide for a number of years and increasingly providing sophisticated business process services previously a mainstay of advanced Western economies.[24]

Table 3.7 projects the continued lead of the same group of countries codeveloping their access structure to the global digital network. Based on a relative projection of subscribers per 100 inhabitants, the data presented here provide further evidence for our previous finding of a distinct set of geographic groups emerging in the digital commercial system. The Nordic European countries on the forefront of mobile telecommunication technology innovation, i.e., Finland, Norway, as well as Sweden, find their equivalent group in a small number of Asian states, namely South Korea, Taiwan, and Japan. Both groups provide not only crucial clusters of innovation in mobile telecommunication technology but also increasingly a bridging function between the main two means of access to the global digital network, digital mobile tools and PC-based solutions.

In addition the United States and China stand out as countries featuring a single, large market and user-base for both, mobile and PC-based means of access to the global digital network. In addition, however, both also can boast of leading technology clusters in mobile telecommunication technology. In the realm of the PC industry, the emphasis in China remains clearly production-focused (Smith, 2002), whereas the United States still maintains its lead in computer-design and microprocessor innovation (Breshnahan and Malerba, 1999; Langlois and Steinmueller, 1999). This lead is best demonstrated in the continued high rate of innovation of microprocessing power, exemplified in *Moore's law* (after Intel cofounder Gordon Moore).[25]

Biotechnology and Life Sciences

Following in the footsteps of the rise of ICT as a leading sector (and to a large degree now intricately interwoven with this technology) the biotechnology industry can trace its origin in its current form back to the late 1960s and early 1970s. The scientific results enabling genetic engineering techniques built upon more than twenty years of basic research in molecular biology, microbiology, and related fields on DNA (deoxyribonucleic acid), genes, and on cells (McKelvey, 2000, Chapter 5).[26] Indeed, one of the crucial scientific breakthroughs occurred at Cambridge University in 1953 when James Watson and Francis Crick first discerned the double-helix structure of DNA. In the following decades, scientists worldwide struggled with the then harrowing challenge of deciphering and manipulating the billions of molecular components that make up DNA, the master molecule at the heart of all living things (Wolff, 2001, 4).

The genetic engineering techniques developed in the 1970s enabled controlled changes to DNA and followed largely the logic and possibilities that molecular biologists had understood when they possessed the theoretical knowledge but no practical techniques. Alongside basic research unlocking the genetic information of molecules such as DNA, the commercial uses of genetic engineering, mainly for the production of pharmaceuticals, began to develop in the 1970s. Often seen as the start of the new biotech industry, the 1976 founding of the Californian biotech firm Genentech provided a model in which basic scientist and venture capitalists joined together. In general, these firms would sell R&D contracts to established firms in order to develop new scientific knowledge and techniques for the use and adaptation of scientific activities to commercial purposes (McKelvey, 2000, 91–92).[27]

Up until the mid-1980s, most biologists had little use for computers other than to compare DNA sequences and as a communication tool, in the form of electronic mail over the precursor of the Internet. In the late 1980s, however, a significant transformation within the biomedical science finally became a widespread phenomenon, namely the computer-enabled shift from single-gene studies to experiments involving thousands of genes at a time, from small-scale academic studies to industrial-scale ones, and from a molecular approach to life to an information-based one, highly dependent on sophisticated computing and processing power (Zweiger, 2001, x–xi). In a sense, biology was transformed into an informational science. This is development is reflected in the various projects to decode and digitalize the vast

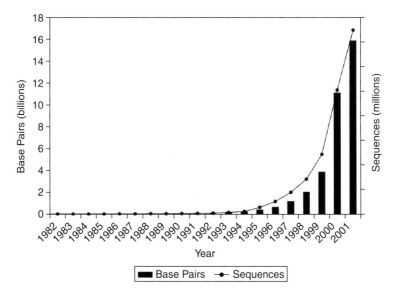

Figure 3.5   Number of Base Pairs (billions) and Sequences (millions) in GenBank Database, 1982–2001

Source: Data from Genetic Sequence Data Bank. 2002. GenBank Growth. National Center for Biotechnology Information (NCBI), U.S. National Library of Medicine (http://www.ncbi.nlm.nih.gov/Genbank/genbankstats.html, accessed March 12, 2002).

amounts of genetic information available for further scientific exploration and commercial exploitation.

Figure 3.5 graphically displays the enormous changes in the amount of available genetic information, showing the rise of digitalized and categorized information about genetic base pairs and sequences stored in a central databank, GenBank. After important introduction of information processing techniques in the late 1980s and early 1990s, the amounts of data rose exponentially, from 680,338 base pairs and 606 complete sequences in 1982, to 101,008,486 base pairs and 78,608 sequences a decade later. Roughly another decade later, biologists had created a sea of biological information, including 15,849,921,438 base pairs and 14,976,310 entire sequences in 2001 in a single data bank.

By now, biology, electronics, and informatics are converging and interacting in their applications, in their materials, and—more fundamentally— in their conceptual approach (Zweiger, 2001; Kelly, 1994). On the hardware side, biochips have compressed thousands of laboratory analyses onto miniscule platforms. A single GeneChip from Affymetrix, the leading maker of microarrays based in Santa Clara, California, now has more than 500,000 interrogation points (The Economist, 2002c).

In addition, the manipulation and duplication of genes and genetic patterns (i.e., cloning and recombination) has become a standardized technical process. The convergence of supercomputers, advanced mathematics and robotics has made possible the fully automatized process of mapping genomes, creating vast amounts of biological data (Enriquez and Goldberg, 2000). These data are now at the center of the most important area commercially in the software side of biotechnology, bioinformatics.

The changes brought about by computers in biology resemble those in the aircraft and car industries in the 1990s, after the arrival of powerful software for CAD (computer-aided design) and CFD (computational fluid dynamics). Engineers embraced the new computational modeling tools as a way of designing products faster, more cheaply and more accurately. In a similar way, biotech firms are now looking to computer modeling, data mining and high-throughput screening to help them discover drugs more efficiently (Cookson, 2002). In the process, biology (and, more specifically, biopharmacy) has become one of the biggest consumers of computing power, demanding petaflops (i.e., thousands of trillions of floating-point operations per second) of supercomputing power, and terabytes (i.e., trillions of bytes) of storage (Economist, 2002c). These vast amounts of computing power are increasingly made possible through grid-computing technology, combining biotechnology with ICT in the form of computing processing power and networking capabilities (Taylor, 2002).

Bioinformatics is a spectrum of technologies, covering such things as computer architecture (e.g., workstations, servers, supercomputers and the like), storage and data-management systems, knowledge management and collaboration tools, and the life-science equipment needed to handle biological samples. Bioinformatics companies sell both software and services for manipulating of all this sort of data. Most do not produce any novel data themselves: they only find ways to transform other organizations' data (Barlow, 1999). Biological data are flooding in at an unprecedented rate and biotechnology is now mainly an information industry.

First, there has been an enormous creation of new biological data (such as DNA sequence data from the various genome-sequencing projects but also all the information that biologists are gathering about metabolic pathways, gene function and proteins). Second, there is chemical data. Most pharmaceutical companies now own, or have access to vast libraries[28] of compounds with potential medicinal value. Third, there is literature-based data (including searchable databases of published research, and access to worldwide patent information). Fourth, there is clinical information. Great effort is put into time-reducing the performance of clinical trials and improving their chances for success. Clinical and toxicity data are becoming crucial in this regard (Barlow, 1999).

An important issue facing any leading sector but especially so in an environment characterized by digital networks, is the problem of standardization. Without the setting of standards, leading sectors cannot develop their full potential and diffuse their core technologies into other sectors to form a new technological style. Bioinformatics is no exception. At the BIO 2001 conference in San Diego, fifty biotechnology, pharmaceutical and IT companies announced plans enable standards for the collaboration of the various cells in the biotechnology tissues. Their new consortium, known as the Interoperable Informatics Infrastructure Consortium or I3C for short,[29] enables researchers to exchange and manipulate data from hundreds of different sources over the Internet (Cookson, 2002). I3C's *Life Science Identifier*, released in mid-2002, defines a simple convention for identifying and accessing biological data stored in multiple formats. Meanwhile, the "Distributed Annotation System," a standard for describing genome annotation across sources, is gaining popularity (The Economist, 2002c). Thus, a crucial step has been taken to follow the first wave of standardization in the ICT sectors to form a new leading sector of the information network economy.

New partnerships between IT and biotech companies are being formed at a very fast rate, as we would expect them to from both, our global system process model anticipating an innovative surge of commercial activity in this area (variation creation in the evolutionary global economic system process, see chapter 2) and organizational model discussed later in the following chapter. The list covers bioinformatics, DNA microarrays (gene chips), data analysis and visualization, chemical and biological library integration, detection of human genetic variation (SNPs), microfluidics, and in silico research. However, almost all the big IT participants are American or Japanese. Large European IT companies are virtually absent from the list (Cookson, 2002).

The most commonly used measure of biotechnology activity employed is the comparison of patents (esp. in the business school literature, see e.g., Enriquez, 2001; Henderson et al., 1999). Henderson et al. (1999, see esp. tables 7.2 and 7.3; see also Enriquez, 2001) have demonstrated the dominance of U.S. activity in this sector during the early period from 1978 to 1993. During this period, the United States claims a share of 36.5 percent of all world patents granted in the biotechnology sector[30] contrasting with 19.5 percent of total world patent share of Japanese, 12 percent share of German, 6.0 percent of French, 5.9 percent of UK, and 4.2 percent of Swiss patentees, respectively. It is important to note that although the United States clearly hosts the majority of biotechnology firms during this period, Japan also features a strong base of firms. However, this "parity" holds true only on a superficial level and a simple firm count comparison.

A closer look reveals a much different picture. Crucial differences exist in the institutional forms of the biotechnology clusters in the various countries listed above. Newly found firms are far more important in the United States and the UK than they are elsewhere, playing a negligible role in Japan, Germany, and Switzerland, whereas the public sector plays a disproportionately important role in France (Henderson et al., 1999, 290–91). This is especially important in respect to the ability to innovate and more general questions of lock-in and technological trajectories (McKelvey, 2000, see case studies, for discussion of the terms, see Chapters 2 and 9), allowing U.S. firms to embrace much more forcefully the coming marriage of ICT and biotechnology.

During the 1990s, the absolute number of U. S. Patent and Trademark Office (USPTO) and European Patent Office (EPO) biotechnology patents has grown substantially in comparison with the total number of patents. Between 1990 and 2000, the number of biotechnology patents granted by the USPTO increased by 15 percent, compared to an increase of just 5 percent for patents, overall. At the EPO, biotechnology patent applications show a very similar trend: between 1990 and 1997, the number of biotechnology patents increased by 10.5 percent, while total patents rose by 5 percent. It is important to note that at both the USPTO and at the EPO the top six biotechnology patentees are identical. Only then a clear geographical bias appears, at the USPTO with Canada and at the EPO with European countries (Beuzekom, 2001, 10–11).

The reliance on patents as a cross-national indicator for sectoral leadership becomes questionable, however, with recent developments in U.S. patenting laws and the associated activity with patentees. To a large degree, this is a consequence of a 1980 U.S. Supreme Court decision (1980), ending a decade long law dispute brought about by General Electric in 1971 (attempting to patent a bacterium that would attack oil spills). Although the bacterium in question was never commercialized, the Supreme Court decision was significant in that it was allowing patents on living organisms and genes. Within two years, more 100 firms had been formed, with annual global sales in the early 1990s exceeding $20 billion (Rathmann, 1993). Since then, the American courts and the USPTO have moved sharply in the direction of strong and broad patent protection in the biotechnology sector (Maskus, 2000, 51–56). Patents have been filed (and issued) covering all potential products of the genetic engineering of a particular plants, animals,[31] or a critical research tool, such as a genetic sequence developed for the use of a specific drug but could also be used an/or required in the development of numerous pharmaceutical products, all of which would be subject to the initial patent (Barton, 1995).

This development has led to a situation, in which the amount of patent requests simply overwhelms the capacity of any of the globally active patent offices and agencies. In 1991 the volume of genetic patent requests on various expressed sequence tags (ESTs) had reached 4,000, a number deemed abnormally high at that time and largely a result of the liberal patent regime of the United States. With the advances of biotechnology and increasing sophistication of analytical tools, genetic patent requests for ESTs exploded in the following five years to reach 22,000. After the development of biotechnology into an information science, the situation became wholly unmanageable: by 1996, the number of patent requests for ESTs had reached 500,000 (Enriquez, 2001, 93–97).

Table 3.8 National Shares (in percentage) of the Total Number of Publications in the Biotechnology and Applied Microbiology NSIOD Journal Category, 1986–1998

Country	1986	1987	1988	1989	1990	1991	1992	1993	1994	1995	1996	1997	1998	Mean
Belgium	1	1.4	1.4	1.1	1	1	1	1	1.6	1.4	1.2	1.4	1	1.2
Canada	9.4	10.5	8.8	7.6	6.3	6.9	6.4	5.9	5.8	6.3	5.1	5.1	3.8	8.2
Denmark	0.6	0.7	0.4	0.5	0.5	0.6	1	0.9	1	1.1	1.2	1.1	1.4	0.8
Finland	1.1	0.9	0.9	0.6	1	1.3	0.8	1.8	1	1.2	0.8	0.8	0.7	0.9
France	7.4	7.1	7	6.1	6.4	6.4	6.9	5.6	6.7	6.9	6.3	7.5	7.3	5.9
Germany	5.4	6.4	6.1	6.5	6.3	6.9	7.3	6.6	6.7	6.8	7.3	6.3	6.9	6
Italy	1.1	1.1	1.3	2.1	1.6	3.8	2.2	4.1	2.5	2.7	2.7	2.7	2.6	2.1
Japan	10.9	10.7	11.3	11.4	12.3	12.6	12.1	13.1	12.7	11.9	10.7	11.6	12.9	12.1
Netherlands	2.2	2.1	2.7	2.1	2.9	2.8	2.6	2.9	2.9	2.8	3.1	3.1	3	2.4
Norway	0.1	0.2	0	0.2	0.4	0.2	0.2	0.3	0.5	0.2	0.3	0.4	0.5	0.2
Spain	1.8	2.2	2.2	2.2	2.4	2.8	2.7	3.6	3.6	4.1	4.9	4.5	4.8	2.6
Sweden	2	1.4	1.7	1.9	1.9	2.2	1.4	1.3	2	1.5	1.4	2	1.9	1.8
Switzerland	1.9	1.1	1.7	1.1	1.2	1.1	1.6	1.9	1.6	1.9	1.8	1.8	1.8	1.5
United Kingdom	12.4	10.2	8.9	7.9	10.1	11	9.7	8.6	9.6	11	8.7	8.6	8.7	9.3
United States	22.9	23.8	28.8	26.5	27	22.8	22.2	21.8	20.5	21.2	21.5	21.8	21	23.9
Other countries	19.8	20.2	16.8	22.2	18.7	17.6	21.9	20.6	21.3	19	23	21.3	21.7	20.3
Total number of papers	1,574	1,889	2,115	2,174	2,347	2,699	2,807	2,845	3,156	3,196	3,161	3,265	3,261	

Source: OECD (Beuzekom, 2001), based on data from NUTEK Sweden.

Note: The total number of publications in the Biotechnology and Applied Microbiology NSIOD journal category in the period 1986–1998 was 34,489.

Given this development, we have chosen here to rely on a different measure to evaluate national sectoral leadership in biotechnology, namely the national share of the total number of biotechnology and applied microbiology publications, as well as the composition of international strategic biotechnology technology alliances.

Table 3.8 provides an overview of the development of the relative national share of publications in the biotechnology and applied microbiology NSIOD journal category between 1986 and 1998. The bibliometric data employed here is based on publications in scientific journals and citations to journal articles. We have chosen this measure here, because it provides a far more conservative estimate of sectoral dominance and leadership than the simple count of biotechnology patents. Whether or not a firm decides to publish an article in a scientific publication depends on several strategic choices. Firms might decide not to publish if they wishes to keep information secret, or they could publish to prevent their competitors from patenting. Thus, publishing papers can reflect the business strategies of corporations rather than the amount of knowledge produced (see discussion in Nilsson et al., 2000).

McKelvey (2000, esp. 157–63) points to this phenomenon in her case study of the pioneering firms in the early biotechnology development, the commercial Genentech group and Baxter and Goodman group of researchers at UCSF (University of California at San Francisco), financed by Kabi and Eli Lilly, respectively. Both, the firms funding and carrying out scientific activities as well as the scientists at universities had reasons for making some of the results of their work public. Despite the high stakes involved in the patenting attempts, both found it was important to establish basic scientific success, whether for the basic scientific or the scientific-economic environment in which they operated.

Thus, assuming that publication strategies are fairly constant over time, the number of papers published by firms and their collaboration patterns can reveal interesting trends in research and development activities. Table 3.8 shows the share of such publications for selected European countries, as well as for Canada, Japan and the United States. The share for most countries has remained stable over time even though the number of biotechnology articles more than doubled, from 1,574 in 1986 to 3,261 in 1998. Together, the United States and Japan account for about a third of all publications in these fields and it is noticeable how the United States holds a constant leadership position in the field. So rather than arguing for a frenzy of activity emerging only in the mid-1990s, establishing a U.S. lead in the sector, we argue here for a

Table 3.9 International Strategic Biotechnology Technology Alliances with at Least One Partner Based in the United States, 1980–1998

	1980	1981	1982	1983	1984	1985	1986	1987	1988	1989	1990	1991	1992	1993	1994	1995	1996	1997	1998
Total U.S. alliances	139	126	200	177	234	235	292	318	367	357	312	287	394	444	497	639	578	497	477
U.S.–Europe	5	6	9	7	14	22	24	28	21	16	11	18	40	42	62	59	75	49	47
U.S.–Japan	6	8	12	7	7	16	14	11	6	6	4	1	5	10	7	6	13	14	6
U.S.–other	3	2	1	0	2	3	0	3	4	5	4	1	5	7	6	6	7	6	2
Intra U.S.	10	12	23	13	28	27	39	36	36	23	13	16	33	57	58	60	53	93	53
Total biotech alliances	24	28	45	27	51	68	77	78	67	50	32	36	83	116	133	131	148	162	108

Source: OECD (Beuzekom, 2001).

continued dominance of the sector, not only in terms of technological and scientific innovation, but also in terms of commercialization of the technology in question.

To substantiate this second argument, we also provide an overview of the development of international strategic biotechnology alliances with at least one partner based in the United States.[32] Table 3.9 lists the number of all U.S. alliances from 1980 to 1998, as well as alliances with U.S. firms involving European, Japanese, and other international partners and alliances of biotechnology firms involving only U.S. firms. The first row gives the number of all U.S. technology alliances between 1980 and 1998 that were included in the CATI database employed as the basis of these data. The following rows list the number of U.S. biotech alliances involving a European, Japanese, or other international partner, alliances involving only U.S. partner, and finally the sum of all biotech alliances as well as the percentage of international alliances.

The total number of U.S. technology alliances has risen from 139 in 1980 to 312 a decade later in 1990, and reach a total of 639 in 1995, although this number has declined to 477 in 1998. Table 3.9 shows that the percentage of all technology alliances in the United States based on biotechnology has followed a cyclical pattern, with an increase in the late 1980s, a decline to 1990, followed by another increase with a peak in 1997. More importantly, however, other than annual fluctuations, there do not appear to be any consistent differences over time in the share of international U.S. biotechnology alliances out of all biotechnology alliances. In addition, intra-U.S. alliances seem to be increasingly favorable as an alternative to ones involving an international partner (especially given the largest direct competitor, Japan). Another important implication is that the U.S. lead in biotechnology has remained relatively constant. In contrast, the share of U.S.-Europe alliances has grown while the share of U.S.-Japan alliances has declined. These data confirm further our argument laid out in earlier chapters of the growing importance of new organizational forms in the external network based iNet economy.

Conclusion

In this chapter, we have provided empirical evidence for the formation of new leading sectors and thus the development of a new phase in the global world system process, emerging in the 1970s and marking the transition from an internal network based structure to one based an external network structures. The key leading sectors driving the development of what we have termed earlier the iNet economy are firmly tied to the development of digital communication networks that provide the infrastructure necessary for networking and e-type organizational structures discussed in the following chapter 4. The leading sectors identified are networking and information and communication technologies (ICTs), as well as biotechnology. We have also demonstrated, how biotechnology has increasingly been turned into an informational science, thus being able to take full advantage of the innovational advances of the first stage of a new K-wave, namely the advances in information processing and networking.

This chapter has also demonstrated the elevated position the United States has assumed in the development of the iNet economy. Compared to its closest competitors from the previous K-wave its loss of relative dominance in previous leading sectors has been well documented (see chapter 3). Our analysis here, however, demonstrates a renewal of leadership in the emerging new leading sectors. In doing so, it lends empirical support to our Phoenix cycle hypothesis of renewed global system leadership as laid out in the previous chapter three. The following chapters will discuss the impact the formation of a new technological style based on these leading sectors has on the core agents in the global complex system, specifically the microeconomic impact on firm structures (chapter 4), and their impact on major power rivalries (chapter 5).

CHAPTER FOUR

Drivers of Leading Sector Change—the Role of States, Organizations, and Individuals

After having examined the evidence for the emergence of new leading sectors and a new K-wave that might feed into a new long cycle, we are now able to draw a broader picture of the emerging new technological style as a result of these changes. This chapter analyzes in depth the currently evolving changes in the inner core of the global system process, the transition to and development of a new technoeconomic paradigm or technological style.

Following a discussion of the role of states in previous and current enterprise systems, we provide an analysis of what is identified here as the iNet economy, based on the complex global system matrix. We thus take into account not only the evolutionary path as manifested in previous technological styles, but also the change in network structures (external versus internal) and the effect of the network structure on the enterprise systems (i.e., the development and impact of technological styles).

The Role of States

Expanding on his identification of trading (as opposed to territorial) states, Rosecrance (1999) develops the concept of *virtual states*. As an outgrowth of a shift toward the dominance of intangible factors for the development of leading sectors

a new form of state is being born: the virtual nation, a nation based on mobile capital, labor, and information. The virtual state

is a political unit that has downsized its territorially based production capability and s the logical consequence of emancipation from
land. Virtual states and their associates would rather plumb the
world market than acquire territory.... The virtual state relies on
mobile factors of production...houses virtual corporations and
presides over foreign direct investment by its enterprises...stimu-
lates, and a degree even coordinates their activities. (Rosecrance,
1999, 4, 6)

Rather than aiming to rely on and extend internal networks of resource
exploitation and production capability, states vying for leadership aim
to specialize in modern technical and research services and high-level
production techniques, deriving income not from the manufacturing
of products, but rather their design, marketing, and financing. The
virtual state is thus simply the organization extension of a smaller sociopolitical (and ultimately cultural) unit, the *virtual cooperation*. Just as
these virtual corporations (discussed in greater detail later) mark an
change from reliance on internal network structures to external one, so
does the rise for virtual state mark the shift of dominance from internal
to external networks in the global system.

From this perspective, what characterizes the current technological
revolution that enables the basis of innovative clustering of the latest
K-wave (or K19 in our count, for which we have shown empirical support in the previous chapter) is not the centrality of knowledge and
information, but the application of such knowledge and information to
knowledge generation and information processing/communication
devices, in a cumulative feedback loop between innovation and the use
of innovation (Castells, 1996; Hall and Preston, 1988; Saxby, 1990). As
pointed out earlier, whereas the leading sectors that developed in former external network–based (i.e., complex regime) systems during
long-cycle six (i.e., the Baltic and Atlantic trade routes (K11) and later
the Eastern trades (K12; see table 3.1) were dominantly maritime in
terms of their physical state, the leading sectors of this external network
system are increasingly digital in nature. As in previous cycles, the
development of a new infrastructure sets the tone of the following leading sectors. It is thus not surprising to see the emergence of a *digital trade
route* in the form of ICT-based digital networks as the precursor of a
more complex digitally based external network system.

The role of states in this context has as a result not changed dramatically. Similar to that of organizations on a microeconomic level,
their main task is to act as facilitators of many of the processes discussed

earlier (innovation, learning, cooperation, but also through their coercive power). States achieve this mainly through the establishment and enforcement of a certain regulatory regime (see previous discussion in chapter 2). The continuation of the role of states, however, should not be confused with the change and transition states themselves have undergone over the course of the development of the global complex system. This transformation has been studied extensively by Spruyt (1994) and needs nor further elaboration here. More recently, Sassen (2006) has added another important contribution to the role of states in terms of their agency in the global complex system.

In *Territory, Authority, Rights*, Sassen, presents a more fully developed criticism of the globalization literature. Sassen argues that critics and proponents of the globalization literature alike miss crucial developments of this process in their focus on established actors and institutional forms and instead argues for the need to situate globalization more concretely and broadly, both in terms of space and place (as marked in the first term of the title, territory), as well as the establishment of new organizing logics, which manifest themselves in new combinations of authority and rights. While she builds on her previous scholarship, this is a novel work—and a most welcome and important contribution to this field as she not merely points out the shortcomings of existing approaches, but provides a well-theorized proposition on how to remedy them.

Sassen is mostly concerned about the lack of existing globalization approaches to escape what she terms the *endogeneity trap* (aiming to understand globalization by confining its study to the characteristics of globalization, i.e., global processes and institutions), arguing instead for an approach that does not focus on either the Y (globalization) nor the X (global process and institutions). Instead, Sassen argues for an evolutionary approach to the study of globalization, albeit never explicitly, explaining globalization through the organizing logic that binds its core elements focusing on the processes and structures shaping the X (and thus the Y). Rather than to focus on the complex wholes (the national and the global) she instead proposes to disaggregate each of them into their foundational components, namely the establishment of territory, authority, and rights, therefore separating these processes from their "particular historical encasements" (Sassen, 2006, 5). In other words, Sassen is pursuing a study of the organizing logic driving the specific combination of these interdependent components that resulted in the establishment of the *national* in order to gain a better idea of the organizing logic behind the establishment of the *global*. What she finds is the critical establishment of certain capabilities or "particular assemblage of specific institutionalizations of territory, authority, and rights," (Sassen, 2006, 404) disaggregated and reassembled together with newly developed capabilities into a new system at certain *tipping points* (particular combination of dynamics and resources that can usher a new organizing logic).

Her main and most provocative finding is a "disaggregating of the glue that for a long time held possibly different normative order together under the somewhat unitary dynamics of nations", which should not be confused with a mere "denationalization" process, but rather identified as a "proliferation of specialized assemblages" with a tendency toward "a remixing of constitutive rules, for instance in the shifts of the private-public division and in the microtransformations of the relationship of citizen to the state an vice versa" as well as the "multiplication of partial systems, each with a small set of sharply distinctive constitutive rules, amounting to a type of simple system" (Sassen, 2006, 422). While not exactly mirroring the medieval world of overlapping domains of authority, territory, and rights, this newly emerging system sheds the overarching *Westphalian* logic for a new one that allows for multiple sets of borderlines (both within as well as across existing national ones), coexisting normative orders that shake-up established meanings of private and public, as well as coexisting and parallel establishments of rights (and wrongs).

In other words, as expected in a global system characterized by an external network environment, the types of facilitation a state performs change significantly. The different tasks a state performs in such a system does not, however, signal a diminished role of the state. As argued later in chapter 5 in greater detail, states merely respond (and therefore reinforce) to the changing *systemic logic*.

Enterprise Structures

As argued previously, the Internet (i.e., the backbone of the digital external network system) serves as a trade route in the sense that the new commodity of the new Internet—information—is transported along its lines. However, information itself is not the only commodity. E-commerce, or the electronically enabled retailing of software, digital books, digital services (e.g., online-brokering and e-banking), and digital outsourcing (e.g., data processing) are now common phenomena. It is reasonable to add the growing number of Web-enabled transactions ("e-business") of analog items and services, both business-to-business and consumer-to-business, to this count. In sum, the Internet already constitutes a significant global digital trade route and is increasingly developing into the central interchange circuit not only for commercial exchange but also for almost any other form of human interrelations.

Its impact, however, goes beyond a mere distributive advancement of external networks. Similar to organizational changes that occurred in earlier external network systems, the Internet enables dramatic organizational change as well. As Castells (2001, 102) points out, "e-Business is not the business that is exclusively conducted online but a new form of conducting business, by, with, and on the Internet." Digital networks thus develop into a truly commercial and organizational central nerve system connecting both, digital (e.g., the Internet, mobile communication networks, etc.) and nondigital (e.g., distributional networks, production facilities, etc.) in nature.

The digital nature (or rather informational basis; see discussion in chapter 3—Network Trajectories) of the system allows for relative ubiquity and low cost of provision and access to the system and thus for a qualitative and quantitative deeper integration than in previous external systems. This is a crucial difference from the previous maritime-bases external system: despite its use and availability as a trade route, the wider impact of the digital nervous system spanning the globe must be seen in its facilitator of organizational and thus institutional change on all level of human interaction, ranging from individual *peer-to-peer exchanges*[1] to exchanges between states and the structure of the global system as a whole (see Singh, 2002).

Harvey (1989) goes as far as to argue that *all* other aspects of late-modern societies, including cultural transformations, are in fact residue effects of this restructuring of the sociospatial logic of modern economies into a new sociospatial axis: as capitalist systems of production mutate to take advantage of globalizing technologies and flexible modes of accumulation (i.e., in our framework the transition to an increasing reliance on external network relationships) in an attempt to find a new *spatial fix*. As our framework emphasizes (see chapter 2), this view would neglect the importance of the coevolution of the dynamic processes laid out in our model. We do, however, agree with Harvey that this change of the sociospatial logic is an important factor and driver of this dynamic process. The main enablers of this change are ICT and the development of *cyberspace* or a digital external network structure (see e.g., Dodge and Kitchin, 2001; Poster, 1995).

Enterprise structures are as much a product of the sociopolitical environment in which they operate, as they are a determinant of those environments (albeit with a significant institutional delay). Therefore, we would expect the current context in which a new enterprise system emerges to resemble more closely that of earlier external network structure phases than the environment characterizing the industrial period. To gain a better understanding of current changes, then, makes it necessary to recall some of the characteristics not only of more recent Fordist enterprise structures. Rather, it is necessary to contrast the organizational structure of current enterprises with enterprises in earlier external network based systems of the commercial maritime phase.

The evolutionary stages of the transformation of business enterprises have been studied extensively and need not much further repetition here.[2] It is useful, however, to recall some of the characteristics of previous enterprise structures in order to gain a better understanding of the importance of the context in which they are situated. Arrighi and Barr, and Hiseda (1999, Chapter 2) in their analysis differentiate between three enterprise systems: (1) the seventeenth century Dutch-style joint-stock chartered companies; (2) the British family business enterprises of the nineteenth century; and (3) a system of vertically integrated, bureaucratically managed, multinational corporations characteristic of the twentieth-century United States. While each system differs from the previous one, they feature nonetheless path-dependent elements as well. Financial tools, capitalization methods, and managerial innovations were not discarded but rather adapted and integrated into the new systems.

The roots of the Western firms more closely associated with the first external network phase lay, if not with ancient Rome, than certainly the Mediterranean revival of the ninth and tenth century (in our model the beginning of the modern global system process). Among the first institutions, not surprisingly, was the so-called *societas maris* or maritime firm.[3] It characterized a partnership of a socius stans, a partner remaining on *the spot*, and a *socius tractator*, who left in person on the ship and was usually entered on a trip to trip basis.[4] Mainly located in port cities, they remained relatively simple and project-based in structure, were relatively numerous, but also short-lived. As a structural model, however, they proved vital.

Later on, the large firms of the inland Italian cities, the so-called *compagnia*, proved far more important as individual organizations. Their main feature was their ability to integrate previously independent and multifaceted trading networks. This was largely the result of their ability to accumulate and provide enough capital to ensure large enough network structures of their own to connect them to existing other, and larger commercial networks. Thus, they adapted to the increasingly complex global system environment by providing a hitherto underdeveloped bridge between the long existing maritime external network system with the largely separately existing territorial internal network structures.

It is important to recall this development here. The rise of the Western trading companies was made possible by the fact that they could focus on establishing links, tapping into existing commercial network structures in the East, rather than having to built extensive territorial and commercial internal networks of their own. As Braudel (1992c, 447) notes

> The local trade which formed the foundation for the European success, giving it regular structures to build on, was evidence of the vigor of a pre-existing economy, built to last. During the centuries of exploitation, the Europeans had the advantage of being faced with rich and developed civilizations, with agriculture and artisan manufacture already organized for export, with trading links and efficient intermediaries everywhere.

The success of the great merchant companies during the seventeenth century, manifested in the history of firms such as the Dutch VOC or the English East India Company,[5] was made possible by the culmination[6] of several factors: (1) The rise of capitalization through joint-stock arrangements and thus high-intensity capitalist activity; (2)the granting of special privileges by the states in which they originated; and (3) the appropriation of entire sectors of overseas trade by these companies (i.e., monopoly rights). What made the VOC so successful was its ability not only to create a bridge between the existing commercial networks (which others had done long before, albeit on a much smaller scale) but also to keep its chosen trading goods exclusive. It thus provided a unique match to the increasingly complex nature of the global external network system, superseded by the British successes in expansion of the geographical reach and organizational capabilities of its firms through its control of the Amerasian trade and increasingly control of production.

Britain is also the place in which the transition from a focus on an external network environment to a focus on internal network creation is most visible. As we have argued earlier, Britain was able to maintain its leadership position in the global system because of this transition and its ability to develop parallel economies. As Nef (1943) points out, Britain had long been one of the main industrial centers of the European-centered world economy. In a global system characterized by an external network environment, however, this proved to be no advantage.

It was only possible for Britain to achieve a global leadership position by replacing the Dutch as the central commercial entrepôt (in both cases mainly through their metropolitan cities of London and Amsterdam, respectively). It was during the first (long) cycle of British leadership that its industrial capabilities grew to emerge as the basis of its renewal of leadership of the global system. In the words of Arrighi et al. (1999, 61):

> It was only in the course of the eighteenth century that the expansion of England's own entrepôt trade and massive governmental expenditure during the Napoleonic Wars turned British industrial capabilities into . . . an instrument [of national aggrandizement].

The shift toward mechanization of production within the home state rather than the previous reliance on the outsourcing of production and a shift away from service-oriented leading sectors to production-oriented ones (see previous discussion of network environments) was to a large degree made possible by the investments from the former into the latter (see Arrighi, 1994; also Arrighi et al., 1999).

The argument of a reversal of emphasis from external networks to internal networks one might at first seem at odds with the conventional view of industrialization as a starting point of a world economy now truly global in reach and connection. Hobsbawm (1975) for example argues that during the latter half of the nineteenth century even the most remote parts of the world began to be linked together by means of communication which had no precedent in terms of its dependency and regularity, capacity of transportation systems (both for goods and people) and especially the speed of exchange (see also McNeill and McNeill, 2003).

As stated in our model, this argument is consistent with the explanation presented here. For indeed, it was during this period (of the punctuation of the global complex system process) that a new economic phase to a significant degree based on new communication structures emerged. We do, however, disagree with the conclusion Arrighi et al.

offer, in that "the British world-trading system thus became an integrated system of mechanized transport and production that left little room for national self-sufficiency" (Arrighi et al., 1999, 62). The driving force behind the creation of internal networks was less the creation of national self-sufficiency in the sense of economic isolationist independence but rather the self-sufficiency or supremacy in the newly emerging production-oriented leading sectors. This intent, of course, did not differ much from those of earlier strives of leading sector domination. What did change, however, was the nature of those leading sectors.

The global economic evolution in our model reflects the then still existing need for and potential in the creation of a global economic network until the punctuation of the system around 1850 (in its center, starting roughly a hundred years prior and ending about a hundred years later). Leading sectors during this phase were sectors that provided an extension of the network, both in terms of its reach and complexity. Once the global commercial system was firmly established, however, these (external) commercial networks turned into a widely available and nonexclusive commodity (as all leading sectors eventually do). With integration came also unprecedented levels of commercial pressure for domestic economies.

Taken together with the rise of new levels of mechanization and power sources, and with external networks increasingly commoditized, internal network creation became crucial for the exploitation of the potential of the newly formed global marketplace. O'Brien (2003; see also Riello and O'Brien, 2004) summarizes this point rather well, ascribing the transformation of the particular sectors of the British economy that generated unbalanced growth and competitive advantage in the global commercial system to the combination of several forms of *power*:

> For my argument, power refers to: (a) energy, derived from coal; (b) to coercion, flowing from massive and sustained investments by the Hanoverian state in the Royal Navy; (c) the deployment of state and monopoly power behind the establishment of a cotton textile industry in England and (d) to geopolitical and geoeconomic outcomes of nearly a quarter of a century of warfare, flowing from the French Revolution. (O'Brien, 2003, 17)

These sources of power are rather familiar drivers of development during the evolution of the global system process (see esp. the previous discussion in chapter 2). O'Brien's factors of (b) coercion (as reflected in a strong military and especially navy to obtain global reach capability), and (d) the importance of the Napoleonic Wars (the *macrodecision* in our model) are all but regular features of the long cycles of the global system process, as are new power sources (see also Freeman and Louçã, 2001). Also, as we have seen in our earlier discussion, state-involvement not only through the granting of monopoly rights has also been crucial during earlier cycles. Thus, what marks the important difference of the industrialization phase of the global system process is not the combination of factors leading to its domination, but rather the change in the nature of the leading sectors.

By 1851 (the time of the Great Exhibition), the *new British economy* (representative of Britain's second long-cycle dominance during long-cycle 8 (LC8, see table 3.1) was characterized by: (1) a low proportion of the national workforce engaged in agriculture, compared to industry and service; (2) the use of coal as the dominant source of energy; (3) the concentration of manufacturing activity in large new northern towns such as Manchester, Liverpool, Glasgow, Birmingham, and Bradford; (4) the organizational change in the form of factories as places of work, concentrated production, and as efficient organizational forms for the supervision and control of labor; (5) the mechanization of textile production, basic metallurgy, and transportation first through the canal system and later railways; (6) the large competitive advantages enjoyed by the British textile, cast iron, and pottery production (as well as shipbuilding) industries; and overall (7) the Victorian kingdom's extraordinary share of world trade in manufactured goods and services (see O'Brien, 2003, 13; see also Freeman and Louçã, 2001).

The different geographical location of the new leading sector industries (located in the north rather than the traditionally commercial dominant south) made possible the parallel development of leading sectors, both previous ones (during the first phase of British global system process dominance) and newly emerging ones. In addition, the different natures of these sectors, a shift from service oriented global commercial system creation to mechanized, mass-production oriented industries, reversed the main direction of flows within the global commercial system.

Whereas previous leading sectors were dependent on the possible flows from outside of the main commercial centers (during this phase mainly located in Western Europe) and redistributive in nature, with the commercial network now in place, the predominance of industrial manufacturing reversed the directions of flows. This reversal was characterized by the shift from external networks to the importance of internal networks, embodied in the creation of internal networks such as the canal system and later railways (in addition to other important internal logistical infrastructure advancements such as the improvement of road networks, etc.).

As Britain had to cede her leadership position eventually, her successor, the United States, advanced the control and creation of internal networks and the mass-manufacturing process. The U.S. dominance of the global system, however, also marks a new transition phase and the return to an external network based system. As we have argued earlier, it is during this punctuation phase of the global system process that the information technologies that constitute the new backbone of the global commercial system (rather than the previous maritime one) evolved (see Hall and Preston, 1988; see also Modelski and Thompson, 1996; Thompson, 2000a, Chapter 11; Hugill, 1999; also Hugill, 1993). This is important to keep in mind, as it shows a repetition of the pattern observed of the emergence of the previous, maritime-based commercial external network system during the first four K-waves of the Chinese dominance of the global system process.

For states competing for global leadership, vertical integration became the crucial factor during this punctuation phase. This focus on the development of vertical organizational integration had implications not only for state organization as a whole (with states becoming stronger and more inclined to be organizational more active rather than outsourcing territorial control to agents such as the large trading firms), but also the territorial expansion of the state (to ensure access to resources and markets).

On a microeconomic level, this extensive creation of internal networks was later taken to a new organizational extreme through the creation of highly vertically integrated organizations during the first long cycle of global political dominance of the United States. This organizational extreme was embodied in the creation of a Fordist industry and thus the development of a new technological style and later, as a logical extension, through its creation of multinational firm structures that embodied this new reversed direction of flows (see Chandler, 1977; Chandler, 1990; 1965; 1964; see also Best, 2001). The rise of a new external network–based global commercial system has thus significant implications for the microeconomic organizational structure of firms, to which we turn now.

New Enterprise Structures in the
Informational Network Economy

In order to better comprehend the role of organizations as agents in the global complex system process, we offer here a framework that allows us to theorize organizational behavior in its evolutionary development as laid out in our complex global system matrix. The organizational form of firms is conceptually an important subject of study, as it represents the overall logic shaping not only a firm's strategy, but also its structure and management processes into an effective whole.

Authors like Schumpeter (1989) and more recently for example Dosi, Nelson, and Winter (2000) have argued that organizational change is as much the result of the pull of market forces as it is influenced by the *push* of organizational innovation from within firms. In each historical area, market forces *pull* forth new organizational forms, as managers try to adapt to the new market structure by rearranging assets and resources to produce the products and services customers are willing to purchase.

At the same time, however, the change in the market structure is also the effect of the push-forces of managerial and organizational innovation resulting in experimental new organizational structures, which in turn can stimulate the creation of new markets and/or products and services. The evolution of firm structures thus resembles the typical pattern observed for the evolution of the global economic system, and ultimately the global system as a whole. A common approach found in the literature concerned with new forms of organizational structures in the informational network economy is the B/C matrix.

B/C Matrix

Previous organizational models of firm structure have focused on the hierarchical structural arrangement within firms. Consumers feature mainly (if at all) as an element of a market, the main determinant of the specific organizational structure chosen. Changes brought on by the emergence of digital networks have shifted the focus on markets and geographical location (at least in terms of organizational structures of firms) to the external relationship structures of firms. The B/C matrix describes the main role of firms in the iNet economy as that of mediators between either businesses (B) or consumers (C) united in one, digital, and virtual sphere, usually referred to as the Internet (see discussion in chapter 3). Four possible combinations exists: (1) B-to-B, (2) B-to-C, (3) C-to-C, and (4) C-to-B (see figure 4.1).[7]

	Business	Consumer

Business	*B-to-B*
	MRO hubs (operating supplies, systematic
	  sourcing, horizontal focus)
	Yield managers (operating supplies, spot
	  sourcing, horizontal focus)
	
	Catalog hubs (manufacturing inputs,
	  systematic sourcing, vertical focus)
	Exchanges (manufacturing inputs, spot
	  sourcing, vertical focus)
	EMS (to-order-manufacturing; e.g.,
	  Flextronics)
		B-to-C
		e-Tailers (e.g., Amazon)
		Direct sellers (e.g., Dell)

Consumer	*C-to-B* Bidder markets (e.g., Priceline)	*C-to-C* Auctions (e.g., eBay)

Figure 4.1   B/C Matrix of Organizational Interaction Forms
Source: B-to-B categories based on Kaplan and Sawhney (1999, 3–4).

B-to-B firms are those that provide services from businesses to business (e.g., maintenance, repair, and operating (MRO) hubs; yield managers organizing operational supplies and manufacturing inputs; virtual exchanges, as existing exchanges organizing the reselling of network capacity or energy; and electronic manufacturing services, such as Flextronics[8]). Generally, this form of electronic commercial exchange is the most advanced form already in place and widely in use.

B-to-C exchanges are the most conventional form of electronic commercial exchanges and usually referred to as *e-business or e-commerce*. Examples include Amazon.com, the most successful (and by now profitable) business based on this model and direct sellers and manufacturers, such as Dell Computers. Replacing *bricks-and-mortar retailers* (i.e., vendors with a physical presence), these businesses transport the classic retailing model into the virtual reality of the *cyberspace* of the Internet. They rely thus not only on a virtual storefront (accessible through a computer or wireless devices able to access the global digital network), but also on virtual forms of communication, payment methods, delivery (in the case of digital-based products, such as software or services), and carrier-based delivery of goods (in the case of physical goods).

C-to-C exchanges are among the most popular forms of digital exchanges and were also among the first to be profitable (as for example in the case of eBay, an online auction platform). Most often, C-to-C exchanges take the form of auctions, in which one person or group offers a good under certain conditions and buyers match either the offer or outmatch each other to purchase the good. C-to-C exchanges, however, can also include peer-to-peer (also referred to in the literature as *P2P)* exchanges that do not involve the commercial exchange of goods, but rather take the form of free e or near-free exchanges of digital goods or services, such as the now-extinct (and reborn as a music download) Napster service, that offered its users access to music files stored on networked computer hard drives.[9]

C-to-B virtual market places are compared to the other exchanges still somewhat rare. This might be a result of the early success in patenting its business model of *reverse bidding* by one of the first C-to-B market places, Priceline.[10] This model has proven particularly important as an outlet for selling commodity-like items, such as transportation capacity (e.g., flights), directly to consumers rather than in bulk to retailers or as packaged items. The main advantage provided by C-to-B market places is the digitalization and automation of the formerly relatively complex price-finding mechanism of consumers with knowledge over their price elasticity searching for a price match for a given good.

This matrix, while useful for distinguishing between multiple organizational structures as they unfold in the new digital commercial system, proves too limited for our purposes. The shift away from a purely intrafirm perspective to the external relationships of firms may prove fruitful to describe and discuss the shift between firm-customer relationships and roles. It comes, however, at the cost of deeper analytical insights into firm hierarchies and internal organizational structures.

Another problem with this framework is the overemphasis on technology as the main determinant of organizational structure. Although we can identify a significant shift toward ICTs as core operands of firms and thus in extension their organizational structure, as well as a strong trend toward automation in the day to day operational set up of firms, this does not replace human agency as a central driver of firm strategy and organizational setup.

The role of technology has not changed as fundamentally the nature of firm-operation and -organization as some of the consultancy and business school literature may suggest. Technology still remains largely a tool and enabler of human agency. Its significant impact on factors of production (including, and maybe most importantly so, human labor) must not be confused with its impact on agency. ICT technologies follow parameters defined and enabled by human agency. Earlier transformations into new technological styles provide a good reminder of the role of technology on the process of transformation. For example, the mechanization of production had a fundamental impact on the organizational structure of production and the role (and livelihood) of individual weavers, both in England as well as in production-facilities far away.

However, it did not make obsolete the role of human agency. Rather, it transformed this role, made possible new forms of agency and thus occupations as well as the organizational forms of individuals, larger groups, and the development of a technological style as a whole. In the same vein the impact of ICTs provide a new playing field for human agents, enabling new forms of organization and new roles (in terms of labor as a production input). They do not, however, replace human agency, only factor inputs of human labor.

Insights into organizational change thus prove not only useful to business school students and academics interested in business structures. They are also important for our study at hand. As argued earlier, firms are as much a reflection of the socioeconomic and—political environment in which they operate as much as determinant factors in its formation. Therefore, the identification and analysis of firm structures provide us with important insights into the technological style (in the Perezian sense) in which not only firms, but agency in general takes place.

Therefore, instead of the matrix discussed above we propose a new framework here, here referred to as a *cellular approach*. A cellular approach allows us not only to understand the impact of the network structure of the global world system on organizational behavior, but also the evolutionary development of the organizational structures over the past millennium, our time frame for the development of the globalization process.

A Cellular Approach

Cellular structures as a form of social organization have been discussed in the literature since the 1960s (for a review, see Mathews, 1996). More recently, Miles et al. (1997; see also Thore, 1999) have put forward a model of organizational evolution that involves the concept of cellular firms as "living, adaptive organizations" (Miles et al., 1997, 12).

Similar to biological multicellular organizational forms, these cellular firms are made up of cells (e.g., self-managing teams, autonomous business units, etc.) that can operate on their own but in interaction with each other (through information- and knowledge-sharing as learning organisms) can produce a more potent and competent (business) mechanism.

While agreeing with this description of cellular firms, we expand here the concept of cellular organization of firms to include all organizational structures of firms as they have evolved over the last millennium. In doing so, we pay particular attention to the difference in composition of the matrix (or extracellular) structure and its impact on the cellular organization within *tissues* (or multicellular aggregations). Here we shall argue that the network structure of the global world system (external in its expanding phase and internal during its punctuation phases) acts as an ecology of organizational structures (in this context: enterprise structures). Just as the ecology of the outer-cell environment (i.e., the matrix) affects the formation structure of the cells themselves in natural tissues, we shall see that the network structure of the global world system process affects the formation structure of economic enterprises.

Cells in our model are the smallest unit. They are characterized by its self-sufficiency and can thus act as independent units outside of the organizational structure. They range in size from an individual free agent (see e.g., Pink, 2001) over teams and groups to business units to an entire corporate firm, for example independent contract-manufacturers, raw-material suppliers, external advisors, or freelance artists. Figure 4.2 graphically summarizes the major features of the two cellular organizational structures, (i) the *e-type* (predominant in internal network structures), and (ii) the *m-type* (predominant in external network environment).

Given the need, cells communicate and interact with each other, forming new combinations and structures, creating so-called *tissues*. These tissues consists of the cells themselves and their outside, the so-called *matrix*. This matrix consists of mainly two groups of proteins, here referred to as system network-structure enablers: (1) *structural proteins,* and (2) *adhesive proteins*. Structural proteins enable external network relationships through fiber connections between the individual cells. This means, that cells can be dispersed but nonetheless integrated through *gap junctions.*

Fiber connections in this model are the equivalent to long-distance maritime trade routes in the (commercial maritime system phase), or cells networked through digital communication networks (in the digital commercial phase). Adhesive proteins on the other hand create a very different matrix structure. Here, internal network relationships are dominant. The cells are connected through close organizational and physical proximity (the equivalent *membrane connection* in biological cells). Adhesive proteins integrate cells either closely through *adhering*

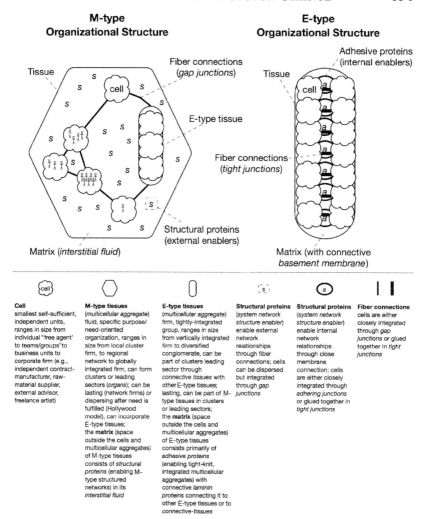

Figure 4.2   Cellular Organizational Structures

junctions or glue them together to form blocks of cells in *tight junctions*. The resulting tissues are, however, able to connect with other tissues (of either kind) in a nonadhesive manner through so-called connective *laminin* proteins. Tight-knit organizations of this kind can thus be part of a more loosely organized larger multicellular organization.

E-type tissues are firm, tightly integrated groups, with a strong emphasis on internal networks and a high degree of internal clusters of specialization. They range in size from a vertically integrated firm to a fully diversified conglomerate and can also form entire sectors (including leading sectors) through clusters held together by "connective tissues" with other e-type tissues. These tissues are usually longer lasting and although they also respond to certain needs are not as flexible as m-type tissues. As mentioned above, e-type tissues can be part of m-type tissues in clusters or leading sectors. We can identify three main internal network–dominated e-type tissues most prevalent during the industrial phase in our model, namely (1) functional tissues, (2) divisional tissues, and (3) matrix tissues (for discussion of structural evolution of these organizational forms, see Miles et al., 1997; see also Best, 2001, Chapter 2).

M-type tissues (i.e., multicellular aggregates) are fluid, specific purpose/need-oriented organizations. They range in size from the local cluster firm, over regional networks to a globally integrated firm. M-type organizations can, in combination with each other, form clusters and at times even entire leading sectors. M-type tissues can be lasting organizations (e.g., network-firms, long-term alliances, etc.) or dispersing after the need that created their organization has been fulfilled (the so-called Hollywood model see, e.g., Kao, 1996). They can also incorporate e-type organizations that are operating in a different matrix-structure and form a distinctive organizational structure.

A typical example of an m-type tissue would be a design cluster of an automobile producer located in three different continents but networked over computer-networks not only to each other but also to dedicated (and independent) manufacturers (e.g., Flextronics), who then produce physical products from the digital blueprints they receive online. In the following section we shall discuss some of the m-type tissues prevalent in external network environments, contrasting newly emerging tissues of the digital commercial system with tissues existing in the maritime commercial system.

Comparison between Past and Present
Enterprise Structures

The purpose of the tissue model developed here is to allow an analysis that spans long periods of time and to allow a comparison of firm structure before the period of what is commonly referred to as industrialization in a single set of typologies. We have argued earlier, that the main differentiation of organizational structure is that between external and internal networks, reflected in the m- and e-types of our tissue model. If viewed from a long-term perspective, internal networks remain an aberration, rather than then the basis of enterprise structure as suggested by models that view the industrialization phase as the origin of the modern global system. To show that this is indeed the case, we shall briefly demonstrate the similarities that exist between preindustrial organizational structures with those emerging in the informational network economy.

Aggregator Tissues

Despite its similarity to existing traditional forms of firm organization,[11] aggregator tissues nevertheless deserve a unique category amongst m-type tissues. Aggregator tissues, such as Amazon.com, the online retailer, organize and orchestrate the distribution of goods, services, and information. What distinguishes them from their physical counterparts is the reliance on and use of their informational platform. With the increased digitalization of information it is increasingly possible for aggregators to focus less on the tangential aspects of their business model (i.e., the physical storage, presentation, delivery, etc.) but to become mainly information processors.

The success of Wal-Mart, the U.S. retailing chain, is an example of this development. The competitive advantage of Wal-Mart is its information processing capability that even outstretches the most advanced systems of the U.S. military. Given its vast informational processing power, Wal-Mart is able to identify consumer demand in real time while meeting this demand immediately through links with their suppliers. This real-time processing allows the firm to take advantage not only of relatively low stocking costs, but also superior demand satisfaction through availability and low prices. Without the availability of the vast amounts of information in digital form and available in a networked environment, Wal-Mart would find it impossible to process the information adequately.

Other firms, such as Orbitz, the online travel solutions provider, rely to an even lesser degree on physical outlets, freeing them to focus on their core business of informational processing (i.e., identifying and formulating customer needs, provision of meeting this demand, etc.). The case of Amazon.com makes clear, however, that the digital commercial system is still only emerging. Although some distributive tissues (see below) do exist, Amazon.com still had to build from scratch important parts of its aggregator tissue it would have preferred to source out.

Distributive Tissues

Physical network-providers, such as national postal systems, UPS, FedEx, or any other form of logistics supply providers are playing an increasingly important role as complements to other firms in digital dadni and aggregator tissues. In addition, digital network providers, such as telecommunications providers, Internet Service Providers (ISPs) are essential elements of these new organizational forms in the global digital commercial system.

The transition from enterprises based on internal networks to external network–based organizational firm structures is exemplified in the transformation of the Hollywood culture industries, which are on the forefront of organizational change of enterprises.[12] During the early half of the twentieth century, the early film industry relied as much on Fordist manufacturing principles as any other modern industry in the United States.

Similar to the other industries, a small number of studio giants, including Warner Brothers, Paramount, Metro-Goldwyn-Mayer, and Twentieth Century Fox, were in control of most of the film industry.[13] Characterized by a hierarchical and centralized structure, designed to control directly every aspect[14] of the production process—from the writing of scripts to the final distribution of the products—these studios were prototypes of the e-type based tissues of the industrial system. As Storper points out,

> The internal organization—or technical division of labor—in each phase of the labor process became increasingly similar to that of true mass production, where routinization and task fragmentation were the guiding principles. (Storper, 1989, 278)

Forced into a severe reorganization of its production processes by two major external shocks (antitrust legal deregulation and the rise of television) the film industry evolved from a production-oriented industry into an experience-centered (and thus service-oriented) one. Emerging in the 1950s, the new network system of film production was a response to the need to bring together diverse talent to each unique film project and to pool risks in case any one product failed to earn the hoped for revenues. Each film now is an independent enterprise on its own, often with budgets similar to medium-sized regular companies.

For each project, a team of specialized production companies and independent contractors as well as the creative and acting personnel. All tasks along the value-chain of an entertainment production (including not only movies, but also TV productions, shows, and to an increasing degree digital games)—from scripting, casting, set design, cinematography, costuming, sound design and mastering, editing, film processing, and so on—are being fulfilled by independent, small, and highly specialized cells[15] combined in a m-type tissue for the duration of a project (whether or not resulting in a final product, i.e., a film, game, or show).

This does not imply, that the major studios have lost their dominant position in the industry as a whole, but rather the shift in the organizational structure of production. Now primarily focusing on their role as *orchestrators* of external network–based enterprises (mainly through their connection of financial prowess and distribution control), the vertical disintegration and the shift to network or cell-structured forms of organization were consciously pursued goals to allow the major studios (or rather the remnants) to better generate product while minimizing financial risks (see Aksoy and Robins, 1992, 9).

Champagne Fairs and eBay—Agora Tissues

Another increasingly important emerging form of organizational structure in the digital commercial system is what is here referred to as the *agora tissue*.[16] Its main value proposition is the provision of liquid markets matching buyers with sellers with a unique and digitalized price discovery mechanism. Given the increasingly low cost of obtaining pricing information in the digital commercial system it is not surprising that agora tissues emerged already as a viable and important organizational enterprise form, as exemplified in one of the best-known examples, the online auctioneer eBay.

Agora tissues include (1) open markets, such as Monster.com, an employment Web site, enabling two private agents to negotiate one-to-one in a structured environment; (2) sell-side auctions, e.g., eBay, with one seller providing an offer to an unlimited number of buyers; (3) buy-side auctions, for example, Priceline, where a single buyer may receive offers from several sellers; and (4) digital exchanges, such as Nasdaq or various commodity-trading exchanges (e.g., telecommunication, electricity, etc.).

In most cases the facilitators of agora tissues only act as standard setters and controllers and not as intermediaries who take control and possession of goods for resale. They represent to a large degree the adaptation of the most prevalent form of commercial intercourse in earlier external network environments, taking advantage of the possibility of automation in the digital commercial system. The further expansion of everyday digitalization enables the transformation of commercial information into commercial knowledge at relatively low cost and maybe more importantly without human intermediaries. This development can be witnessed today for example in the development and increasing use of "smart tags" (standardizing commercial information), both attached to physical goods, as well as digital information (in the form of the new Internet XML code).[17]

It is interesting to notice the many commonalities between existing agora tissues during the previous external network environment, in the commercial maritime system, and their current cousins emerging in the digital commercial system. Many aspects that laid the foundation for the success of one of leading sectors during Genoa's leadership in the global system long-cycle three (LC3, see table 3.1), the Champagne fairs, also apply to the success of its modern-day successors, such as eBay, PayPal (a financial clearing Web site now owned by eBay), Priceline, or half.com (also purchased in 2001 by eBay). For the duration of the Champagne fair, foreigners were placed under the protection of the local *seigneur*. In addition, financial arrangements that allowed for a smoother flow of transactions (and thus lower transaction costs), especially for the number of international merchants attending the fair. Thus, the most important aspects of the fair were the setting of commonly applied standards and rules, their enforcement, and the provision of critical liquidity, both financially and in terms of participants. Eventually, this system emerged into a system of *permanent fair* in the trading merchant cities most closely attached to the commercial maritime network system (see Buzan and Little, 2000, 310–11; see also de Ligt, 1993; Kindleberger, 1993).

The success of eBay as one of the most profitable first major enterprises of the digital commercial system with a near monopoly in its sector is largely rooted in the similar premises it offers to its visitors. By setting a common set of rules and standards and providing both user- and provider-driven control and enforcement of these rules, eBay was able to emerge as the main global digital agora tissue. Not surprisingly, a major function of the agora remains the problem of financial settlement. Users have a multitude of options to settle their claims, but a few options have emerged as the most popular forms. At first offering a rival system to the most popular for of financial settlement between commercial parties, organized by PayPal, eBay later acquired the firm and provides now major financial services in addition to its provision of a "digital fair." The firm has also extended its market place through the acquisition of half.com, a similar digital agora that uses a different form of price-finding mechanism (sellers put in bids for their objects, and buyers can pick the ones that suits them best) but now offers a digital agora combining the two formerly separate market spaces.

Outsourcing in the Commercial Maritime and Digital Commercial Systems—Dadni Systems

The core of digital dadni tissues consists of an enterprise in the center providing the organizational structures and directs the firm network to produce a tightly integrated value proposition. This mediator might for example design core technologies in internal networks, as well as develop the necessary coordination capabilities to enable the external networks providing all other elements of the value-adding process, such as manufacturing, fulfillment, and onsite customer service. This is the most advanced form of m-type tissues and exists in various forms, mostly known as a modular structure widely today. In its most common form, modularity refers to the design of products and product components, enabling firms to extend the options of cooperation with external firms and create wide-ranging digital dadni tissues with a wide range of flexibility in terms of its possible partners.

This m-type tissue is thus an evolution from the modularity principle known as the *American System of Manufacturing* that for the first time, around the early 1800s, enabled open networks of firms by creating standardized components that allowed interchangeability in the production process (see e.g., Best, 2001, 25–28). As Sanchez (2002) points out, the benefits of modular thinking extend beyond product strategies, however, and include new approaches to creating more flexible organizations and improving the management of supply chains and outsourcing (for an empirical analysis of this process see e.g., Worren et al., 2002; see also Andersson et al., 2002).

In effect enabling a digital dadni tissue to function as effectively as an e-type internal network structured one, the concept of modularity works not only with physical components but can also be used to create more flexible, configurable processes. Not only the product or service itself, but also the process of making a product or delivering a service can be separated into various functional activities. Through the definition and subsequent standardization of interfaces between the value-adding activities create such a modular process architecture or in our framework digital dadni tissue. Different versions of each activity can then be mixed and matched in a well-coordinated process design (see e.g., Gulati et al., 2000).

Digital dadni tissues are characterized by their creation of value chains that design, produce, and deliver products or services to meet a specific set of customer needs. One of the core functions of digital dadni tissues is thus the identification and definition of needs and the ability to translate those needs into matching them through the design and creation of solutions. Just as in the case of e-type tissues, the value chains within digital dadni tissues transform, through a sequence of steps, raw materials (whether atoms in the case of physical products or bits in the case of digital value creation) into finished goods and service.

What differentiates the two is not the outcome but rather the process of the value-adding organization. Rather than controlling each step (or significant portions of it) of this process through internal networks of control, as is typically the case in e-type tissues (i.e., Fordist firm structures), firms in the center of digital dadni tissues play the role of context providers. Their main role is to define standards and goals and the coordination of the integration of value contributions from parts of the network, such as third-party designers and technologists, parts suppliers, assemblers, distributors, resellers, and other partners (Tapscott et al., 2000, 95).

More traditional approaches to the creation of digital dadni tissues are the various forms of well-established and widely employed strategic alliances firms engage in. The work of authors such as Doz and Hamel (1998) and Brandenburger and Nalebuff (1996) provides new models of interorganizational cooperation based on alliances, featuring clusters of common activities in the center of various relationship networks, with the primary aim of sharing knowledge and the combination of distinct centers of core competencies.[18] Other authors have developed similar arguments, for example Gomes-Casseres (1996) who uses the term *constellations*, Dunning (1997a) who speaks of the *centerless organization*, or Moore (1996) who argues for the development of *business ecosystems*.

Classic examples of such organizations increasingly seeking product and organizational standardization include IKEA, the Swedish furniture chain, or any modern global car manufacturer such as GM, Ford, or Volkswagen and Cisco Systems, which will be discussed in greater detail in a case study below. Important new elements of the digital dadni system include dedicated manufacturing units, so-called Electronic-Manufacturing Services (EMS), such as Flextronics.

The dadni system emerging in the first British leadership phase during seventh long cycle (LC7, see table 3.1) is remarkably close to the system employed by firms such as Dell Computers or Cisco System, and thus referred to here as digital dadni systems. The English East India Company pioneered a system today widely known as *outsourcing*. Company employees contracted so-called dalals, middlemen or brokers, to procure cloth, forwarding them a portion of the purchase price as an advance, after the two parties had agreed on musters and prices. The dalals functioned as independent agents and would in turn again outsource the production of the cloth to paikars, rural agents who supplied local weavers with the necessary means to produce the cloth and were also responsible for the delivery of the agreed upon amounts and quality of the cloth (sorted and valued by the dalals, see Barr, 1991).

This system of independent agency to form a system for the production of the cloth than traded by the English East India Company and imported and distributed in Europe, is a classic example of an m-type tissue in our model. It also resembles modern day production system featured by organizations such as Cisco or Dell's *on-demand* manufacturing system of ICT equipment. A similar current system engaged in textile production is the digital dadni tissue of Li & Fung, a Hong Kong–based trading company (sorted and valued by the dalals Brown et al., 2002). Li & Fung makes no products of its own, but rather "orchestrates" the production of goods by others, drawing on a vast global network of highly focused providers to arrange for private-label manufacturing, primarily on behalf of U.S. and European clothiers.[19] For a specific product or client, Li & Fung assembles a customized set of specialized providers to handle everything from product development to the sourcing of raw materials, production planning and management, and, eventually, shipping. As soon as problems occur at any stage of the complex process along the network, the company can quickly shift an activity from one provider to another. Rather than squeeze supply chain costs by tightly integrating activities, Li & Fung gains efficiencies through the specialization of suppliers and the creation of loosely coupled processes as the building blocks of a networked company (on other examples, see also Häcki and Lighton, 2001; Castells, 1996; Miles and Snow, 1994). Now as then, the assembly of m-type tissues emerges as the most successful form of production in an external network environment.

Role of Individuals

After having revisited the new roles of states as well as enterprise structures, it is now also necessary to view the effects of the transition to an informational network economy have on individual agents in the latest stage of the complex global system process. As previously discussed, a common phenomenon of organizational change in the informational network economy is the difference in size of organizations: average firms, especially those partaking in external network–based enterprises, feature a much smaller number of employees (a trend that is reflected in the average number of employees in all firms, whatever the overall size). It is not uncommon in today's external network–based enterprises to find a number of individual agents acting as sole acting and often highly specialized nodes within such organizations.[20] In the following section we shall discuss the influence these changes have on the role of labor in general as well as the individual worker.

Knowledgework(ers)

Drucker (1999) describes the change from employees of an organization, working full-time and being dependent on the organization for their livelihood and their careers as *subordinates* with no or low skills to knowledge workers (or *associates*) who posses greater skills than their coordinator. Whereas the majority of people who work for an organization may still be employees of the organization, a very large and steadily growing minority (though working for the organization) are no longer its (full-time) employees:

> Even if employed full-time by the organization, fewer and fewer people are "subordinates"—even in fairly low-level jobs. Increasingly they are "knowledge-workers." For, once beyond the apprentice stage, knowledge workers must know more about their job than their boss does—or else they are no good at all. In fact, that they know more about their job than anybody else in the organization is part of the definition of knowledge workers. (Drucker, 1999, 18)

The responsibility for the productivity of workers shifts from the organization to the individual knowledge workers themselves, which requires a certain amount of autonomy. As a result, continuing innovation and learning becomes part of the work, the task and the responsibility of knowledge workers rather than the organization. According to Drucker, the greatest difference to the older economic paradigms (manual-worker productivity to knowledge-worker productivity), however, is the shift in their respective economics: Whereas economic theory has treated (manual) workers as a cost, knowledge workers must be considered a capital asset (Drucker, 1993). For Drucker, knowledge does not simply become another resource along with the traditional factors of production (such as labor, land, and capital). Instead, knowledge becomes the central and greatest single asset of any organization. As a result, the means of production are no longer in possession of the organization but of the individual knowledge worker, with a growing number of knowledge workers (technologists) combining both, knowledge-work and manual work (Drucker, 1999, 148–49).[21]

At first, it might seem surprising then that knowledge work is listed as a property of the informational network economy here, when, for example, innovation is not. Hardly any factor has remained as consistently important to the economic system as the factor work. Its change from cost to asset, however, marks one of the greatest shifts from the old to the new socioeconomic paradigm.

Entrepreneurialism

Entrepreneurialism becomes an important property of the informational network economy in several aspects. As Castells (1996, 204) points out, the new technological style rearranges the organization of the production system around the principles of maximizing knowledge-based productivity through the development and diffusion of information technologies. This fosters the development of the necessary infrastructure of human resource agents (knowledge workers) and the communications infrastructure that enables the networking between those agents and the "resurgence of self-employment and mixed employment status" (Castells, 1996, 200).

As we have argued earlier, knowledge becomes the central asset of any organization, which also means that the means of production are no longer in possession of the organization but of the individual knowledge worker and changes their status from laborer to capitalist. As a result, knowledge workers become entrepreneurs, with their knowledge as their central capital. Marketing this asset replaces their status from employee to free agent, and knowledge workers are increasingly forced to manage themselves as a business (Davis and Meyer, 1998, 151).

One good example of this development is the constant job-hoping of programmers in Silicon Valley. Another example is the above-discussed change from big movie-producing studios to project-based production of movies in Hollywood. This example best illustrates the changes the organization undergoes in the informational network economy. Rather than providing the whole infrastructure for the moviemaking process (capital, human resources, and technology), movie studios are becoming organizers of networks, connecting independent agents individually for each new project (TV-production, movie, game, etc.).

This molecularization forces each of the agents to become or at least act as individual entrepreneurs rather than static parts of an organization even if the knowledge workers remain in a longer-term (rather than project-based) legal relationship with the organization.

Networking

Michael Borrus and John Zysman (1997a) describe cross-national production networks as the production organization counterpart to *Wintelism*. Cross-national production networks exemplify the consequent disintegration of the industry's value chain into constituent functions that can be contracted out to independent producers wherever those companies are located in the global economy.

Cross-national production networks are the result of an increasingly fine division of labor and lay the basis of its further development. The networks permit firms to weave together the constituent elements of the value-chain into competitively effective new production systems, while facilitating diverse points of innovation. In addition, cross-national productions networks have turned large segments of complex manufacturing into a commodity available in the market (Borrus and Zysman, 1997a). In other words, modern technology made possible the fusion of production- and communication-networks and manufacturing as a result has become a service or widely available commodity.

EMS enable highly flexible production arrangements (see case study in next chapter). For example, Solectron and Flextronics, two leading EMS providers, each have two dozen strategically located factories around the world, allowing them to fly in an entire production line from another location if demand in one market surges (see also case study in chapter 6). The Internet allows a high degree of financial and technical integration between customers and suppliers. Electronics firms enjoy complete access to their contractors' books for their products. Hewlett-Packard, for example, can check on the Web in real time whether its printers are being made properly, and immediately act if they are not. Contractors have direct and up-to-the minute access to their customers' sales information. Some clients at Flextronics' Mexican plant send files with design changes fed into the production robots using a data network (Economist, 2000).

As was pointed out earlier, this development leads to a shift from a focus on economies of scale to economics of networks (Shapiro and Varian, 1999, 173). Among the key concepts that are at the heart of economics of both, virtual and real (i.e., physical) networks are positive feedback and network externalities.

Positive feedback is characterized by its particular dynamic. After an initial threshold, or *critical mass*, is reached it reinforces initial success with exponential further growth and destroys competition in the same manner (Shapiro and Varian, 1999, 176–77). The key assumption is that as more agents choose one technology rather than the other, it becomes increasingly likely that others will subsequently choose the successful version of the product or technology.

The choice of version by any agent has a direct impact on the probability that all subsequent agents will choose this rather than its rival: positive (or self-reinforcing) feedback takes place (Ormerod, 1998, 22). When two or more firms compete for a market with strong positive feedback, only one winner, the creator of the new standard, can emerge in an S-shaped curve with three phases: (1) flat during launch; (2) steep rise during takeoff as positive feedback kicks in; followed by (3) leveling off as saturation is reached (Shapiro and Varian, 1999, 178). This, of course, is the same S-shaped effect we are familiar with from the complex system processes on various levels (macro and micro).

Real networks (e.g., railroad tracks, fiber cables) or *virtual networks* (e.g., Apple Macintosh users, subscriber to AOL's chat software) exhibit positive consumption and production externalities. A positive consumption (or network) externality signifies the fact that the value of a unit of the good increases with the number of units sold. Although at first counterintuitive to economic theory (as market demand slopes downward) it has been shown that the value of a unit of the good increases with the expected number of units to be sold (Economides, 1996).

Depending on the network, the externality may be direct or indirect. When customers are identified with components, the externality is direct. For example, in a typical two-way network, such as the local telephone network, there are n (n-1) potential goods. An additional (n+1th) customer provides direct externalities to all other customers in the network by adding 2n potential new goods through the provision of a complementary link to the existing links. Thus, the demand slopes downward but shifts upward with increases in the number of units expected to be sold (Economides, 1996, 680).

Networking, however, not only takes place between *product definition companies* (Borrus and Zysman, 1997a) and other individual producers in the newly defined value chain (or rather network). As we have argued earlier, networking becomes increasingly important within organizations or even between individual agents. Knowledgeworkers, working in high-performance team structures, become integrated into organizational networks of clients and servers that reach out to customers, suppliers, affinity groups, and competitors connecting through the Internet.

Conclusion

This chapter has analyzed evolving changes in the inner core of the global system process, the macroeconomic transition to and development of a new technoeconomic paradigm or technological style. After a discussion of the role of states as major agents in the complex system process, followed by a look at previous enterprise systems, it has laid out the network trajectories of what is identified here as the iNet economy, based on the complex global system framework. The recent development of this new technological style is based on external network structures, similar to those dominant during earlier commercial maritime phases of the global system development.

What distinguishes the current system, however, is its digital and information-based character. Many parallels exist between earlier commercial maritime phase systems and the current digital commercial system as far as the logic of the external network structure is concerned. The emphasis on information, and since the beginning of the new long-cycle phase around 1970 primarily in digital form, has important implications for the newly emerging leading sectors of this new phase. The following chapter will discuss the impact on this new technological style on the global political process as exemplified in major power rivalries.

CHAPTER FIVE

Drivers of Leading Actor Change—Interstate Rivalry at the Systemic Level

So far we have focused on the innermost core of the global system development, namely the development of new leading sectors and their role in the process of development of new technological styles. In addition, we looked at the impact of external or internal network structures of the global complex system on the development of leading sectors and consequently technological styles in greater detail. This chapter extends this analysis to include the coevolving political global system process unfolding in long cycles of sociopolitical leadership tied into the repeated pattern of socioeconomic renewal as captured in the K-waves and subsequent long cycles at the inner core of the global system process.

A good way to empirically evaluate the evolution of the political global system as identified in our complex global system framework is through the study of major power rivalry.[1] The complex global system framework requires an unusually long timeframe for empirical and quantitative studies. Fortunately, existing numerous studies of major power behavior provide the necessary long-term data for such an analysis. Thus, this chapter examines more closely the issue of international conflict, and more specifically the question whether we should expect the number of rivalries in the twenty-first century to rise, to remain steady, or even to fall and why so in order to test the validity of our proposed framework.

After a brief discussion of the rivalry concept, this chapter uses the earlier introduced categorization of contexts in the form of global long-cycle environments and extends them by identifying long-cycle rivalry environments in which interstate rivalries take place. Combining the framework of the leadership long cycle and the concept of rivalries it identifies global long-cycle environments that determine to a large degree the way rivalries are established, how they "behave," and how they end.

Rivalry Environments in the Global Complex System

An interest in rivalries arises mainly out of the fact that a few pairs of states are disproportionately associated with the disputes and wars that naturally are of great concern in international relations. The likelihood of becoming involved in conflict with all other states is not equally distributed amongst all the actors: some states seem to be more likely to engage in conflict relations with certain other states.[2]

Individual decision-makers base their choices on their understandings of what strategies have or have not worked in the past with a particular rival. This means that they must take into account the possible future consequences of their current strategies and actions involving rivals (or even possible future rivals). The longer these conflict sequences endure, the more they take on a life of their own, a phenomenon Diehl and Goertz call *lock-in* (Diehl and Goertz, 2000, 167). We can therefore view specific conflicts not as independent phenomena but have to take the context in which they occur into account as well.

This chapter introduces a categorization of these contexts in the form of global rivalry environments. Diehl and Goertz applied the natural science model of natural equilibrium to the concept of rivalries. They develop an "equilibrium model of enduring rivalries" (ibid., 132), stating that states (after an initial major shock) rapidly lock in to enduring rivalries, which then change little until their quick demise (partly caused by another major shock).[3] This implies that rivalries create a certain stable (if conflictual) environment. Whenever this environment experiences a sudden and major shock, it forces the actors to accommodate to this shock until it develops a new equilibrium or environment.

Here, we take an even broader view of this process. Combining the framework of the leadership long cycle to capture the political global process development within the global system development and the concept of rivalries we are able to identify global long-cycle environments that determine the way rivalries are established, how they "behave," and how they end. Just as major shocks cause the equilibria[4] of interstate rival behavior to rearrange and create a new stable environment, so do major global shocks create a phase of transition after which a new global environment is established in which the rivalries occur. Each global rivalry environment sets the stage on which the individual rivalries take place.

Rivalry Concept

Diehl and Goertz (2000, 4) define rivalry as "a relationship between two states in which both use, with some regularity, military threats and force as one in which both sides formulate foreign policy in military terms," although they think it possible to broaden this definition for rivalries to exist without violent interactions. In an earlier work, Goertz and Diehl point out to the competitive nature of rivalries, because it involves the division of scarce goods, whether tangible in nature or less tangible goods such as reputational or ideological considerations (Goertz and Diehl, 1992, 153).

Vasquez points to the hostile nature of rivalries: Rivals perceive value in relative terms and believe that the gain for one involves to some extent a loss for another which in turn affects their relative position in the dyadic relationship. Gains and losses affect the future of the rivalry, therefore the rivals evaluate outcomes in terms of their impact on the rivalry itself rather than in terms of their intrinsic value (Vasquez, 1993, 76).

Most conceptualizations also include the occurrence of a certain number of militarized intestate disputes within a given period of time (Bennett, 1996; Hensel, 1996; Diehl, 1998). The inclusion of a dispute-threshold, however, might limit our understanding of it. The occurrence of disputes can tell us something about the intensity and escalation of a given rivalry, it is less useful, however, as an indicator of its existence. Therefore, the conceptualization of a rivalry should only use this indicator as a measure of intensity, not for the measurement of its duration. The definition of rivalry applied in this chapter is based on Thompson's (2000b; Thompson, 2001b) conceptualization of strategic rivalries.

Strategic Rivalries

Conflicts lie at the heart of rivalries. Based on the perception of the actors, conflicts are about real incompatibilities in attaining tangible and intangible goals. Disputes about territory, influence and status, and ideology, are at the core of conflicts of interest at all levels of analysis, but especially between states. Strategic rivalries might be thought of as the reverse image of the cooperative special relationships on a conflict-cooperation continuum. Three selection criteria are of special significance. All actors must regard each other as:

1. competitors;
2. the source of actual or latent threats that pose some possibility of becoming militarized; and
3. as enemies.

The condition of mutuality is critical in the sense that only few countries, especially in the case of major powers, are viewed as competitors "boxing in the same league." This means that competitors may be viewed as both, either too strong, or too weak to be to be considered a genuine and possible threat. In addition, enemies may be viewed as significant threats without being regarded as competitors. If they are not regarded as both, enemies and as competitors, at the same time they cannot be regarded as rivals but simply as opponents or adversaries.

In addition, a critical criterion for identifying rivalries is their nonanonymity. Actors only regard enemies who are also considered valid competitors as rivals. Applying this definition, we are able to identify forty-one strategic major power rivalries over the course of nearly five hundred years (1494–2000, see table 5.1).[5]

Thompson (2000b, 9) marks three main types of strategic rivalry: they are either (1) spatial; (2) positional; and/or (3) ideological in nature. Spatial rivalries are characterized by the contests over the exclusive control of territory. Positional rivalries are contests over relative influence and status, either in the world system at large and/or in regional

Table 5.1   Major Power Rivalries

Major Power Rivalries (Time Period)

Austria-France (1494–1918)
Austria-Ottoman Empire (p1494–1918)
Austria-Piedmont/Italy (1848–1918)
Austria-Prussia (1740–1870)
Austria-Russia I (1768–1780)
Austria-Russia II (1790–1918)
Austria-Spain I (1701–1725)
Austria-Spain II (1733–1793)

Continued

Table 5.1 Continued

Major Power Rivalries (Time Period)

Britain-France I (p1494–1716)
Britain-France II (1731–1904)
Britain-Germany I (1896–1918)
Britain-Germany II (1934–1945)
Britain-Italy (1934–1943)
Britain-Japan (1932–1945)
Britain-Netherlands (1651–1688)
Britain-Russia (1716–1956)
Britain-Spain I (1568–1667)
Britain-Spain II (1701–1793)
Britain–United States (1783–1904)

China-USSR (1958–1989)
China–United States (1949–1978)

France-Prussia I (1756–1763)
France-Prussia II (1792–1955)
France-Italy (1881–1940)
France-Netherlands (1668–1748)
France-Russia I (1732–1756)
France-Russia II (1792–1894)
France-Spain (p1494–1700)

Germany-United States I (1889–1918)
Germany-United States II (1939–1945)

Italy-Russia (1937–1943)

Japan–United States (1900–1945)

Ottoman Empire–Russia (1668–1920)

Portugal-Spain (p1494–1581)

Prussia-Russia I (1744–1807)
Prussia/Germany-Russia II (1890–1945)
Prussia-Sweden (1648–1813)

Russia/USSR–Japan (1873–1945)
Russia-Sweden (1600–1724)

USSR–United States (1945–1991)

Source: Rivalry data provided by William R. Thompson.

Notes: Major power definition based on Levy (1983), Rasler and Thompson (1994), and the Correlates of War data project.
p indicates that the rivalry has a prior start date.

subsystems. The main issues at stake in ideological rivalries are the relative superiority of (economic, political or religious) belief systems. However, this does not imply that these main types are mutually exclusive. A rivalry may well encompass all three types simultaneously (but not necessarily so).

Commercial Rivalries

This categorization omits another important type of rivalry, namely those rivalries that are primarily commercial in nature. So far, no clear definition has emerged that distinguishes a strategic rivalry from a commercial one, although this certainly would be a useful undertaking in order to get a better understanding of the dynamics involved in the rivalry process. Naturally, a complete separation of commercial and strategic elements of a rivalry is impossible to achieve and does not reflect the nature of both, strategic and commercial rivalries. For example, the bargaining position and threat potential of a country is in large parts determined by its economic strength and capability (Sen, 1984, 67).

At the same time, seemingly pure commercial threats involve political consequences as well (Modelski, 1999, 157). Its ability to enforce unilateral decisions of its own, or to resist those of rivaling countries, limits and defines the position of an actor in the rivalry process. It is, however, possible to identify rivalries that are primarily commercial in nature, and others that are mainly based on strategic considerations. In other words, what ultimately distinguishes a commercial and strategic rivalry is the end and the means the rivalry pursues, that is economic dominance or political primacy.

Levy extends the definition of rivalry to include nonmilitarized interstate disputes as well. He argues, that economic rivalries usually involve sustained, hostile, and nonanonymous competitions (his criteria for rivalries) just as much as strategic rivalries do, and thus should count as rivalries as well (Levy, 1999, 174). Most studies perceive rivalries only as strategic and militarized competitions between states and trivialize the domestic factors, such as commercial interests and their influence on national policy. However, as Hitch and McKean (1960) have shown, military problems are essentially economic problems involving the allocation of scarce resources to competing objectives. As Levy points out, commercial rivalries are an important form of competition for power, status, and wealth in international politics and should not be left out in our study of the rivalry process (Levy, 1999, 174).[6]

Again, mutual recognition as rivals is the most important criterion for identifying commercial rivalries. A commercial rivalry is distinguishable from mere commercial competition among states by the fact that both actors regard each other not just as (1) competitors but also as (2) enemies in a commercial sense at the same time. Enemies in this context are competitors that are perceived as a significant threat to ones core commercial interest or leading sector(s) with the ability to destroy or significantly influence the structure of commercial activity of an actor. However, they must also be seen as viable competitors and thus a real threat. In addition, (3) the source of actual or latent threats in a commercial rivalry must have the potential to develop into a *commercial war.*[7]

Analogous to the strategic kind, commercial rivalries might be thought of as the reverse image of the cooperative special relationships on a conflict-cooperation continuum. The possible consequences or stakes the actors face, in other words the left side of the rivalry conflict-cooperation continuum, in a commercial rivalry are commercial disputes or ultimately a commercial war, as opposed to militarized disputes or as a final consequence, a military war between the strategic rivals. In other words, commercial rivalries are distinct from strategic rivalries because both their means and ends are primarily economic.

Commercial rivalries (just as a strategic ones) can be spatial, positional, and/or ideological in nature. Rivalries can also be commercial and strategic at the same time. However, commercial rivalries exist independently of strategic ones and vice versa. The ends of commercial rivalries are primarily economic in nature. This does not imply that political considerations have no role in them. However, the primary goals of the rivals remain commercial, whereas in strategic rivalries they are political (spatial, positional, or ideological in nature). Likewise, the means of commercial rivalries are economic. This makes a more narrow definition of "political" necessary—military threats are political means, whereas changes in tariff policy are not (Conybeare, 1987, 4).

In addition to the means and ends, the stakes involved mark the most important difference between commercial and strategic rivalries. Whereas strategic rivals face militarized life-and-death conflicts as a possible ultimate consequence, commercial rivals engage merely in a commercial war about certain commercial interests.[8] The definition of commercial wars applied earlier distinguishes commercial wars from two other kinds of conflict: (1) wars, where economic means are facilitated to support political and/or military ends; and (2) wars where political (including military) means are used to achieve economic ends (ibid., 1).

The Relationship between Commercial
and Strategic Rivalry

Most of the criticism regarding the distinction between commercial and strategic rivalries centers on their similarity. Commercial rivalries are assumed simply a subset or type of strategic rivalries. If that would be true, we would be hard pressed to find cases that can be identified as commercial but not strategic major power rivalries or major power strategic rivalries that are not commercial in nature as well.

A good example, however, of a major power rivalry primarily commercial in nature is the commercial rivalry between Japan and the United States starting after the late 1960s (Rapkin, 1999; Harding and Lincoln, 1993). Few people would describe those two countries as strategic rivals in this time period. Nevertheless, ample evidence exists for a commercial rivalry between Japan and the United States (Rapkin, 1999). The same could be argued for a number of states now united in the European Union (mainly the two largest economies within the EU, Germany and France) and their relationship with the United States. Whereas wide-range political cooperation and even a security-infrastructure in form of the North Atlantic Treaty Organization (NATO) between most of the member states of the EU exists, it is not too far fetched to identify the EU and the United States as commercial rivals.

Lacking an accepted measure and thus a listed set of commercial rivalries over an extended period we include only strategic rivalries in our empirical analysis here. However, this does not diminish the importance of acknowledging the importance of commercial rivalries for the study of rivalries in general.

Figure 5.1 plots the total sum of all major power rivalries from 1494 to 2000, as well as the occurrence of global wars and the timing of the hypothesized rivalry environments. We observe relatively low numbers of actors engaging in major power rivalries from the late fifteenth century on until the number or rivalries increases significantly in the eighteenth century (after an initial short-term increase in the latter half of the seventeenth century).[9] In the case of major power rivalries, the stakes involved are almost always commercial and political in nature. Why then is it important to separate the two? The global economic political environment in which the major power rivalries take place has a significant impact not only on the nature of the commercial, but also on the strategic rivalry.

Copeland (2000; see also Copeland, 1996) highlights this relationship in a similar fashion. Copeland aims to combine liberal theory

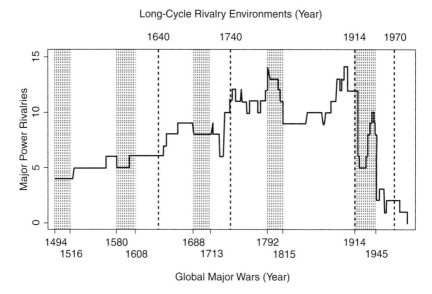

Figure 5.1   Major Power Rivalries, Major Power Wars, and Rivalry Environments, 1494–2000

Source: Rivalries based on data in table 5.1. Major Global Wars based on data in table 5.2. Rivalry Environments based on data in tables 5.3 and 5.4.

(interdependence will increase the costs of rivalries) with a realist perspective (high interdependence will foster rivalries) and adds to the variable of level of interdependence a second causal variable, the expectation of future trade. This enables us to determine under what conditions interdependence will drive actors toward stronger or less stronger engagement in rivalries. Copeland argues that if trade expectations are positive, dependent states will be more inclined toward peace. If, however, such states are pessimistic about future trade, fearing a cutoff of vital goods or the continuation of current restrictions, the negative expected value for trade will push them toward a more aggression, provided they have the military means (Copeland, 2000, 15).

The critical aspect is the emphasis on the trade expectations rather than current trade: In an environment characterized by the reliance of most major powers on access to the global commercial network, we can assume a positive outlook of trade expectations (or better—commercial intercourse within the global network) of the actors seeking access to the commercial network. (In case at least one of the actors does not primarily seek access to it, this assumption does not hold anymore.) Commercial rivalries will certainly erupt, yet are less likely to evolve into strategic ones, as a result of the nature of *cooperative competition* in this environment. In an environment, however, marked by a stronger reliance on internal networks and greater stress of independence rather than interdependence we can assume a less positive trade expectation for vital goods of the actors (such as commodities). The relatively high cost of engagement in a major power rivalry will be discounted for the even higher cost of nonaccess to vital goods and disruption of the internal network. Commercial rivalries in this setting will be much harder to separate from strategic rivalries and (owing to the relatively lower cost of engagement in a strategic rivalry) more likely to appear together.

Global System Rivalry Environments

As we have demonstrated in our previous chapters, the interaction of markets and other environmental conditions (from an evolutionary perspective) account for much of the economic and political history of the modern world. Markets affect the structure of societies and the political framework at the domestic and the international levels just as much as they are affected by them: they dissolve social structures, alter political relations, and stimulate both scientific and technological advance (Gilpin, 1987). To get a better understanding of rivalries between states we must therefore not only include strategic components as listed in the definition given earlier, but also economic ones. In the words of Sen (1984), ultimately the motivation for rapid industrial change is almost invariable of a military nature.[10]

These rivalry environments themselves are stable and only change after shocks in the form of major paradigm shifts in the world system occur. By applying the leadership long-cycle framework as our analytical tool to capture the political global system process within the complex global system framework to the concept of rivalry, we are able to identify the timing, the character, and the transitional phases from one rivalry environment to another.

External Network–based Environments

Rivalries in an environment characterized mainly through external networks will be predominately marked by *cooperative competition*. In a network- and service-based economy, the actors are bound by the necessity to cooperate to a certain degree and have to find a balance between the amount of competition they are willing to tolerate and the level of cooperation that does not erode their strong economic and political position. Commercial rivalries can be bitterly fought in such a setting, but at the same time the likelihood of commercial rivalries developing into evenly bitterly fought strategic ones will be limited by the risk to endanger the connection to the economic network controlled in large part by a small group of major powers.

A major power engaged in a strategic rivalry would be forced to create alternative external networks (i.e., networks involving actors outside their direct political influence). This *economic deterrence* (Rosecrance, 1992) limits the number of major powers willing and able to engage in a number of strategic rivalries, as the contending rivals must either be able to control important elements of the commercial network or establish alternative networks of their own.

Internal Network–based Environments

In an environment mainly based on industrial production and character-ized by the aim of economic independence (and thus the creation of internal networks), commercial rivalries will me much different in nature and far more directly intertwined with strategic rivalries. The number of actors that are able to engage in both types of rivalries (commercial and strategic) at the same time rises significantly. If, owing to the change of the nature of the leading sectors from predominately flow-oriented ones (trade and services) to stock-oriented leading sectors (manufacturing), the importance of tangible factors (land and manufacturing) rises in importance to intangible ones (free commercial flows and capital) "coop-erative competition" changes into *hostile competition.*

Without the need to build entire alternative external networks the aim of obtaining similar leading sector industries as other major power rivals (and thus only internal economic networks) can be obtained with some economic repercussions (e.g., in the form of initially higher prices) but not nearly as many as in network-based economies. The control over internal networks of production is far less costly achievable than control over external commercial networks, both in economical as in political terms.

Whereas the value-gain (as expressed in additional capabilities and thus gained power) of actors in a commercial network environment is dependent on the access to the global commercial network, the value-gain and (relative) power in an industrial environment is built on independence. Therefore it is not surprising, that the number of actors with the will and the ability to engage in both, commercial and strategic rivalries increases significantly in such an environment. In other words, the distinction between commercial and strategic rivalries in combination with a study of the global economic context in which those rivalries take place enables us to get a better understanding of the dynamics of rivalries. The most interesting issue then is not to simply identify commercial rivalries as opposed to strategic ones but the reasons why and under what conditions commercial rivalries can transform into strategic rivalries. The complex global system framework allows us to combine the strategic and economic aspects, dynamics, and interactions of interstate competition applicable to the concept of rivalry for an empirical test of the proposed model of the development of the global political process.[11]

Major Shocks

Major shocks in this understanding are major political shocks, or a dramatic change in the international system or its subsystems that fundamentally alters the processes, relationships, and expectations that drive nation-state expectations (Diehl and Goertz, 2000). As the level of analysis here is the global world system, we must include the most significant major political shocks of that system, that is, major global wars.

Table 5.2 summarizes the major global wars that have occurred during the time from 1494 to 1990. It also lists the major participants and the time period in which they took place as well as the corresponding K-wave. We know from the leadership long-cycle model (Rasler and Thompson, 1989; 1994) that those wars occur in a regular pattern and involve the major global powers. Five global wars are identified: the Italian and Indian Ocean Wars (1494–1516), the Dutch-Spanish Wars (1580–1608), the Wars of the Grand Alliance (1688–1713), the French Revolutionary and Napoleonic Wars (1792–1815), and World War I and II (1914–1945). These wars were fought by coalitions of global and other types of powers, as identified in table 5.3. They are included because they exemplify at our level of analysis the type of dramatic change defined above as major political shocks driving the change in rivalry behavior.

At the same time, we have argued that the same expectation holds true for the environments in which the rivalries take place (i.e., global rivalry environments). Here a major shock is not so much exemplified by militarized contests, but through a shift from one global system

Table 5.2   Major Global Wars, 1494–2000

Global War	Major Participants	Time Period (K-waves)
Italian and Indian Ocean Wars	Portugal/Spain (+ England) versus France	1494–1516 (K10)
War of Dutch Independence	Netherlands/England/France versus Spain	1580–1606 (K12)
Wars of Grand Alliance	Britain/Netherlands versus France (+ Spain)	1688–1713 (K14)
French Revolutionary and Napoleonic Wars	Britain/Russia versus France (+ Netherlands/Spain)	1792–1815 (K16)
World Wars I and II	United States/Britain/Russia[USSR]/ France versus Germany (+ Japan)	1914–1945 (K18)

Source: Adapted from Rasler and Thompson (1994, 17).

environment to another and thus major economic shocks in the form of changes in the global network structure. Therefore, our evolutionary framework takes into account two types of major shocks: major power wars (broadly endogenous to the global political process development) and changes in the network structure of the global system (exogenous to the process).

The Effects of Industrial Production-based and Commercial Maritime-based Rivalry Environments

As pointed out earlier, rivalries influenced by a network-based environment will be predominately marked by cooperative competition. That is, in an external network- and service-based economy actors are to a certain degree dependent on other actors in the global economic system, not only economically but as a result of this interdependence also politically. Major powers participating in the global commercial network are forced to find a balance between the amount of competition they are willing to tolerate and the level of cooperation that does not erode their major power position. This limits the number of major powers willing and able to engage in strategic rivalries, as the contending rivals must each be able to control and maintain the commercial network or establish alternative networks of their own.

Thus, in eras where most major global powers are connected in a global commercial network, rivalries amongst major networked (i.e., connected to the global commercial network) powers will be marked by cooperative competition owing to the higher levels of interdependency and the higher costs of engaging in a major power rivalry. Rivalries involving nonnetworked major powers, however, will be less costly and thus more likely than rivalries involving only networked major powers to occur.

In contrast, rivalries between major powers rooted in a system of internal networks will be larger in number and more prevalent in environments marked by hostile competition. Most of the industries predominant in the industrial rivalry environment, such as iron and steel, chemical, textiles, machinery, and transport equipment had also strategic significance for the production of military goods. This is of course, not a new phenomenon. Ships in the maritime trade environment were as much prone to *dual-use* as technologies in the industrial rivalry environment.

The difference between the core or leading sectors in the maritime network (or for that matter the digital network environment) and the industrial rivalry environment is, as Sen (1984, 7) pointed out the dual strategic significance for military self-sufficiency and national economic independence held to provide the rationale for the desire to acquire this group of industries. Major powers in this environment try to establish internal rather than external networks, in order to, as Rosecrance (1999, 6) puts it, "to excel in all economic functions, from mining and agriculture to production and distribution" (see also previous discussion in chapter 2 on network trajectories).

This emphasis on self-sufficiency and national economic independence characterizing the industrial environment stands in stark contrast to the necessities of a network- and service-based environment as found in the maritime trade and the digital network environments.[12]

Table 5.3 lists the leadership long cycles and the corresponding set of K-waves as identified in our model (see table 2.1 and figure 2.3) with the addition of the first half of the new leadership long-cycle ten (LC10). The hypothetical global system rivalry environment types are based on the leading sectors in each K-wave. The leading sectors reflect the main nature of the world economy during the phase in question. Figure 5.1 graphically represents these rivalry environments in the same time frame. Following our discussion on the impact of external and internal network structures on rivalries in the global complex system, we can identify three major rivalry environments: (1) the first global complex system rivalry environment stretching from the long cycles dominated by the Italian city states and the Oceanic Trade long-wave; (2) a second

Table 5.3   Global Complex System Rivalry Environments, 1190–2000

Global Complex System Rivalry Environments	Leadership Long Cycles (with Corresponding K-waves)	Rivalry Environment Type	Predicted Takeoff	Predicted High-Growth
Environment 1	LC3 Genoa	*External Networks*		
	K5	Maritime Trade Network	1190–1220	1220–1250
	K6		1250–1280	1280–1300
	LC4 Venice			
	K7	Maritime Trade Network	1300–1320	1320–1355
	K8		1355–1385	1385–1420
	LC5 Portugal			
	K9	Maritime Trade Network	1430–1460	1460–1494
	K10		1492–1516	1516–1540
	LC6 Dutch			
	K11	Maritime Trade Network	1540–1560	1560–1580
	K12		1580–1609	1609–1640
Transition (Ex > In)	LC7 Britain I			
	K13	Transition Phase	1640–1660	1660–1688
	K14		1688–1713	1713–1740
Environment 2	LC8 Britain II	*Internal Networks*		
	K15	Industrial Production	1740–1763	1763–1792
	K16		1792–1815	1815–1850
	LC9 United States I			
	K17	Industrial Production	1850–1873	1873–1914
Transition (In > Ex)	K18	Transition Phase	1914–1945	1945–1973
Environment 3	LC10 United States II	*External Networks*		
	K19	Digital Commercial Network	1973–2000	2000–2030
	K20		2030–(?)	(?)–(?)

Source: Leadership Long Cycle based on Thompson (2000a, 12) with modifications.

environment characterized by the dominating internal network structure during Industrial Takeoff long-wave phase; and (3) a third global complex system rivalry environment characterized by the return to a complex regime and external network structures with the beginning of our hypothesized Information long-wave emerging with K-wave nineteen (K19).

First Global System Rivalry Environment

From long-cycle three (LC3) to long-cycle six (LC6) we see leading sectors predominately based on the global maritime trade network (see table 5.3). Major types of strategic rivalries in this period are very much characterized by the nature of the long-cycle rivalry environment. Spatial rivalries in the first global system rivalry environment will be in one way or another affected by the need to exercise some control over the maritime trade network. This involves either the creation of an alternative external (i.e., involving other external actors) trade network or the ability to exert control over the existent network. Positional rivalries in the first system will be fights over the share of influence over the maritime trade network.

The meaning of *resources*, and the rivalry over them, is also predominately characterized by the maritime nature of this global system rivalry environment as discussed earlier. Intangible factors such as the establishment of commercial flows and the ability to exert control over the network and its various main nodes gain in importance over tangible assets, such as natural commodities. This explains why relatively small nations such as Portugal, the Netherlands, and earlier the two city-states Genoa and Venice were able to take a leadership position in the world system.[13]

In the same manner, rivalries over access will involve the contest over territorial space connected to the maritime trade network (i.e., their nodes). That is, the requirements to "play in the same league" and thus be perceived as both, a competitor and enemy will involve naval capabilities for major powers enabling them to engage in rivalries characterized by this maritime-based environment. At the same time, however, as argued earlier, a major feature of networks include the necessary element of basic cooperation and interdependence of the members of the network. This means that disputes over the share of influence over the network can only be successful if they do not at the same time destroy the value of the network that is defined by the numbers of actors connected to it.

In other words, sea-routes are only valuable to those who control them if the goods shipped through them can be obtained and distributed. This causes a significant degree of interdependence amongst the actors. It also highlights the need for at least a minimum level of cooperation coexistent with rivalries over, say, access. No country was able to control (or in other words, internalize) all the nodes of the global maritime trade network. Therefore, it had to cooperate to a certain degree to be able to establish a functioning trade network (based on an external network involving actors outside the direct control). In order to achieve a competitive advantage in the ability to provide the intangible good of trade flows cooperation was a necessary element.

Only those countries that threatened the control over their position and role in the commercial network (and thus the competitive advantage) needed to be regarded as both, commercial and strategic rivals. The number of countries able to do so remained fairly low. The global leadership of each long cycle is therefore not surprisingly attained by major powers that base their capability predominately on their naval capability. We can therefore characterize the period from K-wave five to twelve (K5-K12) and the corresponding long-cycle three (LC3) to long-cycle six (LC6) as the first global system rivalry environment or the maritime trade network environment.

Transition from External to Internal Network Environment

During the following long-cycle seven (LC7) we witness a transition from a maritime-based to a more industrialized environment (see table 5.3). Naval capability still remains important; what defines potential threat to rivals, however, becomes more and more industrial in nature. Leading sectors in the following period are predominantly based on industrial capability. However, as the change from a maritime to an industrial character is only emerging in this long cycle, the period from the eleventh to twelve K-wave (K11–K12) during long-cycle seven (LC7) is defined here as a transition phase.

Second Global System Rivalry Environment

During the entire long-cycle eight (LC8) and until roughly the middle of long-cycle nine (LC9), industrialization emerges as the dominant factor determining the character of this second global system rivalry environment (see table 5.3). The change of the nature of the leading sectors reflects also on the character of the second global system rivalry environment. A clear shift from intangible (flow-based) to tangible (land-based) factors, such as manufacturing capabilities, occurs.

Naval capability does not cease to be an important factor of power in this time period (see Rasler and Thompson, 1994). However, the meaning of what constitutes a spatial rivalry in the second global system rivalry environment changes. The important territory contested no longer reflects the maritime character of the previous environment but the new determinant of power, industrial capability. As Sen (1984, 7) points out, many of the industries developing during this phase are also of strategic significance for the production of military goods or what determines power in both strategic and commercial rivalries during this phase.

Whereas the first global system rivalry environment is characterized by its network nature, the second global system rivalry environment is very different in nature as a result of the transition to a dual strategic significance for military self-sufficiency and national economic independence (see Sen, 1984, 7). In short, we would expect this to change of the character of the second global system rivalry environment to have an effect on the rivalries taking place within this rivalry environment as well.

Positional rivalries in the second global system rivalry environment will no longer be disputes over the share of influence over the trade network but capability of industrial production and dominance in demand markets. The type of competed resources will also be predominately characterized by the industrial nature of the second global system rivalry environment. In the same manner, access rivalries will no longer be predominantly over access to the trade network but over access to raw materials necessary for production capability.

Transition from Internal to External Network Environment

The following K-wave (K18) marks a second transitional phase (see table 5.4). The character of the industrial production environment is still highly visible in this transition. At the same time, however, something new emerges. We witness a shift away from the emphasis on self-sufficiency and industrial production to a more connected and interdependent global economy (see e.g., Keohane and Nye, 1989).

Third Global System Rivalry Environment

In fact, the new environment that emerges out of this transition to a new leading sector with a network- rather than industrial production-character in the following K-wave (K19) for which we have provided evidence here is in many ways similar to the maritime trade network-based character of the first global system rivalry environment. However, owing to the digital nature of the network, the main emphasis of the global commercial network in this new environment lies on the worldwide integration of production processes and less on trade. Although similarities to what Kenneth Barr has termed the "regime of factories abroad" (Barr, 1991, 82) in the maritime trade network exist, the activity in the first global system rivalry environment is marked more by the exchange of goods rather than the integration of production processes. The changes wrought by digital communication networks and the relative ease and low cost of global transportation has made a far more highly integrated global production process possible. We would expect the emergence of a new the third global system rivalry environment predominately based on this digital network beginning in K19, the first K-wave of the new long-wave taking shape in the global system process.

Hypotheses

From the previous discussion of the connection between the global system environment and rivalries as well as the distinction of commercial rivalries from strategic rivalries, it is possible to develop the following hypotheses:

H1: The number of strategic major power rivalries is most likely to be dependent on the rivalry environment in which these rivalries take place.

Every economy is a hierarchical structure composed of dominant cores (leading sectors) and a dependent periphery (Gilpin, 1975). This economy can be mainly centered in the national realm (i.e., under direct political and commercial control).[14] Major powers in such an environment aim to rely on internal networks. These internal networks are characterized through their core and periphery structure within a national economy (including areas outside the physical borders of a country but under its full economic and political control) based on the principle of self-reliance and economic independence. The number of major powers willing to engage in one or more strategic rivalries increases, as the cost of participation (loss of integration into network) decreases.[15] Thus, we can state the following hypothesis:

H2: In internal network–based environments, more major powers are likely to engage in strategic rivalries. As a consequence, the number of strategic major power rivalries will be higher than in external network–based environments.

The hierarchical structure of economies, however, can also extend to the international realm (i.e., involving external actors). In contrast to internal network–based world economies, external network–based economies are characterized by the need for cooperative competition with external actors that are outside the direct political and commercial control of the economy of major powers, although major powers as the cores of the world economy can exert significant influence and thus have indirect influence on these outside actors.

The costs for networked major powers of engaging in strategic major power rivalries in such an environment are significantly higher: major powers engaging in strategic rivalries with other major powers risk exclusion from the commercial network and must either be able to insure this access through political and military means or be able to install alternative external networks. The trade expectations in such an environment are necessarily high, so that, in accordance with Copeland's trade expectation theory (Copeland, 1996) rivalries will be less likely to occur between networked major powers. Thus, the number of major powers willing to engage in major power rivalries will be significantly lower than in environment characterized through internal network–based economies.[16]

H3: In external network–based environments, fewer major powers will engage in major power rivalries. As a consequence, the number of strategic major power rivalries will be lower than in internal network–based environments.

Table 5.4 summarizes the global system rivalry environments and their predicted main characteristics in terms of the numbers of actors (that is the number of major powers with the potential to engage in a rivalry), the rate of volatility of the number of rivalries during the global complex system rivalry environments, and the likelihood of escalation from commercial to strategic rivalry depending on the descriptions of the global system rivalry environments above.

During the first global system rivalry environment we would expect a situation where only a few major powers exist that are capable of engaging in a rivalry within this environment. At the same time, we would expect that fact to reflect on the volatility of the number of rivalries. Major shocks will not have as much of an impact because of

Table 5.4 Main Characteristics, Global Complex System Rivalry Environments, 1190–2030

Global Complex System Rivalry Environments	Main Characteristics	Time Period (K-waves)
Commercial Maritime System Rivalry Environment (RE1)	low number of actors; low volatility; low likelihood of external network rivalries; high likelihood of internal network rivalries	1190–1640 (K5–K12)
Transition Phase (TRE)	increased number of actors; high volatility; low likelihood of external network rivalries; high likelihood of internal network rivalries	1640–1740 (K13–K14)
Industrial Production System Rivalry Environment (RE2)	high number of actors; high volatility; high likelihood of internal network rivalries	1740–1914 (K15–K17)
Transition Phase (TRE)	high number of actors; high volatility; high likelihood of internal network rivalries	1914–1970 (K18)
Digital Commercial System Rivalry Environment (RE3)	medium number of actors; low volatility; low likelihood of external network rivalries	1970–(?) (K19–K?)

Source: K-waves based on Modelski and Thompson (1996).

the limited number of actors. Also, because of the relatively high rate of interdependency within this environment, we would expect the threshold for commercial rivalries to develop into strategic ones to be relatively high, or put differently we would expect the number of actors engaging in a strategic rivalry to be relatively low.

The second global system rivalry environment is identified by its transition character. It is the equivalent to a major war as a major systemic shock leading to a new rivalry environment. Naturally, we expect an increase in both, the numbers of potential rivals and higher rates of volatility because of the unstable nature of this phase.

The first transition phase marks the beginning of a new equilibrium or rather a second global system rivalry environment. We would expect the number of potential and actual rivals to increase, as this phase is marked less by reliance on other actors in the network, but by an increased emphasis on self-reliance. At the same time, the threshold of engaging in a strategic rivalry has somewhat lowered as the main determinant of rivalry potency is now measured in industrial production capability and not in maritime power alone. The increase in actors and the lowering of the threshold of engaging in a strategic rivalry would lead us to expect a greater rate of volatility in the change of number of rivalries. In addition, the decrease in interdependency would lead us to expect an increased likelihood of commercial rivalries changing into strategic ones.

The phase following the second global system rivalry environment is another transitional phase. We would again expect a higher rate of volatility and a change in the number of actors. The description of the third global system rivalry environment is naturally highly speculative. However, judging from the available evidence, we expect a higher rate of interdependency in this phase than in the previous, second global system rivalry environment, similar, if not significantly higher, to the level of the first global system rivalry environment. This leads us to expect the number of potential strategic rivals to decrease. At the same time, and again analogous to the first global system rivalry environment, we would expect a decrease in volatility in the number of rivalries within this phase. The higher rate of interdependency leads us also to expect a lower likelihood of escalation from commercial to strategic rivalries, again for the same reasons mentioned for the first global system rivalry environment.

Empirical Evidence—Descriptive Analysis

In order to put these hypotheses to a test, we can look at the actual numbers of major power rivalries over the period under consideration and compare the expected behavior of rivalries with the observed development over the various long cycles. Figure 5.1 shows the relationship between leadership long cycles and major power rivalries. Based on the major power rivalries as identified earlier (see table 5.1), it displays the development of the combined number of rivalries for each year from 1494 to 2000.

On the top of the chart, the predicted starting dates of the long-cycle rivalry environments are marked. The areas and the dates marked at the bottom of the figure mark the starting and ending points of the major global wars listed in table 5.2, representing the major political shocks discussed earlier. Figure 5.1 graphically indicates that the hypothesized global system rivalry environments are reflected in the data presented here. As we would expect from our first hypothesis, the number of strategic major power rivalries seems to be correlated with the world system environment in which they take place.

The first global system rivalry environment, the maritime trade network environment, is the relatively stable environment we would expect it to be. The major shocks, in this case the Italian and Indian Ocean Wars (1494–1516) and the Dutch-Spanish Wars (1580–1608), do not seem to have a significant impact on the overall number of major power rivalries. The following first transition phase (1640–1740) is marked by higher volatility and also the increased impact of the major shock provided in the form of the Wars of the Grand Alliance (1688–1713). It indicates the behavior of strategic major power rivalries in the next global system rivalry environment, the industrial production environment (the second global system rivalry environment).

Here, the French Revolutionary and Napoleonic Wars (1792–1815) seem to have a significant impact on the overall number of major power rivalries, just as we would expect from our hypothesized relationship between the two. The major shock in the form of global war "settles" a number of disputes amongst rivaling major powers. The effect of the industrial production environment marked by its hostile competition in the commercial realm, however, causes the equilibrium in this environment to be a higher rather than lower number of major power rivalries, and the number of major power rivalries increases to its old high level as we would expect from hypothesis 2.

The following second transition phase is not only significantly shorter than the previous first transition phase but also more intense in its volatility. From a height of twelve major power rivalries prior to the last shock, World Wars I and II (1914–1945), the number of rivalries decreases to only five, and, after a short-lived upswing to eleven major power rivalries, it finally decreases to only two remaining major power rivalries. In the initial stage of the hypothesized new global system rivalry environment, the digital network environment (the third global system rivalry environment), the number of major power rivalries drops even further so that at this point we see no strategic major power rivalry existent anymore, despite the fact that commercial major power rivalries (e.g., Japan-United States) did not fade to exist (Rapkin, 1999).

Judging from our experience in the first global system rivalry environment with its many similarities with the current long-cycle rivalry environment, we would expect this number to increase somewhat in the future.[17] However, the overall number of major power rivalries might be as low or even lower as in the first global system rivalry environment. The increase in commercial (and thus to a certain degree political) interdependency and the resulting rivalry environment marked by cooperative competition explains this phenomenon.

To show that the behavior of major powers engaged in the same commercial network differs from that of nonnetworked major powers, it is useful to compare the rivalry behavior of *networked* (i.e., sea or maritime powers) and nonnetworked (i.e., land powers). Figure 5.2 shows the number of rivalries between two sea powers (sea power rivalries) and the rivalries amongst major powers where at least one of the actors is a land power (land + land/sea power rivalries).

The number of rivalries involving only sea powers is as low as we would expect it to be. Only major powers willing to challenge and (perceiving themselves as) able to compete with the leader of the commercial network are engaged in a strategic rivalry with other networked major powers. Briefly, before the major shock in form of the War of Dutch Independence, three rivalries involving only maritime powers take place at the same time, otherwise only two rivalries, involving sea powers in a fight over regional dominance in the network (Denmark-Sweden) and a

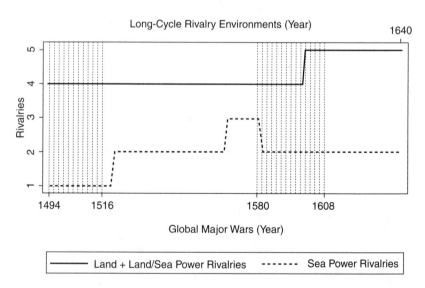

Figure 5.2 Number of Major Power Rivalries in Maritime Commercial Rivalry Environment, 1494–1640

Source: Rivalries based on data in table 5.1. Major Global Wars based on data in table 5.2. Rivalry Environments bases on data in tables 5.3 and 5.4.

challenge to the current leader in the commercial network (Portugal-Spain) take place at the same time and both of them are challenges to the leader of a part of the commercial system.

During the same period, rivalries involving at least one nonnetworked rival are much more likely to take place: we can identify four rivalries involving at least one nonnetworked major power in existence at the same time in this period (see figure 5.2). This suggests that hypothesis 2 (higher number of strategic major power rivalries in internal network–based environments) and hypothesis 3 (lower number of strategic major power rivalries in external network–based environments) hold true.

A closer look at the first transition phase, illustrated in figure 5.3, shows that a change from one environment to another takes place. The two land-based major power rivalries involve both major power rivalries seemingly less correlated to both, the first and second global system rivalry environment. Both rivalries (Austria-France and Austria-Ottoman Empire) are struggles of three major powers competing for the establishment of alternative internal networks (i.e., empires) relatively

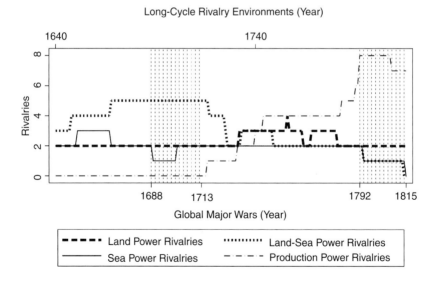

Figure 5.3 Number of Major Power Rivalries in Transition Phase 1 and Industrial Production Phase Rivalry Environment, 1640–1815

Source: Rivalries based on data in table 5.1. Major Global Wars based on data in table 5.2. Rivalry Environments bases on data in tables 5.3 and 5.4.

unaffected by the global rivalry environments affecting most of the other rivalries. Sea power rivalries fade away, as the maritime rivalry environment changes into an environment dominated by industrial production capability (i.e., the second global system rivalry environment).

Rivalries between sea powers and land powers surge initially as the remaining major land powers gain independence from the maritime trade network. This, however, proves a short-lived phenomenon and represents simply "fights of the past." Steadily increasing after 1713, major power rivals competing over industrial production capability reflect the impact of the change in the global rivalry environment. The high number of major power rivalries characterized by this struggle for industrial production capability is consistent with hypothesis 2 (higher number of strategic major power rivalries in internal network–based environments).

Figure 5.4 graphs the development of major power rivalries in the industrial rivalry environment. In the same manner as in the first global system rivalry environment and the first transition phase, the number of rivalries rises before a major shock in form of two major wars (starting in 1792 and 1914). This is hardly surprising in an environment

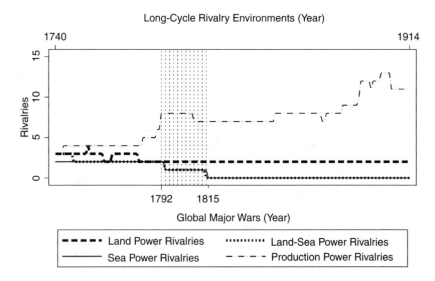

Figure 5.4 Number of Major Power Rivalries in Industrial Production System Rivalry Environment, 1740–1914

Source: Rivalries based on data in table 5.1. Major Global Wars based on data in table 5.2. Rivalry Environments bases on data in tables 5.3 and 5.4.

characterized by hostile competition and low levels of economic inter-dependency. The number of major power rivalries in the first half of this phase remains high and rises after the major shock of the French Revolutionary and Napoleonic Wars.

As the number of actors increases, so does the number of major power rivalries. Countries succeeding in their strive to *catch up* with the major powers are eager to compete as soon as they reach the ability to do so. Again, this seems to provide further evidence for hypothesis 1 (number of strategic rivalries dependent on global system rivalry environments) and two (higher number of strategic major power rivalries in internal network–based environments).

The highly significant drop of the number of major power rivalries in the next second transition phase indicates a shift into the third global rivalry environment (the third global system rivalry environment, see figure 5.5). Repeating the pattern seen in the first transition phase, the stark drop in the number of major power rivalries in the major shock of World War I and II is followed by an initial surge in rivalries that does not last. Rivalries rooted in the industrial production environment fade

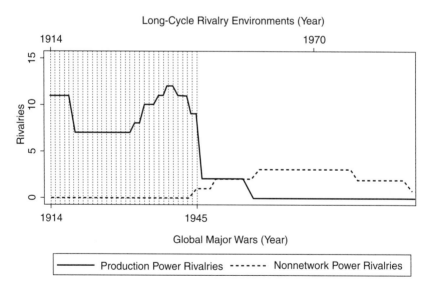

Figure 5.5 Number of Major Power Rivalries in Transition Phase 2 and Digital Commercial System Rivalry Environment, 1914–2000

Source: Rivalries based on data in table 5.1. Major Global Wars based on data in table 5.2. Rivalry Environments bases on data in tables 5.3 and 5.4.

away, just as major power rivalries rooted in the maritime trade network environment did earlier.

This time, however, we see again the effects of an external network–based environment with its characteristic of cooperative competition reflected in the number of major power rivalries after the end of the major shock in 1945 (see figure 5.5). As rivalries rooted in the prior environment die out, the number of rivalries between major powers competing is, as expected, very low.

Judging from the behavior of major powers in the maritime trade network environment this might be changing in the near future, although we can expect the overall number of network-integrated major powers engaged in a rivalry with each other to be very low, as the high level of interdependence in the new digital network environment calls for an even more cautious balancing act between cooperation and competition.

Empirical Evidence—Quantitative Analysis

Our regression analysis confirms these preliminary results. As we face the problem of dependence between events (sum of major power rivalries in t), a negative binomial estimation offers the best way to study the relationship between major power rivalries and the impact of rivalry environments on them. Both transition phases have been omitted since we expect no clear influence on the dependent variable.

All three rivalry environments have been dummied into the dataset. In addition, we have included the sum of major great wars as discussed earlier, since we would expect them to act as *exogenous shocks* with an initial positive effect (increase in number of rivalries) and later negative effect on the number of major power rivalries. Both the shocks themselves and their lag (fifteen years) have been included in the dataset.[18]

The first model (see table 5.6) measures the effect of all three global system rivalry environments, controlling for the sum of all major powers present in the same year, as well as the effects of the external shocks in the form of major great wars and their lag-effect. All variables point in the direction we would expect them too. Except for the first rivalry environment, they are also highly significant (at the $p<.001$ level). During the second global system rivalry environment, the number of expected major power rivalries increases by a factor of 56 percent, whereas in the third environment, the mean number of rivalries in this period decreases by a factor .44 holding all other variables constant.

As we would expect from our hypotheses, the external shocks in the form of major great wars initially causes the number of rivalries to increase (during a shock the expected number of rivalries increases by 14.9 percent) but taking into account the lag-effect of the shocks (fifteen years) we find that they then contribute to a lowering of the number of major power rivalries by a factor of .85, holding all other variables constant.

Table 5.5 shows the impact of these independent variables on the number of possible major power dyads in each year. The result are very similar to those for the number of actual major power rivalries and confirm our conviction that the effect of the rivalry environments and the exogenous shocks are effects on the world system and not just on the particular rivalry dyads.

To control for the impact of the number of major powers in the system, we included the sum of the number of major powers present in each year. The number of major powers present in the system naturally also has a significant effect on the number of major power rivalries. Model 2 (table 5.6) shows the results if we include out control for the number of major powers present in the system each year. For each additional major power in the system the number of major power rivalries increases by 16.5 percent. The impact of the second and the third global system rivalry environment remains highly significant. During the third global system rivalry environment, the expected number of major power rivalries decreases (by a factor of .54) whereas the increase in the second global system rivalry environment remains almost unchanged (beta .4272). The coefficient for the first global system rivalry environment changes its sign and now shows a positive (albeit very small) effect on the number of major power rivalries (beta .0513).

This result is, however, even less significant than in the first model (standard error of .0562). The coefficients for both the external shock and its lag-effect are less significant than in the first model and also smaller (beta of .0822 and −.0781 respectively). In other words, the existence of a shock and its lag initially increases the number of major power rivalries by 8.6 percent and the lag–effect decreases the number of major power rivalries only by a factor of .92.

The effects on the number of possible major power dyads changes however significantly in model 2. The impact of all rivalry environments decreases (although the proportion between them remains relatively stable), whereas the impact the external shock increases markedly (the existence of a major great war increases the number of major power rivalries by 32.4 percent). This however is consistent with

Table 5.5 Summary of Summary Statistics for Major Power Rivalries, Major Powers, Major Power Dyads, and Rivalry Environments

	Statistics	Sum Rivalries	Sum of Major Powers	Sum of Possible Dyads
RE1				
0	N	352	352	352
	Mean	6.3608	6.3182	19.1506
	SD(mean)	2.2891 (0.1220)	0.8546 (0.0456)	5.5158 (0.2940)
	Min/max	1/12	4/8	8/30
	Median	7	6	18
1	N	139	139	139
	Mean	4.7554	5.5396	15.0719
	SD(mean)	0.8151 (0.0691)	0.8100 (0.0687)	3.6028 (0.3056)
	Min/max	3/6	4/7	11/21
	Median	5	5	16
RE2				
0	N	317	317	317
	Mean	4.7571	5.8738	16.1672
	SD(mean)	1.5056 (0.0846)	0.9759 (0.0548)	5.0810 (0.2854)
	Min/max	1/10	4/8	8/30
	Median	5	6	16
1	N	174	174	174
	Mean	8.0000	6.5057	21.3276
	SD(mean)	1.2947 (0.0982)	0.5962 (0.0452)	4.1492 (0.3145)
	Min/max	6/12	6/8	17/30
	Median	8	6	18
RE3				
0	N	470	470	470
	Mean	6.0681	6.1383	18.3532
	SD(mean)	2.0084 (0.0926)	0.9025 (0.0416)	5.2089 (0.2403)
	Min/max	2/12	4/8	8/30
	Median	6	6	18
1	N	21	21	21
	Mean	2.2857	5.1905	10.0000
	SD(mean)	0.6437 (0.1405)	0.6016 (0.1313)	0.0000 (0.0000)

Continued

Table 5.5   Continued

	Statistics	Sum Rivalries	Sum of Major Powers	Sum of Possible Dyads
	Min/max	1/3	5/7	10/10
	Median	2	5	10
Total				
	N	491.0000	491.0000	491.0000
	Mean	5.9063	6.0978	17.9959
	SD(mean)	2.1130 (0.0954)	0.9117 (0.0411)	5.3696 (0.2423)
	Min/max	1/12	4/8	8/30
	Median	6	6	18

Note: RE notes the respective Global Complex System Rivalry Environment.

Table 5.6   Analysis of the Effect of Rivalry Environments on Number of Rivalries per Year

	Model 1			Model 2			Model 3		
	Coef	SE	p	Coef	SE	p	Coef	SE	p
Rivalry Environment 1	−.07536	.0518	0.146	.0513	.0562	0.361	.0370	.0563	0.511
Rivalry Environment 2	.4426	.0457	0.000	.4272	.0465	0.000	.4111	.0466	0.000
Rivalry Environment 3	−.8113	.1480	0.000	−.6222	.1534	0.000	−.6244	.1538	0.000
Sum Major Great Wars	.1387	.0437	0.001	.0822	.0454	0.070	.1015	.0489	0.038
Sum Major Great War lag (15 years)	−.1680	.0460	0.000	−.0781	.0488	0.110	−.0720	.0498	0.148
Sum of Major Powers				.1531	.0256	0.000	.1402	.0266	0.000
Long Cycle Phase C (Coalition)							.0651	.0489	0.184
N-size	491	491	491	—	—	—	—	—	—
Chi^2 (df)	256.73 (5)	284.03 (6)	279.04 (7)	—	—	—	—	—	—
Chi^2 p value	<.0001	<.0001	<.0001	—	—	—	—	—	—

Source: Author's analysis of the data provided in the previous tables.

our expectations; the number of rivalries is affected to a greater extent than the possible number of major power dyads (all likely to become a rivalry), but the results here show that the effect is significant and the systemic effects are important.

The third model (model 3) introduces anther control variable, this time for the impact of the long-cycles phases (as discussed earlier) on the number of major power rivalries at any given year. The results for the rivalry environments do change significantly from the other models and the impact of the external shock and lag becomes more significant. As we would expect, the number of major power rivalries during the coalition phase (with a decline in the power of the system leader) increases by 6.7 percent. This tells us that the rivalry environments have a greater impact on the number of major power rivalries than the long-cycle phases alone-it does indeed matter in what kind of systemic environment rivalries take place.

In conclusion, we can argue that these findings lend further support for our hypotheses laid out earlier. The global system rivalry environment in which they take place affects major power rivalries. The systemic effects of the external shocks (in the form of major great wars) are present and measurable. The same test with another Poisson model (Poisson exponentially weighted moving average model, or PEWMA, see Brandt et al., 2000) yields very similar results and gives further confidence in the results of the analysis of he three models discussed above.

Conclusion

As this chapter has shown, major power rivalries with their roots in the new digital network global system rivalry environment will have a different history and therefore a different future than rivalries rooted in the industrial production long rivalry environment. The global system environments shape the behavior of major power rivalries significantly and must therefore taken into account in the definition of rivalries. As Copeland has shown, the expectations of actors for future commercial intercourse is vital for their rivalry behavior (Copeland, 1996). A major exogenous variable determining those expectations is the rivalry environment in which rivalries take place.

Rivalry environments based on external networks will be characterized by the necessarily positive outlook of the networked major powers in regards to future commercial interactions. In contrast, environments based on internal networks with their stress on independence rather than interdependence will be much more characterized by each individual actors judgment on future commercial interactions. In addition, the cost of engaging in strategic rivalries will be lower than in external network–based environments. Strategic rivalries between major in such a setting are much more likely to evolve than in external network–based environments.

We have many indications that a key to understanding the dynamics of rivalries is their development from commercial rivalries to strategic ones. Again, the different environments must be taken into account when studying rivalries. A commercial rivalry in the industrial production environment has been far more likely to develop into a strategic rivalry than a similar commercial rivalry in the digital network environment. Therefore, findings from previous studies must be reviewed with this knowledge in mind.

This chapter has lend further evidence to the many similarities between the first maritime trade network environment and the new digital network environment. This is especially helpful, since the digital network environment is only starting to evolve now. The integration of Asia as an important node in the global commercial network in the new digital network environment is a return of its importance in the maritime trade network. The cotton of the first global system rivalry environment has become the computer-hardware in the third global system rivalry environments. The gaining importance of nations like India and China, after their decision to become a "networked" rather than "nonnetworked" actor, is another echo of the past.

Thus, we can expect the number of rivalries between networked major powers to be very low. In terms of stability in the world system then it seems to be less a question of *democratic peace*, but more a question of *networked peace* owing to the effects of cooperative competition.

CHAPTER SIX

The Continuation of Change of the Global Complex System—an Outlook on Its Future Development

This study set out to resolve the "contradictory and puzzling process" (see Guillén, 2001a; see also Gilpin and Gilpin, 2000; Giddens, 2000; Held et al., 1999) of globalization as we experience it today. Rather than understanding it as a disruptive process uniquely tied to technological advancements emerging in the twentieth century, we have argued here for a different understanding of current transformations. Globalization should be understood as a developmental process of the global system unfolding over many centuries, increasing in its complexity, both in width and depth, and structured in its form of development. Its developmental structure is in its core the result of human agency and thus follows a similar pattern despite the increasing complexity of the global system and different technologies involved.

However, the most important question for all historically based analysis on globalization is whether the past patterns of global system development still hold true for its current transformation or whether we are indeed witnessing a structurally different development altogether, whether technologically induced or the result of other processes? Is there something inherently novel and/or unique about modern (digital) technologies that renders our insights from past patterns of transformation useless? Is globalization as we experience it today therefore a stage in an ongoing developmental process or a unique occurrence in history?

In order to answer this question, we have offered here a powerful analytical framework that functions across all levels of analysis, across time, and across research traditions, employing an evolutionary approach that draws on existing approaches to provide a systematic and empirically based answer to the origins, timing, and effects of globalization in its current and possible future form. This framework sheds new light on the relationship between complex system development and the development of the global system as a whole (drawing on complex systems theory), uncovering external and internal network structures of global system development.

With the help of this framework, our study has traced the evolutionary pattern of communication and digital technologies and their effect on the development of a new technological style.

As laid out in chapter 2, in this view, globalization comprises a set of coevolving processes: global economic evolution (of trading systems and world markets); global political evolution (of nation-state systems, world power competitions, and international organizations); democratization (i.e., the formation of a potential democratic community); and the creation of a world public opinion (through media and learning processes). The ultimate agents of these processes are individuals and organizations sponsoring and advancing innovation that results in the strengthening of the global layers of interactions. In other words, globalization is an evolutionary process and this requires an evolutionary methodological framework.

Our study shows, that technology plays a crucial, yet nondeterministic role in this transformation, as it has done in previous transformations. It enables, drives, and manifests the development of new technological styles. These technological styles interact and depend for their development (or lack thereof) as much on the social, political, and cultural environment in which they operates as much as they influence these environments. In order to make sense of the implications of the development of a new technological style thus requires not only the identification of the key technologies (making possible and driving the development of new leading sectors) enabling this new socioeconomic environment. It also makes it necessary us to place the role of technology in a broader, historical context.

The framework employed in this study and expanded in its theoretical reach—what we have called the global complex system model—has allowed us to empirically survey the globalization process as a nonstatic and cyclical process with changes (increase) in the level of integration (over time) and the structure of the system. Whereas a repetitive pattern of cyclical change (rise and fall of a sociopolitical leader) does indeed exist, the element of structural change and especially the implications of this structural change on the emerging global system as a whole is a significant and crucial part of this pattern. As we have demonstrated, the rise of the global system can be broken down into several distinct phases and the identification and systemization of these phases and patterns are important for the analysis of the current changes and path-dependent structures of the international political economy.

We do not argue that globalization (i.e., the global system process) in its current stage equals earlier stages at any given earlier point in time. Given our assessment of the development of the global system as an evolutionary, complex system process, only the opposite can be true. The current stage of the global system process is indeed unique and unprecedented in many ways: for example its geographic reach, its complexity, and its level of interconnectedness, to name just a few characteristics. However, the same holds true for earlier stages. The core of this work is thus not so much a study of the outcome of the global system formation process per se, but rather a study of the process itself.

Expanding on previous applications of the evolutionary world politics model, we not only highlighted the similarities between old and the new external network structures of the global system process. We also emphasized differences compared to previous internal-network environments and the implications these similarities have for the development of the political, economic, cultural, and social globalization process (especially in regards to the politicoeconomic impact) in terms of power relations, geographical aspects, and institutional arrangements (with a main emphasis on differing technological styles).

Thus, in presenting, first, the major theoretical explanations for the globalization process, and second, providing a theoretical framework to analyze this phenomenon by adding new theoretical insights to existing approaches in the literature and presenting a variety of methodological approaches to provide empirical analyses to test the theories presented, this book provides a contribution to the field both on a theoretical and on an analytical level.

Implications for Technological Change

The findings of our analysis especially in chapters 3 and 4 have important implications for the question of the role of technological change, both now and for the future. Our model has laid out the importance of the shift from a global system process based on analog information processing technologies to a system based on digital information processing.

This shift has opened up an entire new environment for all agents that partake in the global system process, and has several important implications for both, the agents, as well as the system itself.

As previously demonstrated, the global system as a complex system features self-organization as its main organizational principle. During the initial phase of systemic growth and emergence we have argued that learning, innovation, and institutionalization become critical factors that contribute to the rise of complexity in the system and eventually lead to the shift to a rule-based regime, during which learnt and institutionalized copying mechanisms prove far more effective than innovation and trial-and-error strategies.

With the shift to a new information system (exemplified especially in its storage), however, the environment changes dramatically. As a result, the system that has been too complex to allow for new trials and innovations to be immediately more successful than established patterns of behavior changes. It becomes an entirely new "playing field" in which the old rules and forms of behavior are still effective, yet other coping mechanisms emerge that are even more effective. As in the previous complex regime phase, especially new technologies that facilitate new forms of information processing (again as a result of trial and error, learning, and innovation) prove themselves very effective new coping strategies in a changing world system. This is the result of the new opportunities of agents in a changed information environment.

As we have shown in our study, the critical path in terms of coping strategies of agents is the transfer from information to knowledge. The use of paper currency in Sung China is a good example of such an institutionalized coping strategy. It provided a very effective coping strategy to solve a critical issue (capital transfer) in a very effective manner given analog informational processing technologies. The shift to a digital information highlights the new opportunities that arise for agents to innovate and develop in trial-and-error fashion new forms of capital transfer. This opportunity has been the hallmark of the rise of new forms of capital transfer since the beginning of the first K-wave (K19) in such an environment, that also marks the end of the punctuation of the global complex system process and the shift back to a complex regime.

What distinguishes this study from other analyses of globalization that also emphasize the transition in global forms of capital transfers, is that we place this innovation in a much larger, historical, economic, social, political, and cultural context. This study has argued that the era often considered the beginning of the modern globalization process (i.e., industrialization) has in fact been the opposite. Rather than marking the start of a complex regime, industrialization has been the outcome of the institutionalization of coping mechanisms that emerged out of a system based on analog information processing technologies.

This macrosystem-perspective also allows us to place the recent rise of commercial powers such as China, India, or Brazil into a more appropriate perspective. Some readers might have been surprised to see China mostly featured in the historical discussion, but not as an emerging major competitor to the United States beginning in, say, 2000. This is largely the result of the focus of our study on the first K-wave (K19) of the hypothesized new long cycle (LC10). As we have shown in great detail in our discussion of leading sectors of this new K-wave, the United States has established an early lead in the development of the critical technologies for the establishment of leading sectors and thus emerged as the leader of the global system following past patterns of development.

The Phoenix-cycle hypothesis we proposed has demonstrated that it is possible that the United States might follow in the footsteps of Great Britain in developing two separate centers of leading sectors development as part of the transition from external to internal network structures (in the case of Britain) and now reverting back to a global economy characterized by external network structures. The advantages of backwardness might thus elude the emerging competitors in the critical phase of the emergence of a new K-wave (i.e., around the 1970s in our model).

The recent rise of India as a global business process outsourcing (BPO) destination of choice (ITU, 2006; see also Nasscom, 2007)and the rise of China as major economic and increasingly political power on the world stage in recent years documents the advantages of our model for a better understanding of this rise. As we have shown, the systemic leadership (lasting as a process for about 100 years in the form of a long-cycle) of agents (i.e., states in the modern global system) is based on not one, but two consecutive K-waves that help the emerging leader to lock-in a distinctive technological style, based on critical carrier technologies of the first K-wave.

We have shown, that those carrier technologies involved ICTs and biotechnologies in particular and that the United States was able to dominate the development of those sectors in the time frame of the first K-wave of a (possible) new long cycle (starting in the 1970s and ending in the late 1990s). China, India, and Brazil, have all emerged in recent years as major adopters of such technologies (ITU, 2007; 2006). This is of course what our model would predict, as it reflects the learning and institutionalization processes that make up the evolutionary logic of the global complex system process. Although neither India, nor Brazil or China were able to emerge as major players during the initial development of this carrier technologies, they now have proven very effective adapters and innovators, leading to systemic instability and concentration of systemic capabilities we would predict as part of the development of the long-cycle process (see esp. chapter 5 and the following discussion). The recent rise of both, China and India at this point in time, therefore, lends further credence to our arguments developed here, rather than to contradict them.

In other words, not only do we have plenty of evidence based on the data available to us from the first K-wave of the hypothesized new long-cycle 10, but also do recent technological, economic, and political trends unfold in the direction we have predicted.

Implications for Global System Leadership

Although predictions about the future behavior of major powers and the relationship between them are naturally rather speculative, the many similarities between the first global system rivalry environment and the emerging new, third system are striking. Both environments are characterized through their external network reliance, causing major powers to engage in cooperative competition in order to participate in the global commercial network (or else be forced to built an alternative network). The most apparent similarity between the two environments is the application of the so-called *Venetian model* (Lane, 1973) by the most successful major powers: Not territorial possessions (i.e., land factor) but the control over the commercial network and its nodes (i.e., flow factor) are the key to success in this environment.[1]

As was argued earlier, a key parameter influencing the character of each global system rivalry environment is the level of dependency on the functioning of the commercial network and access to it. For example, the value of the Portuguese enclaves on the area between the East African (Sofala), the Persian (Ormuz), Indian (Goa), and Malay coasts (Malacca)[2] was highly dependent on the demand markets in the Western hemisphere, where all of the commercial rivals of the Portuguese were located. The Portuguese, and for that matter all the major powers seeking access to the commercial network, could only afford to engage in a very limited number of strategic rivalries or otherwise would endanger their access to the global commercial system that was the basis of their major power status.

Comparative advantage (and the establishments of monopolies) in this setting meant in large parts enabling commercial flow through superior technology (shipping technology, maritime techniques, and routes) and thus leadership in leading sectors of this environment rather than complete political control over the commercial nodes which was rather costly and hard to achieve and maintain in the first place (see e.g., Chaudhuri, 1985, 72–73; Steensgaard, 1974). As Pérotin-Dumon (1991) points out, it was not until the nineteenth century that first England, and later the United States, strove to apply the doctrine of total mastery of the seas and monopolistic barriers were permeable at the local level (or outside nodes of the commercial global network). This, again, is reflected in the number involving land-based major power strategic rivalries and strategic rivalries between major sea powers.

Thus, during the first global system rivalry environment only relatively few major powers exist and most strategic rivalries within this environment involve at least one non-networked major power. Strategic rivalries in this environment are limited by the high costs of engagement and mostly limited to direct challenges to the systemic leader in the world system. In addition, we observe lower volatility of the number of rivalries, in large part because of this lower number of actors but also because major shocks seem to have less of an impact as in the following phases. Given that the newly emerging system is even more reliant on external network relationships, we can expect a similar pattern to unfold in the newly emerging third global system rivalry environment, which might be called the digital network rivalry environment.

As pointed out in chapter 3, one aspect of the maritime trade network environment was the ability of global major powers to establish *factories abroad* and in effect outsource the production for example of muslin or cotton products without actual ownership of those production facilities (see Barr, 1991). As a result we can identify a higher proportion of service industries and lower proportions of production or manufacturing capabilities during these phases, in other words a greater reliance on flow-based capital rather than land-based assets at home.

In the same way, the core *virtual head states* (Rosecrance, 1999) in the digital network environment rely for their production capability on body states in the periphery. In both environments, the leading sectors are mostly an expression of the ability to enable the flow in the global commercial system. In the digital environment, however, we observe an even higher rate of interdependency between the major powers

(Cooper, 1980; Keohane and Nye, 1989; Gaddis, 1991), as the level of production integration is far more advanced than in the maritime trade network. Therefore, we would also expect the number of future strategic rivalries in the third global system rivalry environment to be significantly lower than in the previous industrial production environment (the second global system rivalry environment).

This high level of integration and interdependency explains why in the new digital network environment we observe such low numbers of strategic rivalries. The cost of engagement in a strategic rivalry between *networked powers* (i.e., major powers integrated within the world economic system) has risen significantly in relation to the maritime trade network rivalry environment, which explains why we not a single strategic rivalry between networked major powers since the end of the last major shock in 1945 and only very few challenges involving at least one non-networked major power. The need for access to the global commercial network seems to have the effect of what Rosecrance (1992) calls economic deterrence.

Similarly, Golden (1994) argues, that national strategy in the new strategic global environment will have to balance economic and security interests and support approaches that develop international consensus in order to meet the economic challenge of sustaining high and rising levels of national income in the face of intense competition. The key to adaptation to the new environment is to blend cooperation and competition. The combination of convergence in economic performance and the new global environment of the Informational network economy, have altered the nature of regional competition in ways that have profound strategic implications. As a result of changes in industrial organization from the period of the industrial rivalry environment with an emphasis on hierarchical firms to the horizontally organized and virtually networked structured corporations of the digital network rivalry environment cooperative competition becomes the main character not only for the corporate environment but also for the environment in which rivalries take place.

Golden shows, that in this setting of network organizational relationships, national strategy must balance cooperation and competition to achieve national objectives (Golden, 1994, 4). This gives rise to what Rosecrance (1999) calls the *virtual state* where no longer the products of land determine market and power relationships, but mobile capital, labor, and information become the primary major power factors in this new environment. "The virtual state," so Rosecrance, "is a political unit that has downsized its territorially based production capability and is the logical consequence of emancipation from land. Virtual states and their associates would rather plumb the world market than acquire territory" (Rosecrance, 1999, 4). In other words, states in this view will not engage in territorial strategic rivalries anymore, and positional rivalries will (as was the case in the maritime trade network environment) be reduced to a very few challenges to the systemic leader.

The informational network economic environment thus changes the organizing principles for the analysis of power. As Albert Bressand (1989) puts it, power in this context depends more on the ability to influence access and interconnection than on the capacity to enforce borders. Golden (1994) argues that the political and security networks will perform the same kinds of functions as economic organizational networks, that is providing an infrastructure that will enhance cooperation and constrain the nature of competition. Cooperation across the various major actors in the world economic system will be essential to avoid confrontations over the location of network nodes, which would undermine the advantages of global networks. Although it is still possible to influence the location of network nodes, the form of the competition must be consistent with the need to cooperate in constructing and sustaining global political, security, and economic organizational networks. The strategy of cooperative competition will be defined in terms of global organizational networks that provide for enhanced cooperation on technological developments and potential responses to international crises in a framework of shifting ad hoc coalitions and intense economic competition. This is, of course, in many ways very similar to the rivalry environment of the maritime trade network.

One outcome of this change in the context in which major power rivalries take place is the change of the "nature" of rivalries between major powers. The many possible divisions between major powers will be much more likely to find their expression in commercial rivalries than in strategic ones, as the cost of engaging in strategic rivalries of all kind (spatial, positional, and ideological) has risen significantly in the digital network environment. This is reflected in an increasing emphasis on economic competitiveness as a major security and strategic issue (U.S. Congress. House and Senate, 1996). The case of the U.S.-Japan relationship (see Harding and Lincoln, 1993) is a good example for this change of rivalry dynamics between major power nations. Whereas in the industrial production environment the threshold for engagement in strategic rivalries was lower than in the previous maritime trade network environment, the likelihood of a commercial rivalry between two major powers developing into a strategic one, as for example the Anglo-Dutch rivalry in the seventeenth century (Levy, 1999), is even lower in the new digital network rivalry environment, for the reason laid out earlier.

A second interesting aspect is the role of size of an actor in the new rivalry environment. The number of nations considered a major power in the new global system will rise as the "virtual state" gains in importance. Territorial size will be less of a factor in determining the power status of an actor than its role in the global commercial network as (flow-based) intangible assets rise in their value over the value of (land-based) tangible assets. Rosecrance, for example, argues for a renaissance of the powerful city-state in the new form of *virtual states*. Just as in the maritime trade network environment, smaller states can play a major role in a network-based environment. It also comes as no surprise, that nations with a powerful position in the first global system rivalry environment are gaining in importance and strength in the third global system rivalry environment; Sweden and the Netherlands are just two obvious examples.

The shift of what constitutes fitness and thus increased power in the world system can be seen in the cases of China and India. Although rich in traditional land-based assets, they are likely to be regarded not only as a threat but also as a competitor only after they sought access to the global commercial network. At the same time, however, very few major powers will be able to challenge the role of the systemic leader in this changing world system; territorial size will still very much matter for global powers. Global major powers must be able to maintain both internal networks as well as high competence in leading sectors of the informational network economy (and thus strong ties with external networks).

Another effect of the changes in the digital network environment is a growing emphasis on the role of information in security matters, often referred to as *information warfare* (see e.g., Arquilla and Ronfeldt, 1993; Molander et al., 1995; Wall Street Journal, 1995). John Arquilla and David Ronfeldt differentiate between what they call *netwar* (societal-level conflicts waged in part through *internetted* modes of communications) and *cyberwar* (at the military level). Netwar in this context represents a new entry on the spectrum of conflict that spans economic, political, and social, as well as military forms of warfare. In contrast to economic wars that target the production and distribution of goods, and political wars that aim at the leadership and institutions of a government, netwars in this view would be distinguished by their targeting of information and communications. Cyberwar on the other hand involves diverse technologies, notably for command and control, for intelligence collection, processing and distribution, for tactical communications, positioning, identifying friend or foe, and for smart weapons systems. It may also involve electronically blinding, jamming, deceiving, overloading, and intruding into an adversary's information and communications circuits (Arquilla and Ronfeldt, 1993; see also Brewin, 2000; Markoff, 1999a; also Markoff, 1999b).

Unlike most other forms of attack against a major power, it is fairly easy and relatively cheap to engage in information warfare. Similar to the *guerre de course* (privateering) and *vrijbuiters* (freebooters) of the maritime trade network environment, digital *vrijbuiters* offer their services to nations willing to pay for their assistance in information warfare. For example, during the Gulf War in 1990, a group of Dutch hackers (calling themselves *Hackers for Peace*) approached diplomats in the Iraqi Embassy in Paris, offering to foul up the network handling logistics messages between bases in the United States and U.S. military units in Saudi Arabia for a payment of $1 million (Fialka, 1997). The argument, that cyber attacks cannot be regarded as interactions between nations but instead as acts of private individuals, mostly "innocent" teenagers seeking adventure and "reputation" in a digital world, is also ill-founded. The U.S. Air Force, for example, reported a case where (most likely) foreign government agents "mentored" a sixteen-year old British citizen, telling him which military-related computers in the United States to attack, while the young man, known as *Data Stream*, exchanged the information without ever getting in direct contact with his mentor (U.S. General Accounting Office, 1996). A number of other examples of this kind of activity exists (Miklaszewski and Windrem, 1999; National Economic Council [NEC], 1994).

Implications for Global System Development

What unites most of the more recent accounts of the demise of the world system in its current structural form is the puzzling combination of the simultaneous military strength of the United States and its relative decline in economic and political terms. It seems rather peculiar, in this perspective, to witness the economic rise of the triad (and with it a shift of the center of the system further westward and back into the Asian fold in many accounts) without the demise of the existing leader's military capability or at least the rise of a serious challenger or challengers in the short-and even medium-term.

Taken together with the high complexity of the global system, the perceived need for international cooperation not only in economic and sociopolitical, but increasingly also in ecological terms, and its truly global proportions that renders dominance of the world system nearly impossible, the notion of a breakdown of the system and a uncertain future structure seems rather obvious. However, taking our model and the lessons of a prior occurrence of a *Phoenix cycle* with Britain's second leadership of the world system into account, we can not only theoretically explain the current "chaos" but in fact would also expect it to unfold in the manner it currently does. Thus, ours is not an attempt to "twist" existing long-wave explanations to fit current developments, but rather a theoretical extension and clarification based on existing empirical analysis of the historical evolution of the world system.

The rise of Japan, thus, becomes more closely aligned with the rise of France as a challenger to British hegemony during the eighteenth century and resulting in Britain's defeat of the French challenge during the French Revolutionary and Napoleonic Wars and consequently Britain's establishment of her second hegemonic period. This is not to argue for a future war between the United States and Japan, or that Japan is the most likely candidate for the challenge of America's claim for leadership of the world system. Our model does, however, provide some answers several authors, including Wallerstein, raise in order to explain the phenomenon of Japan's economic and especially financial importance in the current world system but its apparent "nonchallenging" behavior in terms of political power. Viewed as a challenge based in the same internal-network structure system, Japan's capabilities seem far greater than if viewed as a challenge to America's lead and rising dominance of the newly emerging external network structure-based new commercial and organizational arrangement.

A number of authors note the similarity between the Dutch systemic structure and the currently evolving system (e.g., Arrighi, 1994; Boswell, 1999), something perfectly consistent with the model applied here. As pointed out, the emerging commercial and organizational structure or technological style resembles in many ways the earlier maritime commercial setting in existence prior to the industrialized phase. To a large degree this is the result of its underlying external network structure. The transformation currently taking place does not, however, mark a simple "return" to an older, previous setting. Prior complexities do not simply dissolve. Thus, elements of the previous industrial system have become integral parts of the new digital commercial system.

But just as in prior cycles, what once was the foundation of leading sectors and the basis of monopoly rents has become a necessary but commoditized element of the value-adding process. The newly emerging leading sectors are not based on the internal network structure of the prior industrial system anymore but rather both producing and products of the external network structure. This transition from an internal network to an external network structure allows for the development of a Phoenix cycle of renewed leadership, out of the ashes of its old hegemonic demise. As was the case in the prior transition from Britain's dominance of the commercial external network structure to an industrial internal one, we cannot expect this transition to progress unchallenged, albeit we would certainly wish for the containment of a future global war and a different form of macrodecision.

Given its long duration, it seems at first surprising that today's transformation of the modern global system should be following past patterns so closely. New information processing technologies make global reach not only possible at a fraction of the cost of past connections but also instant and highly standardized. In addition, as we are witnessing an evolutionary process, the levels of complexity the global system of the twenty-first century are so much greater than anything experienced before. Why then should we still be able to measure the development of new leading sectors and long cycles of political leadership in roughly the same time frames as in earlier stages of global system development?

The answer is simple enough. All of these processes are ultimately driven by human agency and human evolution has in no way matched the speed of technological evolution over the last millennium. As a result, the establishment of a new technological style still requires about one human generation to evolve and one more to manifest itself (until it starts to be replaced by a new emerging style). Many such choices, especially during the last century, might lead us to be skeptical about our ability to live up to this task. The "collateral damage" incurred as the result of the unfolding of the global system development often seems unbearably high.

However, it is important to remind ourselves that far from developing institutional automatisms and thus inevitable paths toward the future, individuals as well as societies (and thus ultimately the global community as a whole) are still able to make choices. These choices determine the environment—in a social, economic, cultural, and also ecological sense—in which our future as mankind unfolds. This book has demonstrated that the past acts indeed as a crucial indicator for the future. Neither does this constitute an embrace of popular notions of *history repeating itself*. Nor does it support deterministic concepts of path-dependent development as a result of certain socioeconomic arrangements (i.e., capitalistic modes of production). Instead, we have argued for a deeper understanding of past developments in order to uncover the structure of the global system developmental process as an evolutionary process. Understanding the relationship between the four coevolving evolutionary processes unfolding in different rhythms is the key for deciphering current transformations in their proper context. A key, that might unlock our ability to make better informed, and therefore sounder choices for our common future.

NOTES

Chapter One Thinking about Globalization—an Introduction

1. The term world public opinion does not mean to imply the existence of a single, uniform globally accepted public opinion but rather an increasing (if largely elite) acknowledgment of matters outside of one's own immediate local environment. See for example, Abu-Lughod (1989); Bentley (1993); Braudel (1992b); Curtin (1984); McNeill (1967; 1982; 1991); Plattner (1989).

2. The concept of technological styles or technological revolutions (based on the term techno-economic paradigm originally) must not be confused with the rather laden concept of capitalism. Whereas capitalism (for a discussion of capitalism in this context, see Wallerstein, 1974; 1980; 1989; see also Amin, 1990) assumes a fixed, unique socioeconomic form of capital, production, exchange, and labor (with the only distinction of systems in the form of proto- or precapitalist systems until its subsequent and inherent demise), the concept of technological styles provides a far more flexible yet systematically rigorous conceptualization of the interconnection between technology, capital, production, exchange, labor, and their embedding in and interaction with social structures (see chapter 2 for a more substantial discussion of the concept of technological styles).

3. In the context of these works, the term flows refers to the movement of physical artifacts, people, symbols, tokens, and information across space and time, whereas networks refer to regularized or patterned interactions between independent agents, nodes of activity, or locations of power (see Modelski, 1972; Castells, 1996; Mann, 1986).

4. For a further account of definitions, see Guillén (2001a, 236; 2001b); Held et al. (1999); Rosenau (1997); Albrow (1997); Kofman and Youngs (1996); McMichael (1996); and Waters (1995). See also the following edited volumes by Hargittai and Centeno (2001), Dunning (1997b), Mittelman (1996), Mander and Goldsmith (1996), Sakamoto (1994), and Featherstone (1990), providing further summaries of the literature.

5. See, for example, Gilpin and Gilpin (2000); Held et al. (1999); Castells (1996); Ohmae (1990; 1995b).

6. See, for example, Fligstein (2001); Doremus et al. (1998); Hirst and Thompson (1999); Krugman (1994); Berger and Dore (1996).

7. See, for example, Meyer et al. (1997); Williamson (1996); Levitt (1983); Bell (1973).

213

8. See, for example, Guillén (2001b); Held et al. (1999); Garrett (1998); Albrow (1997); Boyer (1996); Berger and Dore (1996); Friedman (1994); Stopford et al. (1991); Giddens (1990).
9. See, for example, Vernon (1998); Stryker (1998); Rodrik (1997); Kobrin (1997); Strange (1996); Mander and Goldsmith (1996); McMichael (1996); Ohmae (1995a); Sakamoto (1994); Kennedy (1993).
10. See, for example, Fligstein (2001); Hirst and Thompson (1999); Held et al. (1999); Garrett (1998); Meyer et al. (1997); Albrow (1997); Wade (1996); Sassen (1996); Stopford et al. (1991); Gilpin (1987); Vernon (1971).
11. On the various distinctions of world(-)system(s) with or without a hyphen and in the singular or plural use see Wallerstein (1993) and Chase-Dunn and Hall (Arrighi, 1994).
12. Although rather diverse in its scope and approaches, Frank and Gills identify twelve main "patterns" at the center of world system research (Gills and Frank, 1993).
13. Wallerstein (1974; 1980; 1989) and Amin (1990) argue, that the differentiae specificae of our world system are new since 1500 CE and essentially different from previous times and places (for an early critique, see Braudel, 1992a). For Wallerstein, the differentiae specificae is the ceaseless accumulation of capital. Amin also identifies an economic imperative that is new and unique beginning in the sixteenth century and characterizes the modern capitalist world system thereafter. This is not to argue, that this school argues that there was no form of capitalism before 1500 CE. They do, however, insist that capitalism reached a unique form at this point in history that justifies its unique classification and analytical separation from earlier forms of economic processes. Wallerstein identifies as a result three main aspects that characterize the modern world system emerging in the sixteenth century (for an early critique of this view see, for example, Skocpol, 1977): (1) a core-periphery structure, in which the core economic zone utilizes the periphery for cheap labor and commodities but keeps capital surplus within the core; (2) so-called A/B cycle phases of economic development in which the upward A and downward B economic cycles generate changes of hegemony and of position in the core-periphery structure; and (3) the existence of hegemony-rivalry (political-economic predominance by a center of accumulation regularly contested by one or several challengers during the downswing B-phase). Another importance in the distinction between the world system before and after 1500 CE for Wallerstein lays in his identification of more extended long cycles before 1500 CE. For Wallerstein, the phase from 1050 to 1250 CE marked a time of expansion of Europe (the Crusades, the colonizations), in other words an A-phase, whereas the "crisis" or "great contractions of 11250–1450 [CE]" included the Black Plague, and thus resulted in a downswing B-phase (Wallerstein, 1989).
14. As Buzan and Jones (1981) have reminded us, there is an established tradition of the importance of the analysis of change in the International Relations literature (see also Holsti et al., 1980), but not until the late 1980s and early 1990s have we seen a "return to history" that has, as Knutsen (1992) points out, become somewhat surprisingly dehistoricized in the course of the twentieth century (see also Holsti et al., 1980). Hobson (2001, 5) even states that there is little doubt that much, though not all, of the contemporary International Relations approaches are "historophobic," viewing historical analysis as superfluous or exogenous to the subject matter of the discipline.
15. For realist long-term approaches see, for example, Waltz (1993), in which he argues that for more than 300 years the drama of modern history has turned on the rise and fall of great powers; Gilpin (1987) who applies his form of structural realism to long-term political and economic history; the power transition theories (see e.g., Organski, 1968; Organski and Kugler, 1980; Kugler and Lemke, 1996; see also Doran, 1989); and to some degree also some recent works of the English school of International Relations, for example, Watson (1992; see also Doran, 1989).

16. For early calls from the sociology stratum to bring in, as Skocpol put it, the "international" into historical sociology see, for example, Skocpol (1979); Frank (1967); Tilly (1975); and Wallerstein (1974).

17. See, for example, Jarvis (1989); Halliday (1987; 1994; 1999); Linklater (1990); Buzan et al. (1993); Scholte (1993); Rosenberg (1994); Thomson (1994); Spruyt (1994); Frank and Gills (1993); Ferguson and Mansbach (1996); Hobson (1997; 1998; 2001); Hobden and Hobson (2001).

18. Spruyt (1994), for example, analyzes in his extraordinary study the rise of three new variations emerging in response to economics changes in the late Middle Ages, the development of the sovereign state, the city-league, and the city-state.

19. For example, electrification crowded out other forms of energy engines, such as steam-driven ones, in the early twentieth century. Another well-studied example includes the emergence and rise of the sovereign state, which has proven to be more successful than the city-state or city-league variant of sociopolitical organization. Spruyt (1994) concludes, that in the long run sovereign states displaced city-leagues and city-states. States won because their institutional logic gave them an advantage in mobilizing their societies' resources by which he includes not just economic resources but also institutional and structural ones.

20. See, for example, Borrus et al. (1984); Zysman and Tyson (1983); Zysman and Doherty (1995); Katzenstein (1985); Hall (1986); Kim and Hart (2001).

21. For a discussion, see Nelson and Winter (1974; also Nelson and Winter, 1982, Chapters 1–2); see also Hodgson (1988, Chapters 2–5).

22. See, for example, Dosi et al. (2000; 1988; Dosi and Nelson, 1994).

23. See, for example, Nelson and Winter (1982); Nelson (1987); Saviotti and Metcalfe (1991); Witt (1991); Hodgson (1993); and Andersen (1994).

24. Here we shall focus on the long-wave tradition of long-term change and only point the interested reader to other perspectives on economic change, combining ecological, anthropological, sociological, historical, and economic analyses, such as the well-known work by Polanyi (e.g., Polanyi, 1944; see also Polanyi et al., 1957; Dalton, 1968), developing a three-stage evolutionary model of economic growth and writers such as Jones (1988), taking a very different approach than Polanyi, who argues that demographic change is the driving force of economic change, so the potential for increased intensity of production (laying the foundations of the Industrial Revolution) is not a uniquely Western and late medieval phenomenon, but has indeed existed in many times and places during the existence of the state system worldwide.

25. The following section relies in large parts on the excellent historical review by Louçã (see Freeman and Louçã, 2001, Part I).

26. See also Andersen (1994, Chapter 1). See, however, Hodgson (1993, Chapter 10), who argues that Schumpeter's view of economic evolution differed greatly from that of the pattern of change identified in biological evolution and that therefore Schumpeter's theory cannot be regarded as evolutionary. Freeman and Louçã (2001, 50–51) point out that Schumpeter defined the social process as an intrinsic dynamic disturbance of equilibrium through the creation of novelty (i.e., the innovative mutation), which defines the core of his evolutionary framework. It includes stationary processes of equilibrium (the place of Walras), but also forces and processes moving toward disequilibrium (the place of Marx). It can also be considered organic, since both processes in Schumpeter's view are considered to be compatible, as all the relevant variables are understood to be endogenous to the system (in itself generating movement and change).

27. For a discussion on the application of long cycles and their theoretical and methodological issues, see Duijn (1983); Goldstein (1988); Berry (1991); Freeman and Louçã (2001).

28. See also contributions in Sterman (1987), for example Yakovets (1987); Bruckmann (1987; Freeman, 1987a), Shaikh (1992), and Reijnders (1990; see also Reijnders, 1997; Louçã and Reijnders, 1999) among others.

29. It is important to note in this context Rostow's (1980, 42) argument that these dynamics have to be endogenous: "A satisfactory dynamic theory of production and prices must render substantially endogenous the sequence of major inventions and innovations—the leading sector complexes—as well as the incremental improvements in productivity embraced under the case of increasing return."

30. The SSA school identifies five principal tendencies dominating the trajectory of capitalist development, of which most would also correspond with principles identified by the regulationist school: (1) capitalist accumulation continually attempts to expand the boundaries of the capitalist system; (2) capitalist accumulation persistently increases the size of large corporations and concentrates the control and ownership of capital in proportionately fewer hands; (3) the accumulation of capital spreads wage labor as the prevalent system of production, draws an increasing proportion of the population into wage-labor status, and replenishes the reserve pool of labor; (4) capitalist accumulation continually changes the labor process, both through employers' introduction of improved technologies and new machines and through the imposition of increasingly intensive labor-management systems upon workers; and (5) in order to defend themselves against the effects of capitalist accumulation, workers have responded with their own activities and struggles (Kotz et al., 1994, 11–12).

31. In this view, each Industrial Revolution is composed of two consecutive K-waves. Although more extensive in duration than a century in its entirety (think, for example of the continued existence and importance of railway systems), the life cycle of a technology system goes through several phases (similar to the view expressed by van Duijn). Broadly, these phases can be distinguished as follows (Freeman and Louçã 2001, 146): (1) the laboratory-invention phase (with early prototypes, patents, small-scale demonstrations and early applications); (2) decisive demonstrations of technical and commercial feasibility (with widespread potential applications); (3) explosive takeoff and growth during a turbulent phase of structural crisis in the economy and a political crisis of coordination (as a new regime of regulation is established); (4) continued high growth with the system now accepted as common sense and as the dominant technological regime in the leading countries of the world economy (application in a still wider range of industries and services); (5) slowdown and erosion of profitability as the system matures and is challenged by newer technology (leading to a new crisis in structural adjustment); and (6) maturity, with some renaissance effects possible from fruitful coexistence with newer technologies (but also possibility of slow disappearance).

32. This approach goes beyond the more limited conceptualizations of technological paradigms (Constant, 1980; 1984) and evolutionary technology (see Basalla, 1988; Vincenti, 1990), concentrating more on the scientific and engineering-contexts and communities involved in the evolutionary development of technology, and less as a concept of technological style as a sociopolitical context. According to this view (see Freeman and Louçã, 2001, 121–22), the five-subsystem approach has three central advantages over previous, less macrodynamic oriented approaches. First, the focus of the description lies on the overlapping of subsystems, as their relationship is more adequate to explain reality than the artificially isolated description of each of the subsystems. Second, the focus of analysis lies on the crises and phase transitions from the viewpoint of the lack of synchronicity and maladjustment between subsystems, which defines the time band of major fluctuations. Third, the social conflicts of all types are generated and expressed through the coordination process, that is, by power under all its forms, from the production of legitimacy to strict coercion.

33. In this view
> coordination is the appropriate concept by which to interpret and analyze control systems and cohesive functions in historical development. Coordination, as a social process subjected to complex interactions—and not equilibrium, which is a state— explains the existence of attractors in growth patterns, the weight of social institutions,

and the relation between the economic system and other parts of society....
Coordination explains why disequilibrium processes exist but are constrained, why
different rhythms are mode-locked, and why structural instability persists but does
not drive the systems towards explosion. (Freeman and Louçã, 2001, 120)

34. Freeman's model of the process of the evolutionary development of the global world system
can thus be hypothesized as follows: (1) The social subsystems (i.e., science, technology,
economy, politics, culture) generate a large number of irregular fluctuations, namely cyclical and wave-like movements, with different approximate periodicities. They are caused
either by specific subsystem cycles (political business cycles, technological trajectories,
cultural movements, life cycles of products or industries, etc.) or by the lags and feedbacks
in the intersubsystem connections; and (2) those streams are combined in some bands of
fluctuations by specific coordination processes emerging after structural crises.

35. Some of the crucial suggestions underlying the theoretical framework of this study have
been put forward by Perez (2002). Perez argues that some technology systems (such as information and communication technologies) prove so pervasive that they dominated the
behavior of the whole economy for a number of decades. Putting their stamp on each developing K-wave, they reciprocally influence major social and political changes. For each
long-wave, Perez suggests that one or more key factors (such as iron, coal, steel, oil, electronic chips; Freeman and Louçã prefer the term core inputs) drop so far in price that they
become universally available and give rise to a potentially vast array of new factor combinations. The producers of these key factors, motive branches in her terminology, go on to
become major industries with each successive wave.

36. See also Spruyt (1994), who has shown that change in the constitutive units of the (world or
international) system is only likely to occur after a broad exogenous change, or, in other
words, an environmental shock.

37. See, for example, Spruyt's (1994) convincing development and application of an evolutionary model invoking the role of punctuated equilibrium. For the relevance of adaptation to
environmental change for politics, see Krasner (1984; see also Krasner, 1989). For a discussion of the role of the punctuated equilibrium model, see Somit and Peterson (1992). For a
discussion of the relationship between biological and social evolution, see Runciman (1983,
Vol. 2, 45) and various Chapters in Ziman (2000, especially Part I). Whereas Gould and to
some degree Spruyt focus on the role of exogenous shocks to the system, we differ here in
this respect from this view. Rather than viewing these punctuations as exclusively exogenous, the change of environments in our view is to a large degree also driven by the endogenous process of innovation (not just in technology, but other subsystems as well). In our
view, it is crucial to view this change in the environment (in our case the world system and
its sociopolitical, economic, and cultural subsystems) as the result of feedbacks between the
various systems and subsystems. Thus, exogenous shocks are endogenous processes as well.
Born out of endogenous change in the subsystems, exogenous shocks come into being,
reinforcing and multiplying the endogenous processes of change, given a large enough
change in the environmental structure. We agree, however, with Spruyt's (1994, 25) conclusion, that the

> uneven nature of political change is well captured by the punctuated equilibrium
> model. Given that existing institutions cater to particular interests and reflect spe-
> cific distributions of power, institutions will be "stick." Only when dominant coali-
> tions change, or interests and perceptions shift, will there be an opportunity for
> institutional transformation.

38. In his "general model" (Snooks, 1998b, Chapter 10), Snooks argues for a concept of "great
waves of economic change" and examines his concept using the example of England. In this
view, each of the three great waves—with the first wave lasting from 1000 to 1300 CE, the
second from 1490 to 1650 CE, and the third originating in the 1780s CE—of economic
change that have swept across Europe were the outcome of quite distinct dynamic strategies

(and not an evolutionary development). Whereas the first wave was the outcome of the "conquest" strategy, the second wave was modeled on the "commerce" strategy, with the third and ongoing wave being a result of the "technological" strategy, with each strategy being pursued through investment in the specialized infrastructure, human skills, and institutions required to gain maximum potential.

39. Modelski (2000) argues that each of these structure-building processes at the global level equal one phase (i.e., one-quarter) of an overarching world system period roughly 2,000 years in the making, a democratic community process, lasting about 1,000 years, a global political evolutionary process driven by four long cycles of global politics, and the process of global economic evolution, each consisting of four K-waves. Chapter 2, in this volume, provides a fuller discussion of the model.

Chapter Two   An Evolutionary Theory of Globalization

1. It is important to note that in the context of this study the history of the world system is not viewed as stationary, reproducing, and expanding. This would neither fit an evolutionary perception of its development, nor its actual unfolding (as far as we can trace it from historical and anthropological sources). Rather, it is understood as a process of trial and error, progressing from a condition of potential, over some preliminary stages, toward a more fully developed status, and a future condition yet to emerge. It is thus important for the framework to allow inquires into both, structure and agency (see also Dark, 1998, esp. Chapter 4).

2. For an interesting discussion of this endogeneity trap, see Sassen (2006).

3. For examples of an application of a similar approach, see, for example, Allen et al. (1992; see also Ziman, 2000; but also Shaw, 2000; Scott and Lane, 2000).

4. The terms hypercoherence or catastrophic change refer not to the overall breakdown of the global system process, but rather to the terminology used in chaos- and catastrophe-theory. They represent an option-narrowing as the result of the selection of a new organizational and institutional setting in the global community process. After a relatively short period of internal network structure dominance, the system reverts to an external system structure, setting in motion a new rise of complexity, bringing with it a new phase of externally open systems and consequently in the end leading to a new stage of hypercoherence.

5. See Dark (1998, 116), who also argues that in

> this sense all socio-political systems can be conceived of as also being networks of regimes, organizational linkages, beliefs, cultural values, and other structures. It follows from this that the relationship between the structures, societies, and states means that systems of states cannot be taken as divisible into a discrete dichotomy of "domestic" and "inter-state" politics. These categories represent merely levels of structuring and organization within the systemic whole represented by human socio-political organization.... In the theory of complex socio-political systems . . ., all of these types of political relationship can be seen merely as possible levels in the potential range of nested hierarchies of socio-political systems from the smallest social group to the global system. The system is always a system of systems.

As all these systems, on all levels, are evolutionary in their makeup, they follow the same explanatory logic, implying a fractal-structured system, characterized by "self-similarity," or "symmetry across scale" and a "repetition of structure at finer and finer scales," see Gleick (1987, 100–103).

6. For a broad survey, see Pomper et al. (1998). For a discussion of world history and globalization, see Hopkins (2002). For the concept of global history, see Mazlish (1998), Mazlish and Buultjens (1993); McNeill (1967; 1991) also Braudel (1980; 1994). For a discussion of classic

accounts, especially, Hegel, Marx, Toynbee, and Spengler, see Mazlish (1966), Spengler (1919), also Toynbee (1934).

7. However, note McNeill's (1991, xvii–xix) own comments on this topic.

8. For a comparison of competing approaches to the periodization of world time, see Buzan and Little (2000), especially Chapters 18 and 19. For a discussion of periodizing world history, see Green (1992; 1998). For influential treatments see also Frank (1998); Frank and Gills (1993); Wallerstein (1974); Braudel (1992b; 1994); Mackinder (1904). For a summary of Mackinder's argument, see Sloan (1999). See also the periodization approaches by Dark (1998); Watson (1992); Wilkinson (1993).

9. The concept of democratic community process traces the antecedents, and also the democratic lineage (defined as "the line or succession of societies that have shaped world democratization," see Modelski, 1999, 154) of community at the global system level assuming that such a community can only be built upon democratic (i.e., participatory) foundations in the long run. The term is based on Axelrod's (1984, 154) analysis of evolution of cooperation. The concept does therefore not imply existing democratic societies resembling those of democracies today in the time period under study. Rather, it views the reform movements in Sung China (ca. 1100 CE) and republican experiments in the city states of northern Italy (ca. 1300 CE) as democratic trials (as part of the evolutionary development of variety creation), with the series of social and cultural upheavals as part of the European Reformation centered on the Dutch Republic forming another such trial. It is in liberal-maritime alliance between the Dutch Republic and England that we see a nucleus of a global system based on liberal principles that found rather favorable conditions for further clustering (i.e., more varieties of democratic states) in the mid-nineteenth century, laying the groundwork for a future democratic community as anticipated by Kant and de Tocqueville (see Modelski, 2000, 45–46). For a detailed study of this process from a similar evolutionary perspective, see Spruyt (1994, 45–46).

10. Given the extent of exchanges during this time, interaction took place not only in the form of economic goods, but also as cultural and social ones, as expressed most vividly in religious diffusion and other cultural aspects. The world public opinion does not mean to imply a single world opinion, but rather a growing acknowledgment of matters outside of one's own immediate local environment, shaping the form and boundaries of the evolutionary logic.

11. As pointed out earlier, we wish to address in this study the question of continuation or discontinuation of the global system process as a whole as a result of the impact of digital technologies. Given the extensive time periods in which the global system process as a whole unfolds, it would be purely speculative at this point to discuss this issue in regards to the development of all coevolving processes. However, it is entirely feasible to focus on the inner core of the global system process, the double helix of the economic and political evolution of the system. While placing the development of these process in the larger context of the global system process as a whole, we therefore limit our immediate attention here to these two nested processes.

12. Although the earlier Sung periods (especially the second, southern Sung) could be regarded as maritime in nature, we view them here as part of the experimental variety creation process inherit in evolutionary systems.

13. See for example, Christensen (1997); Gilpin (1996); Freeman and Louçã (2001); Freeman and Soete (1997); Freeman and Perez (1988); Porter (1990); Nelson and Winter (1982).

14. The discussion, as to why China (or rather Chinese leaders) decided against the expansion of their lead during the first occurrence of the co-occurrence of a hegemonic- and systemic crisis is beyond the realm of this work but increasingly receives more attention in the literature (e.g., Levathes, 1996; Pomeranz, 2000; for an alternative account, see Frank, 1998).

15. It is important to note, that our intention here is not to suggest, that only the Venetian or British trading networks existed. Far from it: what characterized the maritime commercial

system was rather a vast multitude of local and regional networks, stretching, as in the case of Asia, vast amounts of geographical space (see e.g., Subrahmanyam, 1996; Frank, 1998). What remains crucial for the rise of the West (as McNeill puts it) as a leading trendsetter (in terms of the global economic and political processes) was the attempt of the network system described here to act as central nodes, connecting the divergent existing networks rather than replacing them.

16. During the high time of Genoese and Venetian trade, it was in Italy where the first systems of "high-finance" emerged (Arrighi, 1994, Chapter 2). It was in Amsterdam, however, that the first stock exchange in permanent session developed, with a volume and density of transactions that outshone all past and contemporary stock markets (Braudel, 1992c; 1992a; Israel, 1989). This feature of a combination of leading sector development and center financing node has characterized all following systems, in external as well as internal network environments alike.

17. Boxer (1979, 51) describes the VOC as a "colossal organization, comparable to one of the modern great multinational firms, when due allowance is made for differences in time, space, and demography." Arrighi, Barr, and Hisaeda (Arrighi et al., 1999, Chapter 2) note that unlike their twentieth-century style versions, join-stock chartered companies were business organizations to which governments granted exclusive trading privileges in designated geographical areas, as well as the right to undertake the war- and statemaking functions needed to exercise those privileges. Again, for an argument of earlier developments of "multinational" (i.e., cross-border active) corporations, see Moore and Lewis (1999).

18. The Dutch were certainly not the only ones to launch enterprises in this new organizational style (in itself an evolutionary outcome of earlier trading enterprises in Genoa and Venice combined with the increased influence of political actors as exemplified in the Portuguese variations). In fact, the VOC's biggest rival, the English East India Company had been created two years before its Dutch counterpart, in 1600, with other English trading companies having been chartered even earlier. Several other states and cities of the Baltic and North Sea, within approximately two decades, followed the Dutch and English lead by chartering their own overseas companies, mainly to gain unmediated access to the rich trading networks of the east (see e.g., Emmer, 1981; Tracy, 1990; 1991). The VOC, however, was the most successful company. Their Asian effort dwarfed the rival English East India Company's attempts, displacing it to less desirable positions in the Indian subcontinent, which, later on, proved to be an advantage for the British (Modelski and Thompson, 1996, 79).

19. It is important to note the emphasis on production networks. Trade flows remained their expansion, both in volume and reach, throughout the entire period, although the center of control and the direction of flows changed substantially as a result of a change in production patterns.

20. As early as 1922, Unwin (1927, 352), for example, has argued that

    one of the largest and most obvious aspects of the Industrial Revolution is the change involved in the direction of world trade in textiles. The flow of piece-goods, which had for a century been westward from Asia to Europe, turned eastward from Europe to Asia...The new factory system of the west displaced, as far as the production of cotton goods was concerned, an older factory system, which we may regard as essentially of the east, and of which the English factories established in India in the early seventeenth century were representative cases.

21. These factories were in turn evolutions of the earlier organizations of the Portuguese Estado da India.

22. On the effect of organizational change on labor, see Hammond and Hammond (1968, Chapter 2), Pollard (1963); also Thompson (1968); on the history of factories in England, see Mantoux (1983); Daniels and Crompton (1920); and Wadsworth and Mann (1968). For a general overview of the literature on the cotton industry Britain, see Chapman (1987).

23. See for example, Arrighi (1994, esp. Chapter 4); also Arrighi et al. (1999, Chapter 2); Freeman et al. (1982); Freeman and Louçã (2001); Gilpin (1975; 1987; 1996; 2001). For a business perspective, see the seminal works by Chandler (1990; 1977; see also Chandler et al., 1968; 2000); also McCraw (1997).

Chapter Three   Drivers of Global Change—Leading Sectors of the Informational Network Economy

1. As we stay mostly focused on events in the common era at this point of the discussion, all years are henceforth CE unless otherwise noted.
2. For a similar argument, see Robertson (1998). Robertson, however focuses more on the importance of the digital computer as the enabler of this information system transformation.
3. Intellectual capital is the term most widely used in the management and legal literature to describe nontangible forms of assets. The accounting and finance literature uses the term intangibles, whereas economists prefer the term knowledge assets. We follow Lev's (2001, 5, 7) example and use the terms interchangeably, defined as nonphysical sources of value (claims to future benefits) generated by invention/innovation (discovery), unique organizational designs, and/or human resource practices. When the claim enjoys legal protection, for example in the form of patents, or copyrights, the asset is usually referred to as intellectual property instead. These intangible assets often interact with tangible and financial assets in the value creation process. They do, however, possess some unique features that make it necessary to study them separately in this context.
4. Maskus (2000, 3) notes that a country's system of IPRs encompasses (1) the standards it enacts to establish a creator's rights to exclude others from exploiting the economic value of his or her inventions or artistic expressions (i.e., defining the scope of patents, trademarks, copyrights, etc.); (2) limitations imposed on those rights for purposes of domestic economic and social policy (e.g., including compelled licensing of technologies to ensure their use, fair use of copyrighted material for educational and scientific advancement, antimonopoly rules, etc.); and (3) enforcement of the rights (i.e., entails administrative and judicial actions by public authorities to safeguard the rights granted).
5. See for example, Schwartz (1999); Gossain and Kandiah (1999); Economist Survey (1999). On brand evaluation see, for example, Tomkins (1999).
6. See, for example, Mansfield et al. (1977) and Bernstein (1989).
7. For example, Interbrand's model of brand evaluation, or Young and Rubicam's BrandAsset Valuator. In the same manner, the R&D scoreboard, produced annually by the UK Department of Trade and Industry in partnership with Company Reporting of Edinburgh, would prove an essential extension to capture the full spectrum of the iNet economy environment.
8. This discussion is largely based on Romer (1994; 1998).
9. Maskus (2000, 1–2) argues, that the TRIPs agreement represents a significant turning point in the global protection of intellectual property, by setting strong minimum standards in each of the areas commonly associated with IPRs, such as patents, copyrights, trademarks, sui generis methods for protecting new forms of technology, and trade secrets. Also, it mandates that countries set up mechanisms for enforcing these stronger IPRs.
10. Maskus (2000) distinguishes between the copyright and trademark complexes, which is technically correct and makes analytical sense in the realms of his study. For our purposes here, it may suffice to combine the two.
11. The following discussion is mainly based on a case study by Westland and Clark (1999, 389–96) and information from the two markets, available at http://www.nyse.com and http://www.nasdaq.com).

12. Most members of the NYSE are registered as commission brokers. These members represent securities firm such as Merrill Lynch that deal with the public at large, gathering orders off the NYSE trading floor. The second largest number of members are registered as specialists. Specialists, designated to maintain a fair and orderly market, are dealers trading from their own inventory of securities and are obligated (on 75 percent of transactions of their own inventory) to trade counter to the market trend. These specialists hold a monopoly to their assigned markets and each security has only one specialist and may be traded only in one spot of the exchange floor. The function of the third group of members, so-called floor brokers, has been largely automated by a system called SuperDOT.
13. Despite the importance of electronic networks, until 1971 (and in nonsecurities markets even until very recently) most over the counter or OTC-trades (i.e., direct trades between two parties) have still been conducted over the phone and only later formally finalized online. In the case of U.S. securities not listed on Nasdaq (up to 50,000 equity issues) this is still the case.
14. The term over the counter has its roots in the nineteenth century when many corporate headquarters and treasurers' offices were located on Wall Street, in other words close to the NYSE and at the traditional locality of commercial financial trading. Investors interested in buying shares in unlisted companies (i.e., securities not traded on the NYSE trading floor) would be unable to do so at the NYSE. He or she could, however, walk to the nearby corporate treasurer's office, and purchase, through a barred window (i.e., over the counter) the shares of that company.
15. The OTC market is the primary market for all debt trading in the United States as well as U.S. government and agency issued, municipal bonds, and money market instruments (e.g., derivates). Off-exchange trading has been uncommon outside of the United States initially. Given the multinationalization of financial institutions and the increasing reliance on global digital networks for financial transactions this has changed. OTC transactions are now also an internationally common form of trading.
16. The history of the development of the internet is well documented and needs no extended repetition here. For in-depth treatments of the development of the internet, see Abbate (1999), Naughton (2000); for brief overview see Castells (2001), Rutkowski (1997), Varian (1997); for development of the world wide web see Berners-Lee and Fischetti (1999).
17. See also Kotkin (2000) who focuses on the change of digital networks on the urban development; see also Fujita et al. (1999) for a formal economic analysis of this development.
18. Sassen (2001) in the second edition of her book, Global City, recognizes these changes and discusses the emergence of a new global urban system (esp. Chapter 7).
19. For a survey of this technological fusion see, for example, Coffman and Odlyzko (2002; International Telecommunication Union [ITU], 2007, esp. Chapter 3; ITU, 2006, esp. Chapter 3).
20. For a quantitative longitudinal analysis of the international telecommunication network, see Barnett (2001); see also for a more current analysis Gunaratne (2002). For a historical analysis of the evolution of the global communication network, see Hugill (1999). For a study of available network capacity, see Coffman and Odlyzko (2002).
21. Digital information is transmitted in little information packets. The technology that allows the splitting and eventual rejoining of the various parts of a message is being handled by so-called switches. With increasing fiberization of telecommunication lines this becomes less of an issue.
22. The Short Message Service (SMS) is the ability to send and receive text messages to and from mobile telephones. The text can comprise of words or numbers or an alphanumeric combination and was created as part of the GSM Phase 1 standard. Each short message can contain up to 160 characters in length when Latin alphabets are used, and 70 characters in

length when non-Latin alphabets such as Arabic and Chinese are used (Simon, 2000). The first short message is believed to have been sent in December 1992 from a PC to a mobile phone on the Vodafone GSM network in the United Kingdom For example in April 1999, users in Europe sent more than one billion SMS messages with some operators reporting 800 percent increases in the number of messages over the previous year (Paltridge, 2000, 63). At the end of 2002, 1 billion SMS messages are being sent in the United Kingdom alone each month (Ward, 2003).

23. The ability to purchase services in form of prepaid mobile phone cards makes it possible to distribute and use this technology not only in areas without established credit systems but also to user groups in advanced economies previously unable to have access to them (i.e., young people and low income groups). It has enabled the diffusion of this technology and thus the means of access to the global digital network to make it nearly ubiquitous in advanced economies and the main means of access in other areas of the global economy. For the example of Uganda, see Minges (2001), see also Franda (2002a, 98 n15). For an example of an advanced economy, see WuDunn (1999).

24. In both cases, the global digital network infrastructure is highly concentrated in (mainly coastal) clusters and by no means evenly distributed. See, for example, Bradsher (2002); Merchant (2002; 2000); Dugger (2000); Shastri and Bajpai (1998). For a comparison between India's and China's global digital network access strategies, see Franda (2002a).

25. In his original paper, Moore (1965) predicted that the number of transistors per integrated circuit would double every eighteen months. He forecast that this trend would continue through 1975. Through Intel's technology, Moore's Law has been maintained for far longer, and still holds true).

26. Using the simplest definition, biotechnology encompasses any technique that employs biological systems for a practical purpose. Given this standard, the roots of biotechnology reach of course back to 8000 BCE, when humans domesticated crops and livestock and first cultivated potatoes for food, and 4000–2000 BCE, when biotechnology first was used to leaven bread and ferment beer, using yeast in Egypt, as well as for the production of cheese and fermentation of wine in Sumeria, China, and Egypt (Biotechnology Industry Organization, 2007).

27. For a discussion of the development of biotech innovation clusters see McKelvey (2000); also Henderson et al. (1999). For a popular account of the impact of biotechnology as a leading sector see, for example, Rifkin (1998). For a discussion of biotechnology as a metatechnology and its role in and effect on international relations, see Braman (2002). For a discussion of the transition of biology into an informational science, see Zweiger (2001).

28. The firm Bayer, for example, has a library of 1.5 mio compounds (Barlow, 1999).

29. Members of I3C include: IBM, Apple, Sun, and Oracle in the computer industry; GlaxoSmithKline and Pfizer in pharmaceuticals; and Millennium and Affymetrix in bio-technology. Academic and public-sector participants range from the U.S. National Institutes of Health to the European Bioinformatics Institute and Beijing Genomics Institute.

30. For generally agreed definition, see Henderson et al. (1999).

31. This process started with the Harvard mouse, created and patented by Phil Leder in 1988. The mouse was highly susceptible to cancer and thus ideal for research purposes; another prominent example includes Dolly, the first successful genetically duplicated sheep.

32. The table is based on the available data from the CATI database maintained by MERIT. These data were released in the National Science Foundation's Science and Engineering Indicators 2000 report. For more information on this database, see http://www.nsf.gov/sbe/srs/seind00/start.htm.

Chapter Four   Drivers of Leading Sector Change—the Role of States, Organizations, and Individuals

1. See, for example, Oram (2001) and Lessig (2001, esp. 134–38).

2. For a discussion of early multinational business formation see, for example, Lloyd-Jones and Lewis (1988); for a classic discussion of the evolutionary development of firms and enterprises, see Braudel (1992c), see also Arrighi et al. (1999); for a discussion of organizational development from the industrial revolution on, see Freeman and Louçã (2001), also Moore and Lewis (1999); for a discussion of early U.S. enterprise development, see for example, Chandler (1965; 1977; 1990), see also Best (2001).

3. Also referred to as the *societas veritas* (i.e., true firm). This firm structure suggest the centrality of the external network context in which it operated (see J. Kulischer, cited in Braudel, 1992c, 434).

4. For original references legally documenting these partnerships, see J. Kulischer cited in Braudel (1992c, 434, n187).

5. For an extensive study of the East India companies see, for example, Steensgaard (1974; 1981; 1982). For other overseas companies see, for example, Tracy (1990; 1991), see also Blussé and Gaastra (1981). For a classic treatment of the matter, see Bonnassieux (1969).

6. A special emphasis must be put on the word culmination, as each of these factors existed long before the seventeenth century. For example, the first recorded English joint-stock company (defined as a company in which shares are not only transferable but also negotiable on the open market), the Muscovy Company founded around 1553, had many precursors, not only in the Mediterranean trading firms of Genoa and Venice, but also in its more state-dominated cousins in Spain and Portugal, as well as the trading companies of the Northern and Baltic area. These organizations also depended to various degrees on the preferences granted by the states in which they originated. Regarding the advanced financial capitalization strategies it should be noted that early tradable shares were available long before this time, for example shares (known as *partes*) in Mediterranean ships and voyages during the fourteenth century or mining shares throughout Europe as early as the thirteenth century. Of special importance for these new commercial capitalization arrangements were the financial innovations developed during the rise of the fairs (especially the Champagne fairs with their Italian connection) and the development of Italian banking of the twelfth and thirteenth century (see Chown, 1994, esp. Chapter 14; see also Bautier, 1971; Pirenne, 1936).

7. There are numerous theoretical frameworks and organizational descriptions based on this concept available. Among the more serious and theoretically based are, for example, McKnight (2001); Kaplan and Sawhney (1999); Thore (1999); Castells (2001, Chapter 3); Smith, et al. (2000); OECD (1999).

8. Flextronics is a company specializing in contract manufacturing. It employs blueprints of designs that are electronically submitted and relies one the use and combination of computer-aided design (CAD) and computer-aided manufacturing (CAM). See, for example, Economist (2000); Brown et al. (2002); also Schary and Skjøtt-Larsen (2001); Alibre (2001).

9. Napster had to cede its service not because of lack of support from its users, but for legal reasons. See for a discussion , Lessig (2001, 164–65, also 130–32 and 164–66). It has since reemerged as a legal music-download service.

10. Priceline calls its core innovation of automating the price-discovery mechanism between consumers and business (with consumers making offers and businesses matching them) buyer-driven commerce and registered it as patent number 5794207 with the U.S. Patent and Trademarks Office.

11. The value propositions of nondigital based retailers and their counterparts in the digital commercial system are the same: selection, organization, price, convenience, matching, and fulfillment. How those factors actually take organizational shape, however, is fundamentally different.

12. For a discussion of the Hollywood model see, for example, Storper (1989); see also Aksoy and Robins (1992); Kotlin and Friedman (1995); Kao (1996); Rifkin (2000, 24–29).

13. In 1944, the big studios earned 74 percent of all domestic cinema rentals and owned or leased 4,424 theaters, that is, nearly one out of every four movie houses in the country (Storper, 1989, 278–79).

14. Storper (1989, 278) notes, that

    the major studios had permanent staffs of writers and production planers who were assigned to produce formula scripts in volume and push them through the production system. Production crews and stars were assembled in teams charged with making as many as thirty films per year. Studios had large departments to make sets, operate sound stages and film labs, and carry out marketing and distribution. A product would move from department to department in assembly-line fashion.

15. Most firms in the film industry employ fewer than ten people (see Kotlin and Friedman, 1995).

16. The term agora refers to the Greek assembly place, which over time emerged into the center for public and especially commercial intercourse. In ancient Greek cities, agoras represented an open space that served as a meeting ground for various activities of the citizens. The name, first mentioned by Homer, refers to both, the assembly of the people as well as the physical setting. The term was applied by the classical Greeks of the 5 BCE to what they regarded as a typical feature of their life: their daily religious, political, judicial, social, and commercial activity. It was located either in the middle of the city or near the harbor, which was surrounded by public buildings and by temples. Colonnades, at times containing shops, or stoae, often enclosed the space. In order to isolate the agora from the rest of the town, statues, altars, trees, and fountains adorned it (Encyclopædia Britannica, 2003).

17. An existing, though rather crude, example of this process can be witnessed in the form of so-called price-bots. This Web-based technology enables automated price comparisons at no cost to the user, dramatically lowering the cost of price-information seeking. See, for example, http://www.pricegrabber.com. Some Web-based merchants even offer comparison prices on their own site (see e.g., http:///www.buy.com or http://www.amazon.com).

18. See also Häcki and Lighton (2001); Pekar (2001); Hammer (1996; also Hammer and Stanton, 1995); Miles and Snow (1994); Ghoshal and Bartlett (1990).

19. The authors refer to such entities as process orchestrators because the key to achievement in this field is the way companies manage processes, not how they structure and monitor outsourcing contracts or implement new ITs in their supply chains.

20. For models of the role of individuals in such tissues, see, for example, Pink (2001); Zachary (2000).

21. See also Katz (2000), Castells (1996; also Castells, 2001, Chapter 4), Cairncross (2002, Chapter 4).

Chapter Five   Drivers of Leading Actor Change—Interstate Rivalry at the Systemic Level

1. The term rivalry has long been part of international relations language but only recently has it become the center of a conceptual understanding of conflictual relationships between nation states. Whereas early work by Finlay et al. (1967) has concentrated on the idea of international enemies and emphasized the potential of war owing to exhibited overt or

latent hostility amongst nations, the concept of protracted conflict (Brecher, 1984; Starr, 1999) emphasized more the temporal duration of conflicts and observed long-series of hostile interactions between nations. Both of these frameworks, however, fell short of the broader conceptualization of rivalry and can be seen as precursors. The term enduring rivalries, as first mentioned in the literature by Wayman (1982), Diehl (1983), and Gochman and Maoz (1984), used to describe rivalries primarily as an empirical set of cases characterized by states clashing in repeated fashion in militarized disputed over a certain length of time. All of these attempts did not really define what is and what is not meant by the term rivalry. They all, however, implicitly contained three dimensions: (1) spatial consistency; (2) duration (or time); and (3) militarized competitiveness or conflict, all which are necessary for a complete conceptualization (see Goertz and Diehl, 1993).

2. Historically, even the strongest major powers face a great challenge in engaging in too many rivalries at the same time. Consequently, actors sometimes feel the necessity to make choices among threatening enemies. Thompson (2000b, 4) points to the example of British decision-makers, who made their choice in terms of which enemies seemed to present the most acute threat to their interests at the end of the nineteenth century. It is this necessity to focus attention on a manageable and reasonable number of rivals that makes it important for us to understand on which basis these decisions are made. Each individual actor of course, first determines what is deemed manageable and reasonable. As argued earlier what is manageable is also dependent on the global economic environment. In a given global security and power situation, major power actors seem to have similar perceptions as to what is necessary to uphold their status and position in this system. The reason for this is the common global system context in which they operate.

3. In their model (or general framework) of enduring rivalries, Diehl and Goertz point out to the existence of what they call punctuated equilibrium (Diehl and Goertz, 2000, Chapter 7). The punctuated equilibrium (originally proposed by Eldredge and Gould, 1972; see also Eldredge, 1985) is a biological theory that replaces the gradualistic evolution of Darwinism with a system that assumes that species are, for the most part, very stable. However, those periods of stability are occasionally disrupted through dramatic environmental shocks, that not only causes the extinction of many species but also allow for the relatively quick development of new species (Raup, 1991). Diehl and Goertz apply this natural science model to their "equilibrium model of enduring rivalries" (Diehl and Goertz, 2000, 132), stating that states (after an initial major shock) rapidly lock-in to enduring rivalries, which then change little and remain in a relatively stable condition until their quick demise (partly caused by another major shock).

4. Analogous to the punctuated equilibrium model in biology that emphasizes the stability of the majority of species throughout most of their lives, the punctuated equilibrium model for rivalries shifts the focus of analysis from crisis and war to strategic relationships and makes apparent the great stability in enduring rivalries (Diehl and Goertz, 2000, 137). Stability in this context does not imply a nonconflictual relationship or changing dynamics within the rivalry-relationship. It does, however, imply stability in the sense that this conflictual relationship remains existent over an extended period of time. Taking the punctuated equilibrium approach one step further enables us to see that not only do individual rivalries develop equilibria, but that major power rivalries themselves are embedded in a global world system environment. This environment influences the character and form and shape of major power rivalries that take place within them.

5. Major powers were defined as such because of their political and military weight in the given period following the guidelines Levy (1983) and Rasler and Thompson (1994) established (see table 5.1).

6. For other discussions of commercial rivalry see Sen (1984), Conybeare (1987), Frederick (1999), Kelly (1999), Levy (1999), Rapkin (1999), and Thompson (2001b).

7. Commercial wars in this context are a category of intense international conflict where states interact, bargain, and retaliate primarily over economic objectives directly related to the traded goods or service sectors of their economies, and where the means used are restrictions on the free flow of goods or services (see Conybeare, 1987, 3). Classic examples of commercial wars are the international bargaining conflicts over agricultural production or recent conflicts regarding the distribution of genetically modified products between the United States and the EU.

8. These commercial wars can at times, involve life-and-death disputes with militarized components and certainly have done so in the past. Ships, for example, often had and still have to be armed in order to make a commercial service possible—the existence of private armies of the East India companies are but one testimony of this need for protection as are high security measures surrounding many modern day firms, particularly in leading sector production items (such as microchips or biotechnologies). To this day, large transporter ships, particularly in the South China Sea retain armed protection and engage regularly in disputes with pirates in the region. Nevertheless, the scale of these disputes cannot be compared to possible militarized wars. As tragic as these occurrences had been for the individuals involved, in terms of our investigation here these incidents must be regarded as increased transaction costs rather than militarized disputes between two rivals.

9. This could be simply a reflection of the increase in the number of actors: an increase in the number of actors would most likely result in an increase of rivalries. This however, is not the case, as the number of major powers active in a given year remains relatively stable from five to seven.

10. As Gilpin points out, the process of concentration and spread has profound political consequences in the international realm. Just as every economy is a hierarchical structure composed of a dominant cores (leading sectors) and a dependent periphery (Gilpin, 1975), it releases powerful forces of economic nationalism, first in the periphery and eventually in the core (Gilpin, 1987, 94). Owing to the process of diffusion, the periphery enjoys the advantage of backwardness: lower labor costs, up-to-date plants, and expanding investment opportunities (Gerschenkron, 1964). Consequently, newly developing cores in the former periphery eventually displace the old core as the growth poles of the system, as demonstrated in the shifts in economic and political leadership in the global system (see earlier chapters for detailed discussion of this process).

11. A separation into broadly exogenous and endogenous effects does not deny the occurrence of interactions effects between these processes.

12. However, this does not imply that trade does not occur anymore in this environment or that it becomes unimportant. Far from it, trade becomes an important factor in rivalries among nation-states. It is not, however, the central basis of the leading sectors as in the maritime trade network environment.

13. It also explains in part why city-states such as Hong Kong and Singapore were able to thrive in the aftermath of World War II mainly because of their early access and integration into the then newly established commercial network.

14. This does not exclude commercial intercourse, such as trade owing to excess capacity, with outside actors. The main emphasis in an internal network–based economy, however, lies on internal exchange built around leading sectors within the internal economy, rather than an integrated economy involving interdependence with external actors. This is reflected in the similarities in the national economic structures of major powers in the world-economy in such a setting (see Sen, 1984).

15. Other costs of engaging in a rivalry are not listed here since they also occur in rivalries in other environments.

16. The number of major powers willing to engage in strategic rivalries is not to be confused with the numbers of major powers in general or major powers potentially able to engage in strategic rivalries.

17. It can be argued that after the change in China's policy toward participation in the global commercial system (away from a nonnetwork power) in the late 1970s a new strategic rivalry between China (now as network power) and the United States has emerged somewhere between the late 1980s and early 1990s (for argument of development of a new rivalry see e.g., Fialka, 1997).

18. This study also tested for other measures of external shocks and used Levy's (1983; see also Fialka, 1997) great power wars (a sum of all great power wars per year) as a control measure; these were however not significant and did not change the outcome of the other variables.

Chapter Six   The Continuation of Change of the Global Complex System—an Outlook on Its Future Development

1. Control in this context does not necessarily imply political and military control, but the ability to ensure the commercial "functioning" of the node as an integrated part of the commercial network. In addition, the Venetian model is not the only national strategy applied by major powers in this environment but the one most likely to lead to national fit in this kind of rivalry environment.

2. See Barr (1991); Wheeler and Pélissier (1971); McAlister (1984); Hess (1978); Pearson (1987); Subrahmanyam (1993); and Diffie and Winius (1977).

REFERENCES

Abbate, Janet. 1999. *Inventing the Internet*. Cambridge, MA: MIT Press.

Abu-Lughod, Janet L. 1989. *Before European hegemony: The world system A.D. 1250–1350*. New York: Oxford University Press.

Aksoy, Asu, and Kevin Robins. 1992. Hollywood for the 21st century: Global competition for critical mass in image markets. *Cambridge Journal of Economics* 16 (1): 1–23.

Albrow, Martin. 1997. *The global age: State and society beyond modernity*. Stanford, CA: Stanford University Press.

Alibre. 2001. *Design anywhere. Build anywhere: The opportunity in global manufacturing*. White Paper. Richardson, TX: Alibre.

Allen, Peter M., and J. M. McGlade. 1987. Evolutionary drive: The effect of microscopic diversity, error making and noise. *Foundations of Physics* 17 (7): 723–28.

Allen, Peter M., and M. Sanglier. 1981. Urban evolution, self-organisation and decision-making. *Environment and Planning A* 21 (2): 167–83.

Allen, Peter M., Norman Clark, and Francisco Perez-Trejo. 1992. Strategic planning of complex economic systems. *Review of Political Economy* 4 (3): 275–90.

Amin, Samir. 1990. *Transforming the revolution: Social movements and the world-system*. New York: Monthly Review Press.

Andersen, Esben Sloth. 1994. *Evolutionary economics: Post-Schumpeterian contributions*. London: Pinter.

Andersson, Ulf, Mats Forsgren, and Ulf Holm. 2002. The strategic impact of external networks: Subsidiary performance and competence development in the multinational corporation. *Strategic Management Journal* 23 (10): 979–96.

Andrews, Edmund L. 1999. Rush is on in Europe for wireless data services. *New York Times*. July 27. http://www.nytimes.com/library/tech/99/07/biztech/articles/27euro.html (accessed June 10, 2007).

Arquilla, John J., and David F. Ronfeldt. 1993. Cyber war is coming. *Comparative Strategy* 12 (1): 141–65.

Arrighi, Giovanni. 1994. *The long twentieth century: Money, power, and the origins of our times*. London: Verso.

Arrighi, Giovanni, Beverly J. Silver, and Iftikhar Ahmad. 1999. *Chaos and governance in the modern world system*. Minneapolis: University of Minnesota Press.

Ashley, Richard K. 1986. The poverty of neorealism. In *Neorealism and its critics*, ed. Robert O. Keohane, 255–300. New York: Columbia University Press.

Auyang, Sunny Y. 1998. *Foundations of complex-system theories: In economics, evolutionary biology, and statistical physics*. Cambridge: Cambridge University Press.

Axelrod, Robert. 1984. *The evolution of cooperation.* New York: Basic Books.

Barlow, Thomas. 1999. Bioinformatics: Rewards in sight as infant science grows up. *Financial Times.* June 24.

Barnett, George A. 2001. A longitudinal analysis of the international telecommunication network, 1978–1996. *American Behavioral Scientist* 44 (10): 1638–55.

Barr, Kenneth. 1991. From Dhaka to Manchester: Factories, cities, and the world-economy, 1600–1900. In *Cities in the world-system,* ed. Reşat Kasaba, 81–96. New York: Greenwood Press.

Barton, John H. 1995. Patent scope in biotechnology. *International Review of Industrial Property and Copyright Law* 26 (6): 605–18.

Basalla, George. 1988. *The evolution of technology.* Cambridge: Cambridge University Press.

Bautier, Robert Henri. 1971. *The economic development of medieval Europe.* London: Thames and Hudson.

Bell, Daniel. 1973. *The coming of post-industrial society: A venture in social forecasting.* New York: Basic Books.

Benedikt, Michael. 1991. Introduction. In *Cyberspace: First steps,* ed. Michael Benedikt, 1–26. Cambridge, MA: MIT Press.

Bennett, D. Scott. 1996. Security, bargaining, and the end of interstate rivalry. *International Studies Quarterly* 40 (2): 157–84.

Bentley, Jerry H. 1993. *Old world encounters: Cross-cultural contacts and exchanges in pre-modern times.* New York: Oxford University Press.

Berger, Suzanne, and Ronald Philip Dore, eds. 1996. *National diversity and global capitalism.* Ithaca, NY: Cornell University Press.

Bernard, Jaques. 1976. Trade and finance in the middle ages, 900–1500. In *The Fontana economic history of Europe: The middle ages,* ed. Carlo M. Cipolla, 38–71. Hassocks, UK: Havester Press.

Berners-Lee, Tim, and Mark Fischetti. 1999. *Weaving the Web: The original design and ultimate destiny of the World Wide Web by its inventor.* San Francisco, CA: Harper.

Bernstein, Jeffrey I. 1989. The structure of Canadian inter-industry R&D spillovers, and the rates of return to R&D. *Journal of Industrial Economics* 37 (3): 315–28.

Berry, Brian Joe Lobley. 1991. *Long-wave rhythms in economic development and political behavior.* Baltimore, MD: Johns Hopkins University Press.

Best, Michael H. 2001. *The new competitive advantage: The renewal of American industry.* Oxford: Oxford University Press.

van Beuzekom, Brigitte. 2001. *Biotechnology statistics in OECD member countries: Compendium of existing national statistics.* Paris: OECD.

Biotechnology Industry Organization. 2007. Guide to biotechnology: Time line of biotechnology. http://www.bio.org/speeches/pubs/er/timeline.asp (accessed September 25, 2007).

Blussé, Leonard, and Femme S. Gaastra, eds. 1981. *Companies and trade: Essays on overseas trading companies during the ancien régime.* Leiden: Leiden University Press.

Bonnassieux, Louis Jean Pierre Marie. 1969. *Les grandes compagnies de commerce: Étude pour servir á l'histoire de la colonisation.* New York: B. Franklin. [Orig. pub. 1892].

Bornschier, Volker, and Christopher K. Chase-Dunn. 1999. Technological change, globalization and hegemonic rivalry. In *The future of global conflict,* ed. Volker Bornschier, and Christopher K. Chase-Dunn, 285–302. London: Sage.

Borrus, Michael, and François Bar. 1994. *The future of networking in the US.* Research paper, Berkeley Roundtable on the International Economy, University of California Berkeley (BRIE).

Borrus, Michael, and John Zysman. 1997a. Globalization with borders: The rise of Wintelism as the future of global competition. *Industry and Innovation* 4 (2): 141–66.

Borrus, Michael, and John Zysman, 1997b. Wintelism and the changing terms of global competition: Prototype of the future? Working paper 96B, Berkeley Roundtable on the International Economy, University of California Berkeley (BRIE). http://brie.berkeley.edu/publications/WP%2096B.pdf (accessed June 10, 2007).

Borrus, Michael, Laura D'Andrea Tyson, and John Zysman. 1984. How government policies shape high technology trade. Working paper 3, Berkeley Roundtable on the International Economy, University of California Berkeley (BRIE).

Borzo, Jeanette. 1999. Will all networks merge into "Webtone"? *CNNfn*. April 30. http://www.cnn.com (accessed May 3, 1999).

Boswell, Terry. 1999. Hegemony and bifurcation points in world history. In *The future of global conflict*, ed. Volker Bornschier and Christopher K. Chase-Dunn, 262–84. London: Sage.

Boxer, Charles R. 1979. *Jan compagnie in war and peace, 1602–1799: A short history of the Dutch East-India Company*. Hong Kong: Heinemann Asia.

Boyer, Robert. 1990. *The regulation school: A critical introduction*. New York: Columbia University Press.

———. 1996. The convergence hypothesis revisited: Globalization but still the century of nations? In *National diversity and global capitalism*, ed. Suzanne Berger and Ronald Philip Dore, 29–59. Ithaca, NY: Cornell University Press.

Bradsher, Keith. 2002. A high-tech fix for one corner of India. *New York Times*. December 27. http://www.nytimes.com/2002/12/27/technology/27RUPE.html (accessed December 27, 2002).

Braman, Sandra. 2002. Informational meta-technologies, international relations, and genetic power: The case of biotechnologies. In *Information technologies and global politics: The changing scope of power and governance*, ed. James N. Rosenau and J. P. Singh, 91–113. Albany, NY: State University of New York Press.

Brandenburger, Adam, and Barry Nalebuff. 1996. *Co-opetition*. New York: Doubleday.

Brandt, Patrick T., John T. Williams, Benjamin O. Fordham, and Brian Pollins. 2000. Dynamic modeling for persistent event count time series. *American Journal of Political Science* 44 (4): 823–43.

Braudel, Fernand. 1972. *The Mediterranean and the Mediterranean world in the age of Philip II*. London: Collins.

———. 1980. *On history*. Chicago, IL: University of Chicago Press.

———. 1992a. *Civilization and capitalism, 15th–18th century: The perspective of the world*. Vol. 3. Berkeley: University of California Press.

———. 1992b. *Civilization and capitalism, 15th–18th century: The structures of everyday life*. Vol. 1. Berkeley: University of California Press.

———. 1992c. *Civilization and capitalism, 15th–18th century: The wheels of commerce*. Vol. 2. Berkeley: University of California Press.

———. 1994. *A history of civilizations*. New York: A. Lane.

Brecher, Michael. 1984. International crises, protracted conflicts. *International Interactions* 11 (3–4): 237–98.

Breshnahan, Timothy F., and Franco Malerba. 1999. Industrial dynamics and the evolution of firms' and nations' competitive capabilities in the world computer industry. In *Sources of industrial leadership: Studies of seven industries*, ed. David C. Mowery, and Richard R. Nelson, 79–132. Cambridge: Cambridge University Press.

Bressand, Albert. 1989. European integration: From system paradigms to network analysis. *International Spectator* 24 (1): 21–29.

Brewin, Bob. 2000. Army dedicates $7 billion to "transformation." *Federal Computer Week*. February 7. http://www.fcw.com/fcw/articles/2000/0207/web-budget-army-02-07-00.asp (accessed February 10, 2000).

Brown, John Seely, Scott Durchslag, and John Hagel, III. 2002. Loosening up: How process networks unlock the power of specialization. *The McKinsey Quarterly* (Special edition: Risk and resilience): 58–69.

Bruckmann, Gerhart. 1987. Will there be a fifth Kondratieff? In *The long-wave debate: Selected papers*, ed. Tibor Vasko. Berlin: Springer-Verlag.

Brynjolfsson, Erik, and Brian Kahin, eds. 2000. *Understanding the digital economy: Data, tools, and research.* Cambridge, MA: MIT Press.

Burgelman, Robert A., and Philip Meza. 2000. AOL: The emergence of an Internet media company. Case Study, Graduate School of Business, Stanford University.

Buzan, Barry, and R. J. Barry Jones, eds. 1981. *Change and the study of international relations: The evaded dimension.* New York: St. Martin's Press.

Buzan, Barry, and Richard Little. 2000. *International systems in world history: Remaking the study of international relations.* Oxford: Oxford University Press.

Buzan, Barry, Charles A. Jones, and Richard Little. 1993. *The logic of anarchy: Neorealism to structural realism.* New York: Columbia University Press.

Cairncross, Frances. 2001. *The death of distance: How the communications revolution is changing our lives.* 2nd rev. ed. Boston, MA: Harvard Business School Press.

———. 2002. *The company of the future: How the communications revolution is changing management.* Boston, MA: Harvard Business School Press.

Cameron, Rondo E. 1989. *A concise economic history of the world: From Paleolithic times to the present.* New York: Oxford University Press.

Castells, Manuel. 1996. *The rise of the network society.* Malden, MA: Blackwell.

———. 2001. *The Internet galaxy: Reflections on the Internet, business, and society.* Oxford: Oxford University Press.

Chandler, Alfred Dupont. 1964. *Giant enterprise: Ford, General Motors, and the automobile industry.* New York: Harcourt Brace & World.

———. 1965. *The railroads, the nation's first big business.* New York: Harcourt Brace & World.

———. 1977. *The visible hand: The managerial revolution in American business.* Cambridge, MA: Belknap Press.

———. 1990. *Strategy and structure: Chapters in the history of the industrial enterprise.* Cambridge, MA: MIT Press.

Chandler, Alfred Dupont, and James W. Cortada, eds. 2000. *A nation transformed by information: How information has shaped the United States from colonial times to the present.* New York: Oxford University Press.

Chandler, Alfred Dupont, Stuart Weems Bruchey, and Louis Galambos. 1968. *The changing economic order: Readings in American business and economic history.* New York: Harcourt Brace & World.

Chapman, Stanley D. 1987. *The cotton industry in the Industrial Revolution.* 2nd ed. Houndmills, UK: Macmillan Education.

Chase-Dunn, Christopher K., and Thomas D. Hall, eds. 1991. *Core/periphery relations in precapitalist worlds.* Boulder, CO: Westview Press.

———. 1997. *Rise and demise: Comparing world-systems.* Boulder, CO: Westview Press.

Chaudhuri, K. N. 1978. *The trading world of Asia and the English East India Company, 1660–1760.* Cambridge: Cambridge University Press.

———. 1985. *Trade and civilization in the Indian Ocean: An economic history from the rise of Islam to 1750.* New York: Cambridge University Press.

Chown, John F. 1994. *A history of money: From AD 800.* London: Routledge.

Christensen, Clayton M. 1997. *The innovator's dilemma: When new technologies cause great firms to fail.* Boston, MA: Harvard Business School Press.

Clark, Norman, Francisco Perez-Trejo, and Peter M. Allen. 1995. *Evolutionary dynamics and sustainable development: A systems approach.* Aldershot, UK: Edward Elgar.

Coffman, Kerry G., and Andrew M. Odlyzko. 2001. *Growth of the Internet*. In *Optical Fiber Telecommunications IV-B: Systems and Impairments*, ed. Ivan P. Kaminow and Tingye Li, 17–56. San Diego, CA: Academic Press.

Colecchia, A., E. Anton-Zabalza, A. Devlin, and P. Montagnier. 2002. *Measuring the information economy 2002*. OECD Directorate for Science, Technology and Industry (DSTI). Paris: OECD.

Constant, Edward W. 1980. *The origins of the turbojet revolution*. Baltimore, MD: Johns Hopkins University Press.

———. 1984. Communities in hierarchies: Structure in the practice of science and technology. In *The nature of technological knowledge: Are models of scientific change relevant?* Ed. Rachel Laudan, 46–59. Dordrecht, NL: D. Reidel.

Conybeare, John A. C. 1987. *Trade wars: The theory and practice of international commercial rivalry*. New York: Columbia University Press.

Cookson, Clive. 2002. Scientific buzz surrounds test bed of ideas in supercomputing. *Financial Times*. May 11.

Cooper, Richard N. 1980. *The economics of interdependence: Economic policy in the Atlantic community*. New York: Council on Foreign Relations/Columbia University Press.

Copeland, Dale C. 1996. Economic interdependence and war: A theory of trade expectations. *International Security* 20 (4): 5–41.

———. 2000. Trade expectations and the outbreak of peace: Détente 1970–74 and the end of the cold war 1985–91. In *Power and the purse: Economic statecraft, interdependence, and national security*, ed. Jean-Marc F. Blanchard, Edward D. Mansfield, and Norrin M. Ripsman, 15–58. London: Frank Cass.

Cox, Robert W. 1986. Social forces, states and world orders: Beyond international relations theory. In *Neorealism and its critics*, ed. Robert O. Keohane, 204–54. New York: Columbia University Press.

Cukier, Kenneth Neil. 1999. Bandwidth colonialism? The implications of Internet infrastructure on international e-commerce. Paper presented at Nineth Annual Conference of the Internet Society, INET '99, San Jose, CA. June 22–25.

Curtin, Philip D. 1984. *Cross-cultural trade in world history*. Cambridge: Cambridge University Press.

Dalton, George, ed. 1968. *Primitive, archaic, and modern economies: Essays of Karl Polanyi*. Garden City, NY: Anchor Books.

Daniels, George William, and Samuel Crompton. 1920. *The early English cotton industry*. Manchester, UK: Manchester University Press.

Dark, K. R. 1998. *The waves of time: Long-term change and international relations*. London: Pinter.

Davis, Ralph. 1954. English foreign trade, 1660–1700. *The Economic History Review* 7 (2): 150–66.

Davis, Stanley M., and Christopher Meyer. 1998. *Blur: The speed of change in the connected economy*. Reading, MA: Addison-Wesley.

Denison, Edward Fulton. 1967. *Why growth rates differ: Postwar experience in nine Western countries*. Washington, DC: Brookings Institution.

Devezas, Tessaleno C., and James T. Corredine. 2001. The biological determinants of long-wave behavior in socioeconomic growth and development. *Technological Forecasting & Social Change* 68 (1): 1–57.

———. 2002. The nonlinear dynamics of technoeconomic systems: An informational interpretation. *Technological Forecasting & Social Change* 69 (4): 317–35.

Devezas, Tessaleno C., and George Modelski. 2003. Power law behavior and world system evolution: A millennial learning process. *Technological Forecasting & Social Change* 70 (9): 819–59.

Diamond, David. 2002. One nation, overseas. *Wired*. June.

Diamond v. Chakrabarty. 1980. 447 U.S. 303.

Dicken, Peter. 1992. *Global shift: The internationalization of economic activity*. 2nd ed. New York: Guilford Press.

———. 1999. Globalization: An economic-geographical perspective. In *Twenty-first century economics: Perspectives of socioeconomics for a changing world*, ed. William E. Halal, and Kenneth B. Taylor, 31–51. New York: St. Martin's Press.

———. 2003. *Global shift: Transforming the world economy*. 4th ed. Thousand Oaks, CA: Sage.

Diehl, Paul F. 1983. Arms races and the outbreak of war, 1816–1980. PhD Diss., University of Michigan.

———. 1998. Introduction: An overview and some theoretical guidelines. In *The dynamics of enduring rivalries*, ed. Paul F. Diehl, 1–25. Urbana-Champaign: University of Illinois Press.

Diehl, Paul F., and Gary Goertz. 2000. *War and peace in international rivalry*. Ann Arbor: University of Michigan Press.

Diffie, Bailey W., and George D. Winius. 1977. *Foundations of the Portuguese empire, 1415–1580*. Minneapolis: University of Minnesota Press.

Dodge, Martin, and Rob Kitchin. 2001. *Mapping cyberspace*. London: Routledge.

Doran, Charles F. 1989. Power cycle theory of systems structure and stability: Commonalities and complementaries. In *Handbook of war studies*, ed. Manus I. Midlarsky, 83–110. Ann Arbor: University of Michigan Press.

Doremus, Paul N., William W. Keller, Louis W. Pauly, and Simon Reich. 1998. *The myth of the global corporation*. Princeton, NJ: Princeton University Press.

Dosi, Giovanni. 1984. *Technical change and industrial transformation: The theory and an application to the semiconductor industry*. London: Macmillan.

Dosi, Giovanni, and Richard R. Nelson. 1994. An introduction to evolutionary theories in economics. *Journal of Evolutionary Economics* 4 (3): 153–73.

Dosi, Giovanni, David J. Teece, and Josef Chytry. 1998. *Technology, organization, and competitiveness: Perspectives on industrial and corporate change*. Oxford: Oxford University Press.

Dosi, Giovanni, Richard R. Nelson, and Sidney G. Winter, eds. 2000. *The nature and dynamics of organizational capabilities*. New York: Oxford University Press.

Dosi, Giovanni, Christopher Freeman, Richard R. Nelson, Gerald Silverberg, and Luc L. G. Soete, eds. 1988. *Technical change and economic theory*. London: Pinter.

Doz, Yves L., and Gary Hamel. 1998. *Alliance advantage: The art of creating value through partnering*. Boston, MA: Harvard Business School Press.

Drucker, Peter F. 1993. *Post-capitalist society*. New York: HarperBusiness.

———. 1995. The information executives truly need. *Harvard Business Review* 73 (1): 54–63.

———. 1999. *Management challenges for the 21st century*. New York: HarperBusiness.

Ducharme, Louis-Marc. 1998. *Amsterdam 1999: Paper 1. Introduction: Main Theories and Concepts*. Amsterdam 1999: OECD Work on Measuring Intangible Investment. Paris: OECD. http://www.oecd.org/dataoecd/45/15/1943178.pdf (accessed September 27, 2007).

Dugger, Celia W. 2000. Web moguls' return passage to India. *New York Times*. February 29. http://www.nytimes.com/library/tech/00/02/biztech/articles/29india.html (accessed June 10, 2007).

van Duijn, Jacob J. 1983. *The long wave in economic life*. London: Allen & Unwin.

Dunning, John H. 1997a. *Alliance capitalism and global business*. New York: Routledge.

———, ed. 1997b. *Governments, globalization, and international business*. Oxford: Oxford University Press.

Economides, Nicholas. 1996. The economics of networks. *International Journal of Industrial Organization* 14 (6): 673–700.

The Economist. 1999. Microfinance in cyberspace. *The Economist.* November 25.

————. 2000. Have factory, will travel. *The Economist.* February 12.

————. 2002a. Computing's new shape. *The Economist.* November 21.

————. 2002b. The fight for digital dominance. *The Economist.* November 21.

————. 2002c. The race to computerise biology. *The Economist.* December 12.

Economist Survey. 1999. Business and the Internet. *The Economist.* June 26. http://www.economist.com/specialreports/displayStory.cfm?story_id=215657 (accessed June 10, 2007).

The Economist Technology Quarterly. 2002. Watch this airspace. *The Economist.* June 20.

Eldredge, Niles. 1985. *Time frames: The rethinking of Darwinian evolution and the theory of punctuated equilibria.* New York: Simon and Schuster.

Eldredge, Niles, and Stephen J. Gould. 1972. Punctuated equilibria: An alternative to phyletic gradualism. In *Models in Paleobiology,* ed. Thomas J. M. Schopf, 82–115. San Francisco, CA: Freeman Cooper.

Elvin, Mark. 1973. *The pattern of the Chinese past.* London: Eyre Methuen.

Emmer, P. C. 1981. The West India Company, 1621–1791: Dutch or Atlantic? In *Companies and trade: Essays on overseas trading companies during the ancien régime,* ed. Leonard Blussé, and Femme S. Gaastra, 71–95. Leiden: Leiden University Press.

Encyclopædia Britannica. "Agora." Encyclopædia Britannica Online. http://search.eb.com/eb/article?eu=4106 (accessed January 27, 2003).

Enriquez, Juan. 2001. *As the future catches you.* New York: Crown Business.

Enriquez, Juan, and Ray A. Goldberg. 2000. Transforming life, transforming business: The life-science revolution. *Harvard Business Review* 78 (2): 96–105.

Ernst, Dieter. 1994. *Inter-firms networks and market structure: Driving forces, barriers and patterns of control.* Research paper. Berkeley Roundtable on the International Economy, University of California Berkeley (BRIE). Berkeley: University of California.

Featherstone, Mike, ed. 1990. *Global culture: Nationalism, globalization, and modernity.* London: Sage.

Ferguson, Yale H., and Richard W. Mansbach. 1996. *Polities: Authority, identities, and change.* Columbia: University of South Carolina Press.

Fialka, John J. 1997. *War by other means: Economic espionage in America.* New York: Norton.

Finlay, David J., Ole R. Holsti, and Richard R. Fagen. 1967. *Enemies in politics.* Chicago, IL: Rand McNally.

Fligstein, Neil. 2001. *The architecture of markets: An economic sociology of twenty-first-century capitalist societies.* Princeton, NJ: Princeton University Press.

Fox, Edward Whiting. 1991. *The emergence of the modern European world: From the seventeenth to the twentieth century.* Cambridge, MA: Blackwell.

Franda, Marcus F. 2002a. *China and India online: Information Technology politics and diplomacy in the world's two largest nations.* Lanham, MD: Rowman & Littlefield.

————. 2002b. *Launching into cyberspace: Internet development and politics in five world regions.* Boulder, CO: Lynne Rienner.

Frank, Andre Gunder. 1967. *Capitalism and underdevelopment in Latin America: Historical studies of Chile and Brazil.* New York: Monthly Review Press.

————. 1998. *ReOrient: Global economy in the Asian age.* Berkeley: University of California Press.

Frank, Andre Gunder, and Barry K. Gills, eds. 1993. *The world system: Five hundred years or five thousand?* London: Routledge.

Frederick, Suzanne Y. 1999. The Anglo-German rivalry, 1890–1914. In *Great power rivalries,* ed. William R. Thompson, 306–36. Columbia: University of South Carolina Press.

Freeman, Christopher. 1983. *Long waves in the world economy.* London: Butterworths.

———. 1986. *Design, innovation, and long cycles in economic development.* New York: St. Martin's Press.

———. 1987a. Technical innovation, diffusion, and long cycles of economic development. In *The long wave debate: Selected papers*, ed. Tibor Vasko, 295–309. Berlin: Springer-Verlag.

———. 1987b. *Technology, policy, and economic performance: Lessons from Japan.* London and New York: Pinter.

———. 1988. Preface to part II. In *Technical change and economic theory*, ed. Giovanni Dosi, Christopher Freeman, Richard R. Nelson, Gerald Silverber, and Luc L. G. Soete, London: Pinter.

———. 1996. *Long wave theory.* Cheltenham, UK and Brookfield, VT: Edward Elgar.

Freeman, Christopher, and Francisco Louçã. 2001. *As time goes by: From the Industrial Revolutions to the information revolution.* Oxford: Oxford University Press.

Freeman, Christopher, and Carlota Perez. 1988. Structural crises of adjustment: Business cycles and investment behaviour. In *Technical change and economic theory*, ed. Giovanni Dosi, Christopher Freeman, Richard R. Nelson, Gerald Silverberg, and Luc L. G. Soete. London and New York: Pinter.

Freeman, Christopher, and Luc L. G. Soete. 1990. *New explorations in the economics of technical change.* London and New York: Pinter.

———. 1997. *The economics of industrial innovation.* 3rd ed. Cambridge, MA: MIT Press.

Freeman, Christopher, John Clark, and Luc Soete. 1982. *Unemployment and technical innovation: A study of long waves and economic development.* Westport, CT: Greenwood Press.

Friedman, David. 1995. Why every business will be like show business. *Inc.* Magazine. March.

Friedman, Jonathan. 1994. *Cultural identity and global process.* London: Sage.

Friedman, Thomas L. 2006. *The world is flat [updated and expanded]: A brief history of the twenty-first century.* New York: Farrar, Straus and Giroux.

FT Information Technology Survey. 1999. The Internet changes everything *Financial Times.* April 9.

Fujita, Masahisa, Paul R. Krugman, and Anthony Venables. 1999. *The spatial economy: Cities, regions and international trade.* Cambridge, MA: MIT Press.

Gaddis, John Lewis. 1991. Toward the post–cold war world. *Foreign Affairs* 70 (2): 102–23.

Galbraith, James K. 1989. *Balancing acts: Technology, finance, and the American future.* New York: Basic Books.

Garrett, Geoffrey. 1998. *Partisan politics in the global economy.* Cambridge: Cambridge University Press.

Gates, Bill. 1999. *Business @ the speed of thought: Using a digital nervous system.* New York: Warner Books.

Gereffi, Gary. 1994. The organization of buyer-driven global commodity chains. In *Commodity chains and global capitalism*, ed. Gary Gereffi, and Miguel Korzeniewicz, 95–122. Westport, CT: Greenwood Press.

Gernet, Jacques. 1996. *A history of Chinese civilization.* 2nd ed. Cambridge: Cambridge University Press. [Orig. pub. 1972].

Gerschenkron, Alexander. 1964. *Economic backwardness in historical perspective, a book of essays.* Cambridge, MA: Belknap Press.

Ghoshal, Sumantra, and Christopher A. Bartlett. 1990. The multinational corporation as an interorganizational network. *Academy of Management Review* 15 (4): 626–46.

Giddens, Anthony. 1987. *The nation-state and violence.* Berkeley: University of California Press.

———. 1990. *The consequences of modernity.* Cambridge: Polity Press.

———. 2000. *Runaway world: How globalisation is reshaping our lives.* New York: Routledge.

Gills, Barry K., and Andre Gunder Frank. 1993. World system cycles, crises, and hegemonic shifts, 1700 BC to 1700 AD. In *The world system: Five hundred years or five thousand?* Ed. Andre Gunder Frank, and Barry K. Gills, 143–99. London: Routledge.

Gilpin, Robert. 1975. *U.S. Power and the multinational corporation: The political economy of foreign direct investment.* New York: Basic Books.

———. 1987. *The political economy of international relations.* Princeton, NJ: Princeton University Press.

———. 1996. Economic evolution of national systems. *International Studies Quarterly* 40 (3): 411–31.

———. 2001. *Global political economy: Understanding the international economic order.* Princeton, NJ: Princeton University Press.

Gilpin, Robert, and Jean M. Gilpin. 2000. *The challenge of global capitalism: The world economy in the twenty-first century.* Princeton, NJ: Princeton University Press.

Gleick, James. 1987. *Chaos: Making a new science.* New York: Viking.

Gochman, Charles S., and Zeev Maoz. 1984. Militarized interstate disputes, 1816–1976: Procedures, patterns, and insights. *Journal of Conflict Resolution* 28 (4): 585–616.

Goertz, Gary, and Paul F. Diehl. 1992. The empirical importance of enduring rivalries. *International Interactions* 18 (2): 151–63.

———. 1993. Enduring rivalries: Theoretical constructs and empirical patterns. *International Studies Quarterly* 37 (2): 147–72.

Golden, James R. 1994. *Economics and national strategy in the information age: Global networks, technology policy, and cooperative competition.* Westport, CT: Praeger.

Goldstein, Joshua S. 1988. *Long cycles: Prosperity and war in the modern age.* New Haven, CT: Yale University Press.

Gomes-Casseres, Benjamin. 1996. *The alliance revolution: The new shape of business rivalry.* Cambridge, MA: Harvard University Press.

Gossain, Sanjiv, and Gajen Kandiah. 1999. Reinventing value: The new business ecosystem. Cambridge Technology Partners. http://www.business@speedofthought.com/experts/value.html (accessed June 1, 1999).

Gould, Stephen Jay. 1980. *The panda's thumb: More reflections in natural history.* New York: W.W. Norton.

———. 1989. *Wonderful life: The burgess shale and the nature of history.* 1st ed. New York: W.W. Norton.

Gould, Stephen Jay, ed. 1993. *The book of life.* New York: W.W. Norton.

———. 2002. *The structure of evolutionary theory.* Cambridge, MA: Belknap Press.

Green, William A. 1992. Periodization in European and world history. *Journal of World History* 3 (1): 13–53.

———. 1998. Periodizing world history. In *World history: Ideologies, structures, and identities,* ed. Philip Pomper, Richard Elphick, and Richard T. Vann, 53–67. Malden, MA: Blackwell.

Greenstein, Shane. 2000. The evolving structure of commercial Internet markets. In *Understanding the digital economy: Data, tools, and research,* ed. Erik Brynjolfsson, and Brian Kahin, 151–84. Cambridge, MA: MIT Press.

Grossman, Gene, and Elhanan Helpman. 1994. Endogenous innovation in the theory of growth. *Journal of Economic Perspectives* 8 (1): 23–44.

Guidry, John A., Michael D. Kennedy, and Mayer N. Zald, eds. 2000. *Globalizations and social movements: Culture, power, and the transnational public sphere.* Ann Arbor: University of Michigan Press.

Guillén, Mauro F. 2001a. Is globalization civilizing, destructive or feeble? A critique of five key debates in the social science literature. *Annual Review of Sociology* 27 (1): 235–60.

———. 2001b. *The limits of convergence: Globalization and organizational change in Argentina, South Korea, and Spain.* Princeton, NJ: Princeton University Press.

Gulati, Ranjay, Nitin Nohria, and Akbar Zaheer. 2000. Strategic networks. *Strategic Management Journal* 21 (3): 203–15.

Gunaratne, Shelton A. 2002. An evolving triadic world: A theoretical framework for global communication research. *Journal of World-Systems Research* 8 (3): 330–65. http://jwsr.ucr.edu/archive/vol8/number3/index.shtml (accessed June 10, 2007).

Häcki, Remo, and Julian Lighton. 2001. The future of the networked company. *The McKinsey Quarterly* 23 (3): 58–62.

Hall, Peter A. 1986. *Governing the economy: The politics of state intervention in Britain and France.* New York: Oxford University Press.

Hall, Peter Geoffrey. 1985. The geography of the fifth Kondratieff. In *Silicon landscapes*, ed. Peter Geoffrey Hall, and Ann R. Markusen, 12–32. Boston, MA: Allen & Unwin.

Hall, Peter Geoffrey, and Paschal Preston. 1988. *The carrier wave: New information technology and the geography of innovation, 1846–2003.* London: Unwin Hyman.

Halliday, Fred. 1987. State and society in international relations: A second agenda. *Millennium* 16 (2): 215–29.

———. 1994. *Rethinking international relations.* Vancouver, Canada: UBC Press.

———. 1999. *Revolution and world politics: The rise and fall of the sixth great power.* Durham, NC: Duke University Press.

Hammer, Michael. 1996. *Beyond reengineering: How the process-centered organization is changing our work and our lives.* New York: HarperBusiness.

Hammer, Michael, and Steven A. Stanton. 1995. *The reengineering revolution: A handbook.* New York: HarperBusiness.

Hammond, J. L., and Barbara Bradby Hammond. 1968. *The town labourer: The new civilization 1760–1832.* Rev. ed. Garden City, NY: Anchor Books.

Harding, Harry, and Edward J. Lincoln. 1993. Rivals or partners? Prospects for U.S.-Japan cooperation in the Asia-Pacific region. *Brookings Review* 11 (3): 6–12.

Hargittai, Eszeter, and Miguel Angel Centeno, eds. 2001. Mapping globalization. *American Behavioral Scientist* 44 (10/Special issue): 1541–774.

Harvey, David. 1982. *The limits to capital.* Oxford: Blackwell.

———. 1989. *The condition of postmodernity: An enquiry into the origins of cultural change.* Oxford: Blackwell.

Hatzichronoglou, Thomas. 1996. *Globalisation and competitiveness: Relevant indicators.* Directorate for Science, Technology and Industry (STI) Working paper OECD/GD(96)43. Paris: OECD.

Headrick, Daniel R. 2000. *When information came of age: Technologies of knowledge in the age of reason and revolution, 1700–1850.* Oxford: Oxford University Press.

Held, David, Anthony McGrew, David Goldblatt, and Jonathan Perraton. 1999. *Global transformations: Politics, economics, and culture.* Stanford, CA: Stanford University Press.

Henderson, Rebecca, Luigi Orsenigo, and Gary P. Pisano. 1999. The pharmaceutical industry and the revolution in molecular biology: Interactions among scientific, institutional, and organizational change. In *Sources of industrial leadership: Studies of seven industries*, ed. David C. Mowery, and Richard R. Nelson, 267–311. Cambridge: Cambridge University Press.

Henry, David, Sandra Cooke, Patricia Buckley, Jess Dumagan, Gurmukh Gill, Dennis Pastore, and Susan LaPorte. 1999. *The emerging digital economy II.* Report. Washington, DC: U.S. Department of Commerce.

Hensel, Paul R. 1996. The evolution of interstate rivalry. PhD Diss., University of Chicago at Urbana-Champaign.

References

Hess, Andrew C. 1978. *The forgotten frontier: A history of the sixteenth century Ibero-African frontier.* Chicago, IL: University of Chicago Press.

Hirst, Paul, and Jonathan Zeitlin. 1991. Flexible specialization versus post-Fordism: Theory, evidence and policy implications. *Economy and Society* 20 (1): 1–56.

Hirst, Paul Q., and Grahame Thompson. 1999. *Globalization in question: The international economy and the possibilities of governance.* 2nd ed. Malden, MA: Polity Press.

Hitch, Charles Johnston, and Roland N. McKean. 1960. *The economics of defense in the nuclear age.* Cambridge, MA: Harvard University Press.

Hobart, Michael E., and Zachary Sayre Schiffman. 1998. *Information ages: Literacy, numeracy, and the computer revolution.* Baltimore, MD: Johns Hopkins University Press.

Hobden, Stephen and John M. Hobson, eds. 2001. *Historical sociology of international relations.* New York: Cambridge University Press.

Hobsbawm, E. J. 1975. *The age of capital, 1848–1875.* London: Weidenfeld and Nicolson.

Hobson, John M. 1997. *The wealth of states: A comparative sociology of international economic and political change.* Cambridge: Cambridge University Press.

———. 1998. Debate: The "second wave" of Weberian historical sociology—the historical sociology of the state and the state of historical sociology in international relations. *Review of International Political Economy* 5 (2): 284–320.

———. 2001. What's at stake in "bringing historical sociology back into international relations?" Transcending "chronofetishism" A.D. "Tempcentrism" in international relations. In *Historical sociology of international relations*, ed. Stephen Hobden, and John M. Hobson, 1–41. New York: Cambridge University Press.

Hodgson, Geoffrey Martin. 1988. *Economics and institutions: A manifesto for a modern institutional economics.* Cambridge: Polity Press.

———. 1993. *Economics and evolution: Bringing life back into economics.* Ann Arbor: University of Michigan Press.

Holsti, Ole R., Randolph M. Siverson, and Alexander L. George, eds. 1980. *Change in the international system.* Boulder, CO: Westview Press.

Hopkins, A. G., ed. 2002. *Globalization in world history.* New York: Norton.

Hounshell, David A. 1984. *From the American system to mass production, 1800–1932: The development of manufacturing technology in the United States.* Baltimore, MD: Johns Hopkins University Press.

Hudson, Heather E. 1998. *Development and the globalization of cyberspace.* The emerging Internet: The 1998 report of the Institute of Information Studies. Washington, DC: Aspen Institute.

Hugill, Peter J. 1993. *World trade since 1431: Geography, technology, and capitalism.* Baltimore, MD: Johns Hopkins University Press.

———. 1999. *Global communications since 1844: Geopolitics and technology.* Baltimore, MD: Johns Hopkins University Press.

Huntington, Samuel P. 1996. *The clash of civilizations and the remaking of world order.* New York: Simon & Schuster.

Innis, Harold Adams. 1950. *Empire and communications.* Oxford: Clarendon Press.

International Telecommunication Union (ITU). 2002. *ITU Internet reports 2002: Internet for a mobile generation.* Geneva: ITU.

———. 2006. *World information society report 2006.* Geneva: ITU.

———. 2007. *World information society report 2007.* Geneva: ITU.

Israel, Jonathan Irvine. 1989. *Dutch primacy in world trade, 1585–1740.* Oxford: Oxford University Press.

Jarvis, Anthony. 1989. Societies, states and geopolitics: Challenges from historical sociology. *Review of International Studies* 15 (3): 281–93.

Johnson, George. 1999. From two small nodes, a mighty Web has grown. *New York Times.* October 12. http://www.nytimes.com/library/national/science/101299sci-internet-anniversary.html (accessed June 10, 2007).

Jones, E. L. 1988. *Growth recurring: Economic change in world history.* Oxford: Oxford University Press.

Kao, John J. 1996. *Jamming: The art and discipline of business creativity.* New York: HarperBusiness.

Kaplan, Steven, and Mohanbir Sawhney. 1999. B2B e-commerce hubs: Towards a taxonomy of business models. Working paper, University of Chicago Graduate School of Business.

Katz, Lawrence F. 2000. Technological change, computerization, and the wage structure. In *Understanding the digital economy: Data, tools, and research*, ed. Erik Brynjolfsson, and Brian Kahin, 217–44. Cambridge, MA: MIT Press.

Katzenstein, Peter J. 1985. *Small states in world markets: Industrial policy in Europe.* Ithaca, NY: Cornell University Press.

Kelly, David S. 1999. Genoa and Venice: An early commercial rivalry. In *Great power rivalries*, ed. William R. Thompson, 125–52. Columbia: University of South Carolina Press.

Kelly, Kevin. 1994. *Out of control: The rise of neo-biological civilization.* Reading, MA: Addison-Wesley.

———. 1999. *New rules for the new economy: 10 Radical strategies for a connected world.* New York: Penguin Books.

Kendrick, John W., Yvonne Lethem, and Jennifer Rowley. 1976. *The formation and stocks of total capital.* New York: National Bureau of Economic Research/Columbia University Press.

Kennedy, Paul M. 1993. *Preparing for the twenty-first century.* New York: Random House.

Keohane, Robert O., and Joseph S. Nye. 1989. *Power and interdependence.* 2nd ed. Glenview, IL: Scott Foresman.

Kim, Sangbae, and Jeffrey A. Hart. 2001. Technological capacity as fitness: An evolutionary model of change in the international political economy. In *Evolutionary interpretations of world politics*, ed. William R. Thompson, 285–314. New York: Routledge.

———. 2002. The global political economy of Wintelism: A new mode of power and governance in the global computer industry. In *Information technologies and global politics: The changing scope of power and governance*, ed. James N. Rosenau, and J. P. Singh, 143–68. Albany, NY: State University of New York Press.

Kindleberger, Charles Poor. 1993. *A financial history of Western Europe.* 2nd ed. New York: Oxford University Press.

Kitchin, Rob. 1998. *Cyberspace: The world in the wires.* Chichester, UK: J. Wiley.

Kitschelt, Herbert. 1991. Industrial governance structures, innovation strategies, and the case of Japan: Sectoral or cross-national comparative analysis? *International Organization* 45 (4): 453–93.

Kleinknecht, Alfred. 1987. Rates of innovation and profits in the long wave. In *The long wave debate: Selected papers*, ed. Tibor Vasko, 216–38. Berlin: Springer-Verlag.

Knutsen, Torbjørn L. 1992. *A history of international relations theory: An introduction.* Manchester, UK: Manchester University Press.

Kobrin, Stephen J. 1997. The architecture of globalization: State sovereignty in a networked global economy. In *Governments, globalization, and international business*, ed. John H. Dunning, 146–71. Oxford: Oxford University Press.

Kofman, Eleonore, and Gillian Youngs, eds. 1996. *Globalization: Theory and practice.* London: Pinter.

Kondratiev, Nikolai D. 1998. About the question of the major cycles of the conjuncture. In *The works of Nikolai D. Kondratiev*, ed. Natalia A. Makasheva, Warren J. Samuels, and Vincent

Barnett. Vol. 1. Trans. Stephen S. Wilson, 23–54. London: Pickering & Chatto. [Orig. pub. 1926].

Kotkin, Joel. 2000. *The new geography: How the digital revolution is reshaping the American landscape.* New York: Random House.

Kotz, David M., Terrence McDonough, and Michael Reich, eds. 1994. *Social structures of accumulation: The political economy of growth and crisis.* Cambridge: Cambridge University Press.

Krasner, Stephen D. 1984. Approaches to the state: Alternative conceptions and historical dynamics. *Comparative Politics* 16 (2): 223–46.

———. 1989. Sovereignty: An institutional perspective. In *The elusive state: International and comparative perspectives,* ed. James A. Caporaso, 69–96. Newbury Park, CA: Sage.

von Krogh, George, Kazuo Ichijo, and Ikujiro Nonaka. 2000. *Enabling knowledge creation.* New York: Oxford University Press.

Krugman, Paul R. 1994. *Peddling prosperity: Economic sense and nonsense in the age of diminished expectations.* New York: W.W. Norton.

Kugler, Jacek, and Douglas Lemke. 1996. *Parity and war: Evaluations and extensions of the war ledger.* Ann Arbor: University of Michigan Press.

Kuznets, Simon. 1940. Schumpeter's business cycles. *American Economic Review* 30 (June): 257–71.

Landes, David S. 1999. *The wealth and poverty of nations: Why some are so rich and some so poor.* New York: W.W. Norton.

Lane, Frederic Chapin. 1973. *Venice, a maritime republic.* Baltimore, MD: Johns Hopkins University Press.

Langlois, Richard N., and W. Edward Steinmueller. 1999. The evolution of competitive advantage in the worldwide semiconductor industry, 1947–1996. In *Sources of industrial leadership: Studies of seven industries,* ed. David C. Mowery, and Richard R. Nelson, 19–78. Cambridge: Cambridge University Press.

Lee, Richard, and Sheila Pelizzon. 1991. Hegemonic cities in the modern world-system. In *Cities in the world-system,* ed. Reşat Kasaba, 43–54. New York: Greenwood Press.

Leiner, Barry M., Vinton G. Cerf, David D. Clark, Robert E. Kahn, Leonard Kleinrock, Daniel C. Lynch, et al. 2003. A brief history of the Internet. Internet Society (ISOC). http://www.isoc.org/internet-history/brief.html (accessed June 10, 2007).

Lessig, Lawrence. 2001. *The future of ideas: The fate of the commons in a connected world.* New York: Random House.

Lev, Baruch. 2001. *Intangibles: Management, measurement, and reporting.* Washington, DC: Brookings Institution Press.

Levathes, Louise. 1996. *When China ruled the seas: The treasure fleet of the dragon throne, 1405–1433.* New York: Oxford University Press.

Levitt, Theodore. 1983. The globalization of markets. *Harvard Business Review* 61 (3): 92–102.

Levy, Jack S. 1983. *War in the modern great power system, 1495–1975.* Lexington, KY: University Press of Kentucky.

———. 1999. The rise and decline of the Anglo-Dutch rivalry, 1609–1689. In *Great power rivalries,* ed. William R. Thompson, 172–200. Columbia: University of South Carolina Press.

de Ligt, L. 1993. *Fairs and markets in the Roman empire: Economic and social aspects of periodic trade in a pre-industrial society.* Amsterdam, Holland: J.C. Gieben.

Linklater, Andrew. 1990. *Beyond realism and Marxism: Critical theory and international relations.* Houndmills, UK: Macmillan Education.

Lipsey, Richard G. 1999. Sources of continued long-run economic dynamism in the 21st century. In *The future of the global economy: Towards a long boom?* Ed. OECD, 33–76. Paris: OECD.

Lloyd-Jones, Roger, and M. J. Lewis. 1988. *Manchester and the age of the factory: The business structure of Cottonopolis in the Industrial Revolution.* London: Croom Helm.

Lohr, Steve, and John Markoff. 1999. Internet fuels revival of centralized "big iron" computing. 1999. *New York Times.* May 19.

Lopez, Robert S. 1987. The trade of medieval Europe: The south. In *The Cambridge economic history of Europe: Trade and industry in the Middle Ages,* ed. M. M. Postan, and H. J. Habakkuk. Vol. 2, 122–45. Cambridge: Cambridge University Press.

Louçã, Francisco and Jan Reijnders, eds. 1999. *The foundations of long wave theory: Models and methodology.* Cheltenham, UK: Edward Elgar.

Mackinder, Halford John. 1904. The geographical pivot of history. *Geographical Journal* 13: 421–37.

———. 1981. *Democratic ideals and reality.* Westport, CT: Greenwood Press. [Orig. pub. 1962].

Makasheva, Natalia A., Warren J. Samuels, and Vincent Barnett, eds. 1998. *The works of Nikolai D. Kondratiev.* Trans. Stephen S. Wilson. Vol. 1–4. London: Pickering & Chatto.

Mander, Jerry and Edward Goldsmith, eds. 1996. *The case against the global economy: And for a turn toward the local.* San Francisco, CA: Sierra Club Books.

Mann, Michael. 1986. *The sources of social power.* Cambridge: Cambridge University Press.

Mansfield, Edwin, John Rapoport, Anthony Romeo, Samuel Wagner, and George Beardsley. 1977. Social and private rates of return from industrial innovations. *The Quarterly Journal of Economics* 91 (2): 221–40.

Mantoux, Paul. 1983. *The Industrial Revolution in the eighteenth century: An outline of the beginnings of the modern factory system in England.* New and rev. ed. Chicago, IL: University of Chicago Press.

Margherio, Lynn, Dave Henry, Sandra Cooke, Sabrina Montes, and Kent Hughes. 1998. *The emerging digital economy.* Report from the Secretariat on Electronic Commerce. Washington, DC: U.S. Department of Commerce. https://www.esa.doc.gov/Reports/EmergingDig.pdf (accessed September 25, 2007).

Markoff, John. 1999a. Blown to bits: Cyberwarfare breaks the rules of military engagement. *New York Times.* October 17. http://www.nytimes.com/library/review/101799cyberwarfare-review.html (accessed June 10, 2007).

———. 1999b. C.I.A. to nurture companies dealing in high technology. *New York Times.* September 29. http://www.nytimes.com/library/tech/99/09/biztech/articles/29cia.html (accessed June 10, 2007).

Martin, Peter. 2002. The bitter battle of platforms. *Financial Times.* June 11.

Maskus, Keith E. 2000. *Intellectual property rights in the global economy.* Washington, DC: Institute for International Economics.

Mathews, John A. 1996. Holonic organisational architectures. *Human Systems Management* 15 (1): 27–55.

Mattelart, Armand. 2000. *Networking the world, 1794–2000.* Trans. Liz Carey-Libbrecht, and James A. Cohen. Minneapolis: University of Minnesota Press.

Mazlish, Bruce. 1966. *The riddle of history: The great speculators from Vico to Freud.* New York: Harper & Row.

———. 1998. Crossing boundaries: Ecumenical, world, and global history. In *World history: Ideologies, structures, and identities,* ed. Philip Pomper, Richard Elphick, and Richard T. Vann, 41–52. Malden, MA: Blackwell.

Mazlish, Bruce, and Ralph Buultjens, eds. 1993. *Conceptualizing global history.* Boulder, CO: Westview Press.

McAlister, Lyle N. 1984. *Spain and Portugal in the new world, 1492–1700.* Minneapolis: University of Minnesota Press.

McCraw, Thomas K., ed. 1997. *Creating modern capitalism: How entrepreneurs, companies, and countries triumphed in three Industrial Revolutions.* Cambridge, MA: Harvard University Press.

McKelvey, Maureen D. 2000. *Evolutionary innovations: The business of biotechnology.* New York: Oxford University Press.

McKnight, Lee W. 2001. Internet business models: Creative destruction as usual. In *Creative destruction: Business survival strategies in the global internet economy,* ed. Lee W. McKnight, Paul M. Vaaler, and Raul Luciano Katz, 39–59. Cambridge, MA: MIT Press.

McMichael, Philip. 1996. Globalization: Myths and realities. *Rural Sociology* 61 (1): 25–55.

McNeill, John Robert, and William Hardy McNeill. 2003. *The human web: A bird's-eye view of world history.* New York: W.W. Norton.

McNeill, William Hardy. 1967. *A world history.* New York: Oxford University Press.

———. 1982. *The pursuit of power: Technology, armed force, and society since A.D. 1000.* Chicago, IL: University of Chicago Press.

———. 1991. *The rise of the West: A history of the human community; with a retrospective essay.* Chicago, IL: University of Chicago Press. [Orig. pub. 1963].

Meilink-Roelofsz, Marie Antoinette Petronella, ed. 1986. *All of one company: The VOC in biographical perspective: Essays in honour of Prof. M. A. P. Meilink-Roelofsz, under the auspices of the Centre for the History of European Expansion, Rijksuniversiteit Leiden.* Utrecht, Holland: HES Uitg.

Mensch, Gerhard. 1979. *Stalemate in technology: Innovations overcome the depression.* Cambridge, MA: Ballinger.

Merchant, Khozem. 2000. India profits from outsourcing. *Financial Times.* July 2.

———. 2002. Indian software sector weathers global storm. *Financial Times.* February 5.

Meyer, John W., John Boli, George M. Thomas, and Francisco O. Ramirez. 1997. World society and the nation-state. *American Journal of Sociology* 103 (1): 144–84.

Miklaszewski, Jim, and Robert Windrem. 1999. Pentagon and hackers in "cyberwar." *MSNBC.* March 4. http://news.zdnet.com/2100-9595_22-513930.html (accessed October 18, 1999).

Miles, Raymond E., and Charles C. Snow. 1994. *Fit, failure, and the hall of fame: How companies succeed or fail.* New York: Free Press.

Miles, Raymond E., Charles C. Snow, John A. Mathews, Grant Miles, and Henry J. Coleman, Jr. 1997. Organizing in the knowledge age: Anticipating the cellular form. *The Academy of Management Executive* 11 (4): 7–20.

Minges, Michael. 2001. Mobile Internet for developing countries. Paper presented at Tenth Annual Conference of the Internet Society, INET 2001, Stockholm, Sweden. June 5–8.

Mintz, Sidney Wilfred. 1985. *Sweetness and power: The place of sugar in modern history.* New York: Viking.

Mittelman, James H., ed. 1996. *Globalization: Critical reflections.* Boulder, CO: Lynne Rienner.

———. 2000. *The globalization syndrome: Transformation and resistance.* Princeton, NJ: Princeton University Press.

Modelski, George. 1972. *Principles of world politics.* New York: Free Press.

———. 1978. The long cycle of global politics and the nation-state. *Comparative Studies in Society and History* 20 (2): 214–35.

———. 1987a. *Exploring long cycles.* Boulder, CO: Lynne Rienner.

———. 1987b. *Long cycles in world politics.* Seattle: University of Washington Press.

———. 1990. Is world politics evolutionary learning? *International Organization* 44 (1): 1–24.

———. 1999. Enduring rivalry in the democratic lineage: The Venice-Portugal case. In *Great power rivalries,* ed. William R. Thompson, 153–71. Columbia: University of South Carolina Press.

———. 2000. World system evolution. In *World system history: The social science of long-term change*, ed. Robert Allen Denemark, Jonathan Friedman, Barry K. Gills, and George Modelski, 24–53. London: Routledge.

———. 2001. Evolutionary world politics: Problems of scope and method. In *Evolutionary interpretations of world politics*, ed. William R. Thompson, 16–29. New York: Routledge.

Modelski, George, and Kazimierz Poznanski. 1996. Evolutionary paradigms in the social sciences. *International Studies Quarterly* 40 (3): 315–20.

Modelski, George, and William R. Thompson. 1988. *Seapower in global politics, 1494–1993*. Seattle: University of Washington Press.

———. 1996. *Leading sectors and world powers: The coevolution of global politics and economics*. Columbia: University of South Carolina Press.

Molander, Roger, Andrew Riddile, and Peter Wilson. 1995. *Strategic information warfare: A new face of war*. Report. Washington, DC: RAND Corporation.

Moore, Gordon E. 1965. Cramming more components onto integrated circuits. *Electronics*. August 19.

Moore, James F. 1996. *The death of competition: Leadership and strategy in the age of business ecosystems*. New York: HarperBusiness.

Moore, Karl, and David Lewis. 1999. *Birth of the multinational: 2000 Years of ancient business history—from Ashur to Augustus*. Copenhagen, Denmark: Copenhagen Business School Press.

Morley, David, and Kevin Robins. 1995. *Spaces of identity: Global media, electronic landscapes, and cultural boundaries*. London: Routledge.

Mueller, Milton L. 2002. *Ruling the root: Internet governance and the taming of cyberspace*. Cambridge, MA: MIT Press.

Nasscom. 2007. *Nasscom strategic review 2007*. Report. New Delhi: National Association of Software and Service Companies.

National Economic Council (NEC). 1994. *Report on U.S. critical technology companies, report to congress on foreign acquisition of and espionage activities against U.S. critical technology companies*. Report. Washington, DC: NEC.

Naughton, John. 2000. *A brief history of the future: Radio days to Internet years in a lifetime*. Woodstock, NY: Overlook Press.

Nef, John U. 1934. The progress of technology and the growth of large-scale industry in Great Britain, 1540–1640. *The Economic History Review* 5 (1): 3–24.

———. 1943. The Industrial Revolution reconsidered. *Journal of Economic History* 3 (3): 1–31.

Nelson, Richard R. 1987. *Understanding technical change as an evolutionary process*. Amsterdam, Holland: North-Holland.

Nelson, Richard R., and Sidney G. Winter. 1974. Neoclassical versus evolutionary theories of economic growth: Critique and prospectus. *Economic Journal* 84 (336): 886–905.

———. 1982. *An evolutionary theory of economic change*. Cambridge, MA: Belknap Press.

———. 2002. Evolutionary theorizing in economics. *Journal of Economic Perspectives* 16 (2): 23–47.

Nelson, Richard R., Sidney G. Winter, and Herbert L. Schuette. 1973. *Technical change in an evolutionary model*. Discussion paper 45. Ann Arbor: Institute of Public Policy Studies, University of Michigan.

Nilsson, Anna, Ingrid Pettersson, and Anna Sandström. 2000. *A study of the Swedish biotechnology innovation system using bibliometry*. NUTEK Working paper. Stockholm: NUTEK.

O'Brien, Patrick Karl. 2003. Reconfiguration of the British Industrial Revolution as a conjuncture in world history. Paper presented at The Other Canon meeting, Venice, Italy. January.

OECD. 1997. *Global information infrastructure—global information society (gii—gis): Policy requirements*. Committee for Information, Computers and Communications Policy Report. Paris: OECD.

———. 1999. *The economic and social impact of electronic commerce: Preliminary findings and research agenda*. Paris: OECD.

Ohmae, Kenichi. 1990. *The borderless world: Power and strategy in the interlinked economy*. New York: HarperBusiness.

———. 1995a. *The end of the nation state: The rise of regional economies*. New York: Free Press.

———. 1995b. *The evolving global economy: Making sense of the new world order*. Boston, MA: Harvard Business School Press.

Oram, Andrew, ed. 2001. *Peer-to-peer: Harnessing the benefits of a disruptive technology*. Sebastopol, CA: O'Reilly.

Organski, A. F. K. 1968. *World politics*. 2nd ed. New York: Knopf.

Organski, A. F. K., and Jacek Kugler. 1980. *The war ledger*. Chicago, IL: University of Chicago Press.

Ormerod, Paul. 1998. *Butterfly economics: A new general theory of social and economic behavior*. New York: Pantheon Books.

Paltridge, Sam. 2000. *Cellular mobile pricing structures and trends*. Working Party on Telecommunication and Information Services Policies report. Paris: OECD.

Pearson, M. N. 1987. *The Portuguese in India*. Cambridge: Cambridge University Press.

Pekar, Peter, Jr. 2001. Alliance enterprise strategies destroying firm boundaries. In *Creative destruction: Business survival strategies in the global Internet economy*, ed. Lee W. McKnight, Paul M. Vaaler, and Raul Luciano Katz, 119–44. Cambridge, MA: MIT Press.

Perez, Carlota. 1983. Structural change and assimilation of new technology in the economic and social systems. *Futures* 15 (5): 357–75.

———. 1985. Microelectronics, long waves and world structural change. *World Development* 13 (3): 441–63.

———. 1986. Structural changes and assimilation of new technologies in the economic and social system. In *Design, innovation, and long cycles in economic development*, ed. Christopher Freeman, 27–47. New York: St. Martin's Press.

———. 2002. *Technological revolutions and financial capital: The dynamics of bubbles and golden ages*. Cheltenham, UK: Edward Elgar.

Pérotin-Dumon, Anne. 1991. The pirate and the emperor: Power and the law on the seas, 1450–1850. In *The political economy of merchant empires*, ed. James D. Tracy, 196–227. Cambridge: Cambridge University Press.

Pink, Daniel H. 2001. *Free agent nation: How America's new independent workers are transforming the way we live*. New York: Warner Books.

Piore, Michael J., and Charles F. Sabel. 1984. *The second industrial divide: Possibilities for prosperity*. New York: Basic Books.

Pirenne, Henri. 1936. *Economic and social history of medieval Europe*. Trans. I. E. Clegg. London: K. Paul, Trench, Trubner.

Plattner, Stuart, ed. 1989. *Economic anthropology*. Stanford, CA: Stanford University Press.

Polanyi, Karl. 1944. *The great transformation*. New York: Farrar & Rinehart.

Polanyi, Karl, Conrad M. Arensberg, and Harry W. Pearson, eds. 1957. *Trade and market in the early empires: Economies in history and theory*. Glencoe, IL: Free Press.

Pollard, Sidney. 1963. Factory discipline in the Industrial Revolution. *The Economic History Review* 16 (2): 254–71.

Pomeranz, Kenneth. 2000. *The great divergence: China, Europe, and the making of the modern world economy*. Princeton, NJ: Princeton University Press.

Pomeranz, Kenneth, and Steven Topik. 1999. *The world that trade created: Society, culture, and the world economy, 1400 to the present*. Armonk, NY: M. E. Sharpe.

Pomper, Philip, Richard Elphick, and Richard T. Vann. 1995. *World historians and their critics.* Middletown, CT: Wesleyan University.

———, eds. 1998. *World history: Ideologies, structures, and identities.* Malden, MA: Blackwell.

Porter, Michael E. 1990. *The competitive advantage of nations.* New York: Free Press.

Poster, Mark. 1995. *The second media age.* Cambridge: Polity Press.

Postma, Johannes M. 1990. *The Dutch in the Atlantic slave trade, 1600–1815.* Cambridge: Cambridge University Press.

Quinn, James Brian. 1992. *Intelligent enterprise: A knowledge and service based paradigm for industry.* New York: Free Press.

Rapkin, David P. 1999. The emergence and intensification of U.S.-Japan rivalry in the early twentieth century. In *Great power rivalries*, ed. William R. Thompson, 337–70. Columbia: University of South Carolina Press.

Rasler, Karen A., and William R. Thompson. 1989. *War and state making: The shaping of the global powers.* Boston, MA: Unwin Hyman.

———. 1994. *The great powers and global struggle, 1490–1990.* Lexington: University Press of Kentucky.

Rathmann, George B. 1993. Biotechnology case study. In *Global dimensions of intellectual property rights in science and technology*, ed. Mitchel B. Wallerstein, Mary Ellen Mogee, and Roberta A. Schoen, Washington, DC: National Academy Press.

Raup, David M. 1991. *Extinction: Bad genes or bad luck?* New York: W.W. Norton.

Ray, George F. 1983. Innovation and long-term economic growth. In *Long waves in the world economy*, ed. Christopher Freeman, London: Butterworths.

Raychaudhuri, Tapan. 1982. Non-agricultural production: Mughal India. In *The Cambridge economic history of India, c. 1200–c. 1750*, ed. Tapan Raychaudhuri, and Irfan Habib. Vol. 1, 261–307. Cambridge: Cambridge University Press.

Reich, Robert B. 1991. *The work of nations: Preparing ourselves for 21st-century capitalism.* New York: A. A. Knopf.

Reichman, J. H. 1994. Legal hybrids between the patent and copyright paradigms. *Columbia Law Review* 94 (8): 2432–58.

Reijnders, Jan. 1990. *Long waves in economic development.* Aldershot, UK: Edward Elgar.

———, ed. 1997. *Economics and evolution.* Cheltenham, UK: Edward Elgar.

Reischauer, Edwin O., John King Fairbank, and Albert M. Craig. 1960. *A history of East Asian civilization.* Boston, MA: Houghton Mifflin.

Rennstich, Joachim K. 2004. The Phoenix-cycle: Global leadership transition in a long-wave perspective. In *Hegemony, globalization and antisystemic movements*, ed. Thomas E. Reifer, 35–53. Boulder, CO: Paradigm Publishers.

Richardson, David. 1987. The slave trade, sugar, and British economic growth, 1748–1776. In *British capitalism and Caribbean slavery: The legacy of Eric Williams*, ed. Barbara L. Solow, and Stanley L. Engerman, Cambridge: Cambridge University Press.

Richardson, G. B. 1972. The organisation of industry. *The Economic Journal* 82 (327): 883–96.

Riello, Giorgio, and Patrick Karl O'Brien. 2004. *Reconstructing the Industrial Revolution: Analyses, perceptions and conceptions of Britain's precocious transition to Europe's first industrial society.* London School of Economics, Economic History Department Working Papers, Working paper 84/04. London: London School of Economics and Political Science.

Rifkin, Jeremy. 1998. *The biotech century: Harnessing the gene and remaking the world.* New York: Jeremy P. Tarcher/Putnam.

Rifkin, Jeremy. 2000. *The age of access: The new culture of hypercapitalism, where all of life is a paid-for experience.* New York: Jeremy P. Tarcher/Putnam.

Robertson, Douglas S. 1998. *The new renaissance: Computers and the next level of civilization.* New York: Oxford University Press.

Robertson, Roland. 1992. *Globalization: Social theory and global culture.* London: Sage.

Rodrik, Dani. 1997. *Has globalization gone too far?* Washington, DC: Institute for International Economics.

Romer, Paul. 1994. The origins of endogenous growth. *Journal of Economic Perspectives* 8 (1): 3–22.

———. 1998. Bank of America roundtable on the soft revolution: Achieving growth by managing intangibles. *Journal of Applied Corporate Finance* 11 (2): 9–14.

Rosecrance, Richard N. 1986. *The rise of the trading state: Commerce and conquest in the modern world.* New York: Basic Books.

———. 1992. Economic deterrence. *New Perspectives Quarterly* 9 (3): 31–35.

———. 1999. *The rise of the virtual state: Wealth and power in the coming century.* New York: Basic Books.

Rosenau, James N. 1995. Signals, signposts and symptoms: Interpreting change and anomalies in world politics. *European Journal of International Relations* 1 (1): 113–22.

———. 1997. *Along the domestic-foreign frontier: Exploring governance in a turbulent world.* Cambridge: Cambridge University Press.

Rosenberg, Justin. 1994. *The empire of civil society: A critique of the realist theory of international relations.* London: Verso.

Rosenberg, Nathan. 1976. *Perspectives on technology.* Cambridge: Cambridge University Press.

Rostow, Walt Whitman. 1952. *The process of economic growth.* New York: Norton.

———. 1960. *The stages of economic growth, a non-communist manifesto.* Cambridge: Cambridge University Press.

———. 1971. *Politics and the stages of growth.* Cambridge: Cambridge University Press.

———. 1978. *The world economy: History & prospect.* Austin: University of Texas Press.

———. 1980. *Why the poor get richer and the rich slow down: Essays in the Marshallian long period.* Austin: University of Texas Press.

Ruggie, John G. 1983. Continuity and transformation in the world polity: Toward a neorealist synthesis. *World Politics* 35 (2): 261–85.

Runciman, Walter Garrison. 1983. *A treatise on social theory.* Vol. 1–3. Cambridge: Cambridge University Press.

Rutkowski, Anthony M. 1997. The Internet: An abstraction in chaos. In *The Internet as paradigm,* ed. Institute for Information Studies, 1–22. Washington, DC: Aspen Institute.

Sabel, Charles F. and Jonathan Zeitlin, eds. 1997. *World of possibilities: Flexibility and mass production in Western industrialization.* Cambridge: Cambridge University Press.

Sakamoto, Yoshikazu, ed. 1994. *Global transformation: Challenges to the state system.* Tokyo: United Nations University Press.

Sanchez, Ron. 2002. Fitting together a modular approach. 2002. *Financial Times.* August 14.

Sassen, Saskia. 1991. *The global city: New York, London, Tokyo.* Princeton, NJ: Princeton University Press.

———. 1996. *Losing control? Sovereignty in an age of globalization.* New York: Columbia University Press.

———. 1997. The new centrality: The impact of telematics and globalization. In *Intelligent environments: Spatial aspects of the information revolution,* ed. Peter Droege, 19–28. Amsterdam, Holland: Elsevier.

———. 2001. *The global city: New York, London, Tokyo.* 2nd ed. Princeton, NJ: Princeton University Press.

———. 2006. *Territory, authority, rights: From medieval to global assemblages.* Princeton, NJ: Princeton University Press.

Saviotti, Paolo, and J. S. Metcalfe, eds. 1991. *Evolutionary theories of economic and technological change: Present status and future prospects.* Philadelphia, PA: Harwood Academic Publishers.

Saxby, Stephen. 1990. *The age of information: The past development and future significance of computing and communications.* New York: New York University Press.

Scammell, Geoffrey Vaughn. 1989. *The first imperial age: European overseas expansion, c. 1400–1715.* London: Unwin Hyman.

Schary, Philip B., and Tage Skjøtt-Larsen. 2001. *Managing the global supply chain.* 2nd ed. Copenhagen, Denmark: Copenhagen Business School Press.

Scholte, Jan Aart. 1993. *International relations of social change.* Philadelphia, PA: Open University Press.

Schumpeter, Joseph Alois. 1933. The common sense of econometrics. *Econometrica* 1 (1): 5–12.

———. 1942. *Capitalism, socialism, and democracy.* New York: Harper.

———. 1989. *Business cycles: A theoretical, historical, and statistical analysis of the capitalist process.* Philadelphia, PA: Porcupine Press. [Orig. pub. 1964].

———. 1994. *History of economic analysis.* New York: Oxford University Press.

Schwartz, Evan I. 1999. *Digital Darwinism: 7 breakthrough business strategies for surviving in the cut-throat Web economy.* New York: Broadway Books.

Scott, Allen John. 1998. *Regions and the world economy: The coming shape of global production, competition, and political order.* Oxford: Oxford University Press.

Scott, Susanne G., and Vicki R. Lane. 2000. A stakeholder approach to organizational identity. *Academy of Management Review* 25 (1): 43–63.

Sen, Gautam. 1984. *The military origins of industrialization and international trade rivalry.* New York: St. Martin's Press.

Shaikh, A. 1992. The falling rate of profit as the cause of long waves: Theory and empirical evidence. In *New findings in long-wave research,* ed. Alfred Kleinknecht, Ernest Mandel, and Immanuel M. Wallerstein, 174–95. New York: St. Martin's Press.

Shannon, Claude E. 1948. A mathematical theory of communication. *Bell System Technical Journal* 27: 379–423, 625–56.

Shapiro, Carl, and Hal R. Varian. 1999. *Information rules: A strategic guide to the network economy.* Boston, MA: Harvard Business School Press.

Shastri, Vanita, and Nirupam Bajpai. 1998. *Software industry in India: A case study.* Development discussion papers. Boston, MA: Harvard Institute for International Development, Harvard University.

Shaw, Martin. 2000. *Theory of the global state: Globality as an unfinished revolution.* New York: Cambridge University Press.

Shy, Oz. 2001. *The economics of network industries.* Cambridge: Cambridge University Press.

Simon, Buckingham. 2000. What is SMS? An introduction to SMS. Mobile Lifestreams. http://www.gsm.org/technology/sms/intro.shtml (accessed December 6, 2000).

Singh, J. P. 2002. Introduction: Information technologies and the changing scope of global power and governance. In *Information technologies and global politics: The changing scope of power and governance,* ed. James N. Rosenau, and J. P. Singh, 1–38. Albany, NY: State University of New York Press.

Sinha, Narendra K. 1953. East India Company investment policy in the eighteenth century. *Bengal Past and Present* 7 (1): 25–44.

———. 1956. *The economic history of Bengal: From Plassey to the permanent settlement.* Vol. 1, Calcutta: Firma K. L. Mukhopadyay.

Skocpol, Theda. 1977. Wallerstein's world capitalist system: A theoretical and historical critique. *American Journal of Sociology* 82 (5): 1075–90.

———. 1979. *States and social revolutions: A comparative analysis of France, Russia, and China.* Cambridge: Cambridge University Press.

Sloan, Geoffrey R. 1999. Sir Halford Mackinder: The heartland theory then and now. In *Geopolitics, geography, and strategy*, ed. Colin S. Gray, and Geoffrey R. Sloan, 15–38. London: Frank Cass.

Smith, Craig S. 2002. China makes progress on chips. *New York Times.* May 6. http://www.nytimes.com/2002/05/06/technology/ebusiness/06FABS.html (accessed June 10, 2007).

Smith, Merritt Roe. 1977. *Harpers ferry armory and the new technology: The challenge of change.* Ithaca, NY: Cornell University Press.

Smith, Michael D., Joseph Bailey, and Erik Brynjolfsson. 2000. Understanding digital markets: Review and assessment. In *Understanding the digital economy: Data, tools, and research*, ed. Erik Brynjolfsson, and Brian Kahin, 99–136. Cambridge, MA: MIT Press.

Snooks, Graeme Donald. 1996. *The dynamic society: Exploring the sources of global change.* London: Routledge.

———. 1997. *The ephemeral civilization: Exploding the myth of social evolution.* London: Routledge.

———. 1998a. *The laws of history.* London: Routledge.

———. 1998b. *Longrun dynamics: A general economic and political theory.* New York: St. Martin's Press.

Somit, Albert and Steven A. Peterson, eds. 1992. *The dynamics of evolution: The punctuated equilibrium debate in the natural and social sciences.* Ithaca, NY: Cornell University Press.

Spar, Debora L. 2001. *Ruling the waves: Cycles of discovery, chaos, and wealth from compass to the Internet.* New York: Harcourt.

Spengler, Oswald. 1919. *Der Untergang des Abendlandes: Umrisse einer Morphologie der Weltgeschichte.* München [Munich], Germany: Beck.

Spruyt, Hendrik. 1994. *The sovereign state and its competitors: An analysis of systems change.* Princeton, NJ: Princeton University Press.

Standage, Tom. 1998. *The Victorian Internet: The remarkable story of the telegraph and the nineteenth century's on-line pioneers.* New York: Walker.

Starr, Harvey, ed. 1999. *The understanding and management of global violence: New approaches to theory and research on protracted conflict.* New York: St. Martin's Press.

Steensgaard, Niels. 1974. *The Asian trade revolution of the seventeenth century: The East India companies and the decline of the caravan trade.* Chicago, IL: Chicago University Press.

———. 1981. The companies as a specific institution in the history of European expansion. In *Companies and trade: Essays on overseas trading companies during the ancien régime*, ed. Leonard Blussé, and Femme S. Gaastra, 245–64. Leiden: Leiden University Press.

———. 1982. The Dutch East India Company as an institutional innovation. In *Dutch capitalism and world capitalism*, ed. Maurice Aymard, 235–57. Cambridge: Cambridge University Press.

Steinbock, Dan. 2001. *The Nokia revolution: The story of an extraordinary company that transformed an industry.* New York: Amacom.

Sterman, John. 1987. The economic long wave: Theory and evidence. In *The long wave debate: Selected papers*, ed. Tibor Vasko, 127–61. Berlin: Springer-Verlag.

Stewart, Thomas A. 1997. *Intellectual capital: The new wealth of organizations.* New York: Doubleday/Currency.

Stopford, John M., Susan Strange, and John S. Henley. 1991. *Rival states, rival firms: Competition for world market shares.* Cambridge: Cambridge University Press.

Storper, Michael. 1989. The transition to flexible specialisation in the U.S. Film industry: External economies, the division of labour, and the crossing of industrial divides. *Cambridge Journal of Economics* 13 (2): 273–303.

Strange, Susan. 1996. *Power diffused: State and non-state authority in the world economy.* New York: Cambridge University Press.

Stryker, R. 1998. Globalization and the welfare state. *International Journal of Sociology and Social Policy* 18 (2–4): 1–49.

Subrahmanyam, Sanjay. 1993. *The Portuguese empire in Asia, 1500–1700: A political and economic history.* London: Longman.

Subrahmanyam, Sanjay, ed. 1996. *Merchant networks in the early modern world.* Vol. 8. Aldershot, UK: Variorum.

Swisher, Kara. 1998. *AOL.com: How Steve Case beat Bill Gates, nailed the netheads, and made millions in the war for the web.* New York: Times Books.

Tapscott, Don, David Ticoll, and Alex Lowy. 2000. *Digital capital: Harnessing the power of business Webs.* Boston, MA: Harvard Business School Press.

Taylor, Paul. 2002. Harnessing hidden reserves of PC power. *Financial Times.* May 1.

Taylor, Peter J. 1995. World cities and territorial states: The rise and fall of their mutuality. In *World cities in a world-system,* ed. Paul L. Knox, and Peter J. Taylor, 48–62. Cambridge: Cambridge University Press.

Thompson, E. P. 1968. *The making of the English working class.* New and revised ed. Harmondsworth, UK: Penguin.

Thompson, William R. 1990. Long waves, technological innovation, and relative decline. *International Organization* 44 (2): 201–33.

———. 2000a. *The emergence of a global political economy.* London: Routledge.

———. 2000b. Wither strategic rivalries? Working paper, Indiana University.

———, ed. 2001a. *Evolutionary interpretations of world politics.* New York: Routledge.

———. 2001b. Identifying rivals and rivalries in world politics. *International Studies Quarterly* 45 (4): 557–87.

Thomson, Janice E. 1994. *Mercenaries, pirates, and sovereigns: State-building and extraterritorial violence in early modern Europe.* Princeton, NJ: Princeton University Press.

Thore, Sten A. 1999. Enterprise in the information age. In *Twenty-first century economics: Perspectives of socioeconomics for a changing world,* ed. William E. Halal, and Kenneth B. Taylor, 131–53. New York: St. Martin's Press.

Tilly, Charles. 1989. The geography of European statemaking and capitalism since 1500. In *Geographic perspectives in history,* ed. Eugene D. Genovese, and Leonard Hochberg, 158–81. New York: Blackwell.

Tilly, Charles and Gabriel Ardant, eds. 1975. *The formation of national states in Western Europe.* Princeton: Princeton University Press.

Tinbergen, Jan. 1983. Kondratieff cycles and so-called long-waves: The early research. In *Long waves in the world economy,* ed. Christopher Freeman, 18–31. London: Butterworths.

Tomkins, Richard. 1999. Assessing a name's worth. *Financial Times.* June 22.

Townsend, Anthony M. 2001a. The Internet and the rise of the new network cities, 1969–1999. *Environment and Planning B: Planning and Design* 28 (1): 39–58.

———. 2001b. Network cities and the global structure of the Internet. *American Behavioral Scientist* 44 (10): 1697–716.

Toynbee, Arnold Joseph. 1934. *A study of history.* London: Oxford University Press.

Tracy, James D., ed. 1990. *The rise of merchant empires: Long-distance trade in the early modern world, 1350–1750.* Cambridge: Cambridge University Press.

Tracy, James D., ed. 1991. *The political economy of merchant empires*. Cambridge: Cambridge University Press.

U.S. Congress. House and Senate. 1996. Report from the Permanent Select Committee on Intelligence: Preparing for the 21st century. An appraisal of U.S. Intelligence. H. and S. 104th Cong., March 1. http://www.access.gpo.gov/su_docs/dpos/epubs/int/pdf/report.html (accessed June 10, 2007).

U.S. General Accounting Office. 1996. *X. Information security: Computer attacks at department of defense pose increasing risks*. Report. Washington, DC: U.S. General Accounting Office.

Unger, W. S. 1982. Essay on the history of the Dutch slave trade. In *Dutch authors on West Indian history: A historiographical selection*, ed. M. A. P. Meilink-Roelofsz, and Maria J. L. van Yperen, 46–98. The Hague, Holland: M. Nijhoff.

Unwin, George. 1927. Indian factories in the eighteenth century. In *Studies in economic history: The collected papers of George Unwin*, ed. R. H. Tawney, 352–73. London: Macmillan.

Varian, Hal R. 1997. Economic issues facing the Internet. In *The Internet as paradigm*, ed. Institute for Information Studies, 23–46. Washington, DC: Aspen Institute.

Vasquez, John A. 1993. *The war puzzle*. Cambridge: Cambridge University Press.

Vernon, Raymond. 1971. *Sovereignty at bay: The multinational spread of U.S. enterprises*. New York: Basic Books.

———. 1998. *In the hurricane's eye: The troubled prospects of multinational enterprises*. Cambridge, MA: Harvard University Press.

Vincenti, Walter G. 1990. *What engineers know and how they know it: Analytical studies from aeronautical history*. Baltimore, MD: Johns Hopkins University Press.

Wade, Robert. 1996. Globalization and its limits: Reports of the death of the national economy are greatly exaggerated. In *National diversity and global capitalism*, ed. Suzanne Berger, and Ronald Philip Dore, 29–59. Ithaca, NY: Cornell University Press.

Wadsworth, Alfred P., and Julia De Lacy Mann. 1968. *The cotton trade and industrial Lancashire, 1600–1780*. New York: A. M. Kelley.

Wall Street Journal. 1995. Pentagon studies of "information warfare." *Wall Street Journal*. July 3.

Wallerstein, Immanuel M. 1974. *The modern world-system*. New York: Academic Press.

———. 1980. *Mercantilism and the consolidation of the European world-economy, 1600–1750*. New York: Academic Press.

———. 1989. *The second era of great expansion of the capitalist world-economy, 1730–1840s*. San Diego, CA: Academic Press.

———. 1993. World system versus world-systems: A critique. In *The world system: Five hundred years or five thousand?* Ed. Andre Gunder Frank, and Barry K. Gills, 292–97. London: Routledge.

Waltz, Kenneth N. 1993. The emerging structure of international politics. *International Security* 18 (2): 44–80.

Ward, Mark. 2003. Mixed messages for mobiles. *BBC News*. January 1. http://news.bbc.co.uk/2/hi/technology/2587247.stm (accessed June 10, 2007).

Waters, Malcolm. 1995. *Globalization*. London: Routledge.

Watson, Adam. 1992. *The evolution of international society: A comparative historical analysis*. London: Routledge.

Wayman, Frank. 1982. War and power transitions during enduring rivalries. Working paper, Institute for the Study of Conflict Theory and International Conflict, Urbana-Champaign, IL.

Westland, J. Christopher, and Theodore H. K. Clark. 1999. *Global electronic commerce: Theory and case studies*. Cambridge, MA: MIT Press.

Wheeler, Douglas L., and René Pélissier. 1971. *Angola*. London: Pall Mall.

Wilkinson, David. 1987. Central civilization. *Comparative Civilizations Review* 17 (3): 31–59.

———. 1993. Civilizations, cores, world economies, and oikumenes. In *The world system: Five hundred years or five thousand?* Ed. Andre Gunder Frank, and Barry K. Gills, 221–46. London: Routledge.

Wilkinson, Julia L. 2001. *My life at AOL.* Bloomington, IN: 1stBooks Library.

Williamson, Jeffrey G. 1996. Globalization, convergence, history. *Journal of Economic History* 56 (2): 277–306.

Witt, Ulrich. 1991. Reflections on the present state of evolutionary economic theory. In *Rethinking economics: Markets, technology, and economic evolution*, ed. Geoffrey Martin Hodgson, and Ernesto Screpanti, 289–311. Aldershot, UK: Edward Elgar.

Wolff, George. 2001. *The biotech investor's bible.* New York: J. Wiley.

Worren, Nicolay, Karl Moore, and Pablo Cardona. 2002. Modularity, strategic flexibility, and firm performance: A study of the home appliance industry. *Strategic Management Journal* 23 (10): 1123–40.

WuDunn, Sheryl. 1999. Forced to compete in wireless technology, Japan becomes a global power. 1999. *New York Times.* July 27. http://www.nytimes.com/library/tech/99/07/biztech/articles/27yen.html (accessed June 10, 2007).

Yakovets, Yuri V. 1987. Scientific and technological cycles: Program and aim-oriented planning. In *The long wave debate: Selected papers*, ed. Tibor Vasko, 230–41. Berlin: Springer-Verlag.

———. 1994. Scientific and technical cycles: Analysis and forecasting of technological cycles and upheavals. In *Economics of technology*, ed. Ove Granstrand, 134–47. Amsterdam, Holland: North-Holland.

Zachary, G. Pascal. 2000. *The global me: New cosmopolitans and the competitive edge—picking globalism's winners and losers.* New York: PublicAffairs.

Zakon, Robert Hobbes. Hobbes' Internet Timeline v8.2. Internet Society (ISOC). http://www.isoc.org/internet/history/ (accessed November 4, 2006).

Zeitlin, Jonathan. 1995. Flexibility and mass production at war: Aircraft manufacture in Britain, the United States, and Germany, 1939–1945. *Technology & Culture* 36 (1): 46–80.

Ziman, John M., ed. 2000. *Technological innovation as an evolutionary process.* Cambridge: Cambridge University Press.

Zook, Matthew A. 2000. The Web of production: The economic geography of commercial Internet content production in the United States. *Environment and Planning A* 32(3): 411–26.

———. 2001. Old hierarchies or new networks of centrality? *American Behavioral Scientist* 44 (10): 1679–96.

Zweiger, Gary. 2001. *Transducing the genome: Information, anarchy, and revolution in the biomedical sciences.* New York: McGraw-Hill.

Zysman, John, and Eileen Doherty. 1995. The evolving role of the state in Asian industrialization. Working paper 84, Berkeley Roundtable on the International Economy University of California Berkeley (BRIE). http://brie.berkeley.edu/publications/WP%2084.pdf (accessed September 25, 2007).

Zysman, John, and Laura D'Andrea Tyson, eds. 1983. *American industry in international competition: Government policies and corporate strategies.* Ithaca, NY: Cornell University Press.

INDEX

agency (*see also*: agents, complex systems)   3–4, 28–31, 35, 48, 54, 62, 137, 148–9, 159, 198, 210, 217
agenda setting phase (*see also*: leadership long-cycle)   40, 48–51
agents   2, 19, 25, 26, 28–9, 33–6, 47, 88–9, 92, 134, 145–6, 149–50, 155, 159–64, 199, 201–2, 212
analog
   as information code   74–8
   capacity as carrier technology   51–3
   technology   111, 123, 139, 199–202
   versus digital   72–4, 77–8, 220, 51–3
anthropological   5, 214, 217
AOL   86–7, 163
Arrighi, Giovanni   54–5, 57, 66, 68, 140, 142–3, 209, 213, 219, 220, 223
Asia   1, 44–5, 48, 53, 56, 63–5, 99, 109, 121, 123, 141, 197, 208, 219

bioinformatics (*see also*: biotechnology, information technology)   126–8
biotechnology (*see also*: information technology)   24, 79, 83, 84, 91, 124–33, 222
   and information technology   91, 127–8
   as leading sector   124–33, 222
Britain (*see*: Great Britain)
Buddenbrook cycle (*see also*: generations)   30–1

capital (*see*: finance)
capitalism   8, 12, 16–17, 44, 54, 212, 213
   as developmental logic   8, 11–13, 16–17
   definition   8, 16, 212, 213
Castells, Manuel   5, 79, 80, 97, 100, 136, 139, 159, 161, 212, 221, 223, 224
cellular approach (*see also*: molecularization, digital dadni system)   149–52
Champagne fairs   41, 56, 64, 84, 155–6
chaos (*see*: complex systems)
Chase-Dunn, Christopher   7, 91, 213
China   46, 49, 51, 55, 63, 123, 124, 169, 197, 201–3, 207, 218, 222, 226, 227
   Sung   51, 55, 63, 201, 218
city states (*see also*: states)   46, 51, 207, 214, 218, 226
clustering (*see also*: innovation)   18–19, 38, 51, 57–8, 65, 70, 87, 92, 97, 136, 218
coalition building phase (*see also*: leadership long-cycle)   40, 49–50, 196
communication   1, 6, 24, 28, 46, 63, 72–8, 81, 89, 90, 91, 93, 94, 97, 99, 100, 102, 106, 109, 110, 111, 121, 123, 124, 133, 136, 142, 147, 150, 154, 161, 162, 183, 199, 208, 216, 221
   as center of new leading sectors   93–124
   systems   72–8

competition (*see also*: rivalries) 2, 15, 27, 38, 39, 46, 47, 71, 76, 78, 79, 86, 163, 170, 171, 174, 175, 176, 177, 178, 184, 187, 188, 191, 192, 197, 199, 203, 205, 206
complex systems 2, 3, 11, 12, 17, 21, 24, 28–35, 44, 47, 50, 51, 53–4, 55, 57–8, 62, 63, 67, 69, 71, 73, 74, 76, 77, 91, 94, 98, 100, 105, 134, 135, 136, 137, 141, 143, 146, 159, 160, 162, 164, 165, 166, 174, 178, 198–203, 209–10, 217, 227
   approach 28–35, 47–68, 165–86
   chaos 32, 34–5, 51, 53, 57, 217
   complex global system 47–62, 67, 68, 69, 135, 141, 146, 160, 164, 165, 176
   complexity 2, 12, 21, 32–5, 51, 53, 63, 74, 143, 198, 200, 201, 209, 210, 217
   hypercoherence 32, 34–5, 51, 53, 217
   theory 11–12, 17–19, 31–6, 174–83
complexity (*see*: complex systems)
computer (*see also*: PC) 18, 77, 78, 81, 86, 90, 94, 98, 99, 123, 124, 125, 126, 147, 148, 152, 197, 208, 220, 222, 223
core (*see also*: periphery, semi-periphery) 7, 8, 9, 25, 204, 213, 218, 226
creative destruction (*see also*: Schumpeter) 12
cyberwar (*see also*: war) 207, 208

dadni system (*see also*: digital, molecularization, cellular approach) 66–7, 154, 157–9
Dell 147, 159
democratic community process (*see*: democratization)
democratization 2, 47, 50–1, 199, 217, 218
determinism and systemic processes 3, 10, 19–20, 29–31, 181, 196, 207, 211

Devezas, Tessaleno 27, 31, 32, 33, 74
digital 2, 3, 4, 22–3, 24, 25, 27, 42, 46, 50, 53, 54, 55, 56, 60, 61, 62, 72–90, 93, 97, 98–106, 106–24, 125, 127, 133, 136, 138, 139, 146, 147, 148, 150, 152, 153, 154, 155, 156, 157–9, 164, 178, 182, 183, 185, 187, 191, 192, 196, 197, 198, 199, 200, 201, 204, 205, 206, 207, 208, 210, 218, 220, 221, 222, 224
   as information code 74–8, 125–8
   capacity as carrier technology 78–81, 93–124
   commercial system 72–90
   dadni system 157–9
   software 78–9, 81, 83, 84, 85, 91, 94, 98, 106, 126, 138, 163
   technology 3, 22, 23, 93–8, 98–106, 106–24, 110, 111, 123, 199
disequilibrium (*see also*: equilibrium, complex systems theory) 11, 214, 216
Dosi, Giovanni 15, 146, 214
Dutch (25, 40, 41, 45, 49, 55, 56, 63, 64–6, 105, 120, 140, 141, 142, 169, 176, 177, 179, 180, 187, 188, 207, 208, 209, 218, 219

East-India Company 66, 84, 141, 159, 219, 223, 226
eBay 147, 155, 156
England (*see*: Great Britain)
enterprise structures (*see*: environment)
enterprise systems (*see*: environment)
environment (as part of evolutionary conceptualization, *see also*: global long-cycle environment) 3, 16, 18, 19, 20, 21, 23, 24, 25, 27, 30, 34, 35, 37, 46, 48, 50, 55, 57, 58, 59, 60, 72, 73, 80, 86, 91, 92, 127, 131, 138, 140, 141, 142, 150, 152, 155, 156, 159, 165, 166, 167, 172, 173, 174–208, 210, 212, 216, 218, 219, 220, 225, 226, 227
   enterprise structures 138–59
   enterprise systems 62–9

global long-cycle 25, 141, 165, 174–83
industrial 55, 175, 178
network 23, 59, 60, 138, 142, 153:
    commercial 53–62, 62–75, 66,
    68, 101, 175; digital 56, 61,
    72–90, 178, 187, 197, 204, 205,
    206, 207; external 138, 140,
    141, 142, 152, 156, 159, 174–5,
    181, 182; internal 60, 175–6,
    181, 182; maritime 55, 61, 181,
    187, 192, 197, 207, 208, 226
rivalry 166–83
eurocentricsm 7
European Union (EU) 84, 85, 105, 172
evolution (see also: agency) 2, 3, 4, 8,
    9–21, 22, 23, 24, 26, 27, 28, 29, 31,
    36, 39, 44, 45, 46, 47, 48, 49, 50,
    51, 53, 54, 58, 59, 60, 62, 68, 69,
    71, 75, 77, 93, 127, 135, 139, 140,
    143, 146, 149, 152, 157, 165, 174,
    177, 199, 200, 203, 209, 210, 211,
    212, 214, 215, 216, 217, 218, 219,
    221, 223, 225
and equilbrium 11–12, 17, 19, 166,
    185, 187, 214, 215–16, 225
as approach 9–21, 26–70
assumptions 27–8
critiqe 19–21
of global system 31–69
possibility space 20, 29, 34, 37, 44,
    45, 46, 48, 51, 79, 168, 215
Evolutionary World Politics Matrix
    (EWP) 4, 21, 24, 36–46, 48, 51,
    53, 54, 72
execution phase (see also: leadership
    long-cycle) 40, 49–50

feedback (see also: evolutionary
    approach) 9, 10, 18, 19, 21, 22, 31,
    86, 97, 136, 163, 216
finance 5, 11, 19, 61, 65, 83, 88, 140,
    155, 156, 157, 162, 209, 219, 220,
    221, 223
role of (capital) 87–90, 140, 155–7,
    162, 209, 223

Flextronics 147, 152, 158, 162, 223
Fordism 3, 68, 238
France 49, 93, 120, 128, 168–9, 172,
    177, 189, 209

generations 30, 31, 38, 48, 51, 57, 58,
    65, 74, 76, 210
and change of systemic leadership (see
    also: agency) 30–1, 56–62
and K-waves 28–31, 51–4
and technology 30–1, 74, 76, 210
theory 30–1
Genoa 41, 45, 49, 55, 56, 64, 101, 156,
    179, 180, 219, 223
Germany 49, 65, 93, 94, 120, 128, 169,
    172, 177
global complex system (see also: global
    system) 22, 24, 28, 29, 33, 35,
    47–62, 71, 74, 94, 137, 142, 146,
    165, 166, 178, 179, 185, 198, 199,
    201, 203
and Evolutionary World Politics
    Matrix 48–54
and long-cycles 30–1, 48–54,
    54–62, 62–9
and nested evolutionary processes 4,
    22, 35, 36, 47, 48, 50, 51, 52, 53,
    54, 61, 68, 69, 71, 217, 218
global long-cycle environments (see:
    environment)
global system (see also: global
    complex system) 2, 3, 4, 9, 21,
    23, 24, 25, 26, 27, 29, 31, 33,
    34, 45, 47, 51, 53, 54, 67, 68, 69,
    71, 72, 73, 74, 75, 76, 77, 78, 84,
    85, 90, 100, 101, 127, 135, 136,
    138, 140, 141, 142, 143, 144,
    145, 146, 153, 156, 160, 164,
    165, 166, 174, 176, 177, 178,
    180, 181, 182, 183, 184, 185,
    186, 187, 188, 189, 190, 191,
    192, 193, 196, 197, 198, 199,
    200, 201, 202, 203, 204, 205,
    207, 208, 209, 210, 211, 217,
    218, 225, 226

global system—*continued*
  definition 3
  development of (*see*: global complex
    system)
globalization (*see*: global system)
Great Britain 65, 67, 93, 102, 120,
  128, 142, 143, 149, 177, 204, 216,
  218, 219, 222

hegemony (*see also*: systemic leadership)
  7, 8, 60, 61, 101, 209, 210, 213,
  218
hinterlands 7, 8, 50, 100, 111
Hollywood model (*see*:
  molecularization)
hypercoherence (*see also*: complexity,
    complex systems) 32, 33, 34, 35,
  51, 52, 53, 217

India 41, 49, 56, 66, 84, 123, 141, 159,
  197, 202, 203, 207, 219, 222, 226
industrial revolution (*see*:
  industrialization)
industrialization 12, 13, 17, 18, 20, 22,
  23, 27, 44, 45, 49, 51, 52, 53, 54,
  55, 56, 60, 61, 62, 66, 67, 68, 72,
  88, 92, 99, 101, 125, 140, 142, 144,
  152, 153, 154, 175, 177, 178, 179,
  181, 182, 185, 186, 187, 189, 190,
  202, 205, 206, 209, 210, 214, 215,
  219, 223
iNet economy (informational network
  economy) 4, 7, 24, 69, 80, 86, 87,
  88, 93, 101, 133, 134, 135, 146, 220
information 1, 4, 5, 6, 24, 25, 32, 34, 45,
  49, 51, 53, 56, 60, 63, 68, 69, 71, 74,
  75, 76, 77, 78, 79, 80, 81, 83, 86, 87,
  91, 93, 94, 95, 96, 97, 98, 99, 100,
  101, 102, 106, 110, 124, 125, 126,
  127, 129, 131, 133, 134, 135, 136,
  138, 139, 145, 146, 149, 153, 155,
  156, 160, 161, 162, 164, 180, 200,
  201, 202, 205, 206, 207, 208, 210,
  212, 220, 221, 222, 224

information technology (*see*:
  information and communication
  technology)
information and communication technology
  (ICT) (*see also*: bioinformatics,
    biotechnology) 24, 42, 78, 85, 91, 92,
  93–8, 100, 101, 106, 107, 124, 126,
  127, 128, 133, 136, 139, 145, 148, 149,
  161, 195, 202, 225
  and biotechnology (*see*:
    biotechnology)
  as leading sector 74–81, 90–3, 93–8
informational (*see*: information)
infrastructure (*see*: structure)
innovation (*see also*: clustering) 2, 8, 9,
  10, 11, 13, 14, 15, 17, 18, 19, 27, 29,
  30, 32, 34, 36, 38, 39, 40, 44, 47,
  48, 50, 57, 58, 63, 64, 68, 69, 72,
  77, 80, 81, 82, 87, 91, 92, 97, 102,
  109, 123, 124, 131, 133, 136, 137,
  140, 146, 161, 162, 199, 201, 215,
  216, 220, 222, 223
intangible assets (*see also*: IPRs) 82, 83,
  88, 207, 220
intellectual property (IP) (*see also*: digital
    technologies, productivity,
    intangible assets, intellectual
    property rights) 82–5, 220
intellectual property rights (IPRs) (*see
  also*: intellectual property,
    intangible assets) 82–5, 220
interconnectedness 3, 37, 46, 99, 200
interdependence 2, 5, 6, 21, 22, 28, 51,
  137, 173, 174, 177, 180, 182, 185,
  186, 188, 192, 197, 204, 205, 226
Italy (*see also*: Genoa, Venice) 49, 51,
  120, 168–9, 218, 219

Japan 73, 89, 93, 94, 97, 106, 121, 123,
  128, 131, 133, 169, 172, 177, 187,
  206, 209

K-waves (*see also*: leading sectors,
    rivalries) 8, 12, 17, 25, 29, 30, 31,

37, 39, 40, 41–2, 53, 54, 58, 62, 63,
    67, 70, 72, 74, 85, 86, 87, 91, 92,
    93, 95, 96, 97, 106, 134, 135, 136,
    145, 165, 176, 177, 178–85, 201,
    202, 203, 215, 216, 217
  and generational cycles   30–1, 52
  as part of global system
    formation   36–47, 47–54,
      56–60, 91–2, 96, 165–86
  definition   12–13
  global system leadership   40–54
knowledgework   160–1, 164
Kondratiev, Nikolai   12, 13

leadership long-cycle (*see* long-cycle,
    agenda-setting phase, execution
    phase, coalition phase,
    macrodecision phase)
leading economy (*see also*: K-waves,
    leading sector)   38, 39, 40, 41–2,
    54, 85, 92
leading sector (*see also*: leading economy,
    K-wave)   3, 4, 8, 9, 13, 14, 24, 25,
    30, 31, 36, 37, 38, 40, 53, 54, 55,
    56, 57, 58, 59, 62, 63, 64, 65, 69,
    72, 73, 74, 83, 84, 85, 86, 90, 91,
    92, 95, 96, 97, 124, 127, 133, 134,
    135, 136, 142, 143, 144, 152, 156,
    164, 165, 171, 175, 178, 181, 182,
    183, 199, 202, 204, 207, 210, 215,
    219, 222, 223, 226
  based on digital technologies   72–81,
    90–133
  concept   13–14
long-cycle (also leadership long
    cycle)   12, 13, 25, 30, 33, 37, 40,
    56, 58, 71, 72, 77, 96, 136, 144,
    156, 164, 165, 166, 174, 176, 178,
    180, 181, 186, 187, 196, 202, 203
  definition and historical development
    of concept   12–14, 37

macrodecision phase (*see also*: leadership
    long-cycle)   40, 49–50, 144, 210

maritime   23, 24, 41, 51, 54, 56, 61, 62,
    63, 64, 67, 68, 82, 84, 97, 136, 139,
    140, 141, 145, 150, 152, 156, 157,
    163, 177–83, 185, 186, 187, 188,
    190, 192, 197, 204, 205, 206, 207,
    209, 218, 226
McNeill, William   28, 40, 42, 44, 45,
    63, 142, 212, 217, 218, 219
microprocessors (*see also*: information
    technology, semiconductors)   91,
    93, 124
Microsoft   79, 81, 87
mobile (*see also*: SMS)   93, 105, 106, 109,
    110, 111, 120, 121, 123, 124, 139
  as part of global digital
    network   120–3, 139
  networks   110, 111, 121, 123
  phones (*see also*: phones)   106, 109,
    110, 111, 221
  prepaid   109, 110, 222
  technology   93, 105, 109, 110, 111,
    120, 121, 123, 124, 222
Modelski, George   2, 8, 21, 22, 23, 25,
    27, 29, 32, 33, 36, 37, 38, 39, 40, 42,
    44, 45, 46, 47, 48, 50, 51, 54, 55, 56,
    57, 58, 59, 63, 64, 69, 72, 74, 91, 145,
    170, 185, 212, 217, 218, 219
molecularization (*see also*: cellular
    approach, Hollywood model)   87,
    162
monopolies   24, 38, 39, 40, 60, 64, 82,
    84, 85–7, 88, 89, 91, 141, 143, 144,
    156, 204, 210, 220, 221
multinational corporations (MNCs)   26,
    140, 145, 219, 221, 223

Nasdaq   88–90, 155, 220, 221
Nelson, Richard   11, 146, 214, 218
Netherlands (*see*: Dutch)
networking   23, 24, 42, 60, 73, 79, 80,
    81, 93–8, 101, 126, 133, 134, 161,
    162–4
networks   2, 4, 5, 15, 22, 23, 24, 25,
    27, 28, 33, 34, 41–2, 44, 45, 46, 47,

networks—*continued*
    48, 51, 53, 54–6, 57, 59, 60, 61,
       62–9, 71–134, 135, 136, 138, 139,
       140, 141, 142, 143, 144, 145, 146, 147,
       148, 149, 150, 152, 153, 154, 155,
       156, 157, 158, 159, 160, 161, 162,
       163, 164, 165, 173, 174, 175, 177, 178,
       179, 180, 181, 182, 183, 184, 185,
       186, 187, 188, 189, 190, 191, 192,
       196, 197, 199, 200, 202, 203, 204,
       205, 206, 207, 208, 209, 210, 212,
       220, 221, 222, 223, 226, 227
    digital   4, 23, 27, 45–50, 60, 75, 80,
       83, 88, 90, 93, 99, 104, 105, 111,
       121, 123, 124, 127, 136, 146,
       154, 178, 183, 187, 192, 196, 197,
       204, 205, 206, 207, 221, 222,
    economies   24, 62–9, 71–134
    externalities   24, 78, 79, 163
    external   2, 15, 23, 24, 33, 34, 53,
       54–6, 57, 59, 60, 61, 62, 63, 67,
       68, 69, 72, 73, 74, 77, 78, 80, 82,
       85, 88, 90, 97, 99, 100, 101, 106,
       110, 111, 133, 136, 138, 139, 140,
       141, 142, 143, 145, 150, 152, 155,
       156, 160, 164, 174–5, 177, 178,
       179, 184, 189, 192, 196, 197, 200,
       202, 203, 204, 209, 210, 223
    internal   2, 23, 24, 25, 33, 34, 53,
       54–6, 60, 61, 62, 66, 67, 68, 72,
       73, 77, 80, 81, 88, 100, 101, 133,
       136, 141, 142, 143, 145, 150, 152,
       153, 154, 157, 158, 165, 174, 175,
       178, 179, 183, 184, 189, 190, 191,
       197, 199, 202, 207, 210, 217, 226
NYSE   88, 89, 90, 220, 221

O'Brien, Patrick   143, 144
organization   2, 16, 17, 18, 19, 22, 24,
    25, 26, 27, 28, 29, 31, 32, 33, 34,
    35, 37, 45, 46, 47, 48, 50, 51, 53,
    56, 57, 58, 59, 60, 61, 62, 63, 65,
    66, 67, 71, 73, 74, 75, 76, 77, 79,
    80, 82, 83, 88, 89, 127, 133, 135,
    136, 139, 140, 141, 144, 145, 146,

    148, 149, 150, 151, 152, 153, 154,
    155, 157, 158, 159, 160, 161, 162,
    172, 199, 201, 205, 206, 209, 214,
    217, 219, 222, 223, 224
outsourcing (*see also*: dadni system,
    digital dadni system)   66, 67, 98,
    138, 142, 145, 157–9, 202, 204

PayPal   156
PC (personal computer) (*see also*:
    computers)   81, 93, 105, 106, 109,
    111, 121, 123, 124, 222
Perez, Carlota   3, 13, 15, 17, 18, 19,
    149, 216, 218
periodization   6, 12, 14, 36, 37, 39–47,
    50, 53, 140, 168–9, 174–7, 218
periphery (*see also*: semi-periphery,
    core)   7, 8, 99, 183, 204, 213, 226
Phoenix-cycle   56–62
phones (*see also*: mobile phones)   78, 81,
    102, 105, 106, 109, 110, 111,
    114–20, 221, 222
Portugal   40, 41, 45, 49, 55, 56, 64, 77,
    169, 177, 179, 180, 189, 203, 219, 223
possibility space (*see*: evolution)
productivity   12, 82, 91, 160, 161, 215
protocols   24, 80–1, 86, 98, 99, 104

railway   18, 42, 56, 67, 144, 145, 163, 215
republics (*see also*: state)   45, 51, 218
rivalries (*see also*: Phoenix-cycle, war)   25,
    55, 69, 165–97, 203, 204, 205, 206,
    207, 213, 224, 225, 226, 227
    between major power states   168–9
    concept   167–74
    commercial   70–1, 72–4
    strategic   167–70, 72–4
    rivalry environments   174–83
Rosecrance, Richard   55, 76, 100, 135,
    136, 175, 178, 204, 205, 206, 207
Rostow, Walt   13, 14, 38, 215

Sassen, Saskia   100, 137, 138, 213, 217
Schumpeter, Joseph   11, 12, 13, 15, 16,
    17, 19, 37, 40, 146, 214

semi-periphery (*see also*: core, periphery) 7, 8

semiconductors (*see also*: microprocessors) 60, 96

ships 44, 64, 65, 226

SMS (short message system) (*see also*: text message) 109–11, 221, 222

software (*see also*: digital) 78–9, 81, 83, 84, 85, 91, 94, 98, 106, 126, 138, 163

states (*see also*: republics, city states, and individual countries) 2, 6, 9, 13, 19, 21, 22, 25, 26, 28, 32, 38, 39, 40, 44, 47, 48, 50, 51, 55, 59, 62, 67, 68, 71, 76, 77, 82, 84, 92, 93, 135–8, 139, 141, 142, 143, 144, 145, 159, 164, 165–83, 199, 202, 204, 205, 206, 207, 213, 214, 215, 217, 218, 219, 223, 224, 225, 226

virtual 135, 205, 206, 207

structure (*see also*: networks) 2, 3, 4, 7, 8, 11, 14, 15, 16, 17, 18, 19, 21, 22, 23, 24, 25, 26, 27, 28, 29, 31, 32, 33, 34, 35, 36, 39, 44, 46, 47, 48, 50, 51, 53, 54–6, 57, 59, 60, 61, 62, 63, 65, 67, 68, 69, 73, 74, 76, 77, 79, 80, 81, 87, 88, 90, 92, 96, 98, 99, 100, 101, 102, 105, 106, 109, 111, 123, 124, 127, 133, 134, 135, 136, 137, 138–64, 165, 171, 172, 174, 177, 178, 179, 183, 184, 198, 199, 200, 202, 205, 206, 209, 210, 211, 212, 213, 216, 217, 222, 223, 224, 226

infrastructure 14, 18, 46, 65, 67, 73, 74, 80, 81, 96, 98, 99, 101, 102, 105, 106, 127, 133, 136, 145, 161, 162, 172, 206, 217, 222

Sung-China (*see* China)

system (*see also*: agency)

global system 2, 3, 4, 9, 21, 22, 23, 24, 25, 26, 27, 29, 31, 33, 34, 45, 47, 51, 53, 54, 67, 68, 69, 71, 72, 73, 74, 75, 76, 77, 78, 84, 85, 90, 100, 101, 127, 135, 136, 138, 140, 141, 142, 143, 144, 145, 146, 153, 156, 160, 164, 165, 166, 174–92, 193, 196, 197, 198, 199, 200, 201, 202, 203, 204, 205, 207, 208, 209, 210, 211, 217, 218, 225, 226

systemic leadership 39–42, 45–7, 56–62, 62–9, 178–80

systemic transitions (*see*: Phoenix cycle)

systemic leadership (*see*: system, *see also*: hegemony)

systemic transition (*see*: system)

technological style (*see also*: technological revolution) 3, 15, 18, 19, 24, 25, 37, 48, 69, 72, 91, 92, 127, 135, 145, 148, 149, 161, 164, 165, 199, 200, 202, 209, 210, 212, 215

technology 3, 6, 9, 11, 13, 14, 15, 16, 17, 18, 24, 28, 37, 38, 39, 58, 60, 63, 73, 75, 77, 78, 79, 82, 83, 84, 85, 86, 87, 91, 92, 93, 94, 95, 96, 97, 101, 102, 106, 109, 110, 111, 123, 124, 126, 127, 128, 129, 131, 133, 148, 162, 163, 199, 204, 212, 215, 216, 220, 221, 222, 224

analog (*see*: analog)

and generational behavior (*see also*: agency) 30–1

bio (*see*: biotechnology)

carrier (*see also*: digital, analog) 18, 31, 147, 202, 203

digital (*see*: digital)

telecommunication (*see also* ICT, phones) 1, 24, 90, 91, 93, 99, 100, 102, 111, 121, 123, 124, 154, 155, 156, 221

telegraph 77, 78, 81, 91

text message (*see also*: text messaging system, SMS) 109–111, 221, 222

Thompson, William R. 2, 8, 21, 22, 25, 29, 36, 38, 39, 40, 47, 51, 54, 55, 56, 57, 58, 59, 63, 64, 69, 72, 91, 145, 167, 168–9, 176, 177, 179, 181, 185, 212, 213, 219, 225

trade (*see also*: networks)   1, 5, 14, 21,
    23, 24, 25, 28, 39, 40, 41, 45, 46,
    48, 49, 53, 55, 56, 62–7, 68, 83, 84,
    85, 88, 89, 90, 97, 128, 136, 138,
    139, 141, 142, 144, 150, 159, 173,
    174, 175, 178, 179, 180, 181, 182,
    183, 184, 187, 190, 192, 197, 204,
    205, 206, 207, 208, 219, 220, 221,
    223, 226
  trade routes   24, 40, 48, 64, 65, 97,
    98, 136, 138, 139, 150

United Kingdom (UK) (*see* Great
    Britain)
United States (US)   25, 40, 42, 45, 49,
    50, 54, 55, 56, 60, 61, 65, 68, 69,
    72, 73, 84, 85, 86, 87, 88, 93, 94,
    95, 96, 98, 99, 100, 102, 105, 106,
    109, 110, 111, 120, 121, 123, 124,
    128, 129, 131, 133, 140, 145, 153,
    154, 157, 159, 169, 172, 177, 179,
    187, 202, 204, 206, 208, 209, 221,
    222, 223, 226, 227

Venice   41, 45, 49, 55, 56, 101, 179,
    180, 219, 223
virtual states (*see*: states)
VOC (Verenigde Oost-Indische
    Compagnie)   65, 141, 219

Wal-Mart   83, 153
Wallerstein, Immanuel   7, 42, 44, 209,
    212, 213, 214, 218
war (*see also*: macrodecision phase,
    rivalries, cyberwar)   4, 11, 13, 27,
    49–50, 58, 81, 142, 143, 144, 166, 171,
    172, 173, 176, 177, 185, 186, 187, 188,
    189, 190, 191, 192, 193, 195, 196, 197,
    207, 208, 209, 210, 224, 225, 227
  global   27, 49–50, 58, 142, 144, 173,
    176, 177, 185, 186, 187, 188, 189,
    190, 191, 192, 193, 195, 196, 197,
    209, 210, 227
Wintelism   81, 162
Winter, Sidney   11, 146, 214, 218
world history   8, 18, 20, 28, 36, 40, 44,
    50, 101, 217

UNIVERSITY OF WOLVERHAMPTON
LEARNING & INFORMATION SERVICES